Sir Henry Pottinger

By the same author

NON FICTION

The Winning Counter
Muirfield and the Honourable Company
St Moritz; An Alpine Caprice
The Court of the Medici
The Secretaries of State for Scotland, 1926–76
The Afghan Connection
Mayo, Disraeli's Viceroy
The Ten-Rupee Jezail (with Sir Patrick Macrory)
Heirs of the Enlightenment
The Real Admirable Crichton

FICTION

Whisky Sour

SIR HENRY POTTINGER

First Governor of Hong Kong

GEORGE POTTINGER

SUTTON PUBLISHING

First published in the United Kingdom in 1997 by
Sutton Publishing Limited
Phoenix Mill · Thrupp · Stroud · Gloucestershire · GL5 2BU

First published in the United States of America in 1997 by
St. Martin's Press · Scholarly and Reference Division
175 Fifth Avenue · New York · N.Y. 10010

British Library Cataloguing in Publication Data
A catalogue record for this book is available from the British Library.

ISBN 0-312-16506-4

TM   ALAN SUTTON™ and SUTTON™ are the
trade marks of Sutton Publishing Limited

Typeset in 10/15½pt New Baskerville.
Typesetting and origination by
Sutton Publishing Limited.
Printed in Great Britain by
Hartnolls, Bodmin, Cornwall.

For Archie William Eldred Pottinger

Contents

List of Plates

List of Maps

Acknowledgements

The main sources for this book have been Ministerial despatches and official records, supplemented by the wealth of memoirs and letters left by those who took part in the campaigns. Recalling Virginia Woolf's caustic observation that one of the aims of biography is 'to make men appear as they ought to be', vices are featured as well as virtues, and an attempt has been made to construct a three-dimensional picture to match Sir Henry's triple career. I am greatly indebted to all who have helped me.

Mr Ben Pottinger Macrory, related through generations to Sir Henry, emulated him in retracing the journey described in his *Travels in Beloochistan and Sinde*. He wore the same disguise, and has confirmed that the attitude of the inhabitants is still much as it was when his ancestor traversed their country at the beginning of the nineteenth century.

Vice-Admiral Sir Peter Berger, with personal experience of the Yangtse on board HMS *Amethyst*, kindly read the manuscript of the China chapters and gave me the benefit of his local knowledge.

Dr R.J. Bingle was, as always, indefatigable in directing me to the more arcane Indian sources, and Mr J.J.G. Browne of Matheson & Co. gave me permission to examine the Jardine Matheson Archives. Mr J. Platt gave me access to the relevant letters in his private collection of Pottinger correspondence, and Mr John Brooke-Little, Clarencieux King of Arms, contributed his authoritative heraldic views.

I am glad to acknowledge the scrutiny of Sir Henry's Ulster family connection carried out by Miss Elizabeth Erskine, and I have also received assistance from Dr Anthony Malcolmson, Mr John Quinn and Mr Ken Bruce of the Public Record Office, Northern Ireland, Mr E. McCauley, Belfast Royal Academy, Mr Gerry Healey, The Linen Hall Library, Mrs Linda Greenwood, Belfast Central Library, and Mrs E. Mountford.

Mr Stephen Rabson, P & O Steam Navigation Co., Miss J.M. Wraight,

Maritime Information Centre, Miss R. Dunne, Trinity College Dublin, and Lt-Col. Anthony Mather, Central Chancery of the Orders of Knighthood, were generous with their time in finding answers to my questions.

To them, and to the staff of the Public Record Office, the India Office Collection, the Cambridge University Library, and the Centre of South Asian Studies, Cambridge, it is a pleasure to offer my thanks.

Finally, without my wife's forbearance and unfailing encouragement, the biography of Sir Henry would not have been completed.

Plates 1 and 3 appear by courtesy of the Oriental Club, other plates by courtesy as follows: 2, 5, 8, 12 and 24, Cambridge University Library; 4 and 6, National Army Museum; 7, Essex Regiment Museum; 10, 11, 14–18, 21 and 22, *Illustrated London News*; 19 and 20, Mr E.G. Howard; 23, Peninsular and Oriental Steam Navigation Company; 26, *The Field*. Plates 9, 20 and 21 come from a private collection.

G.P.

Introduction

Wrath is the first word in the *Iliad*. It was also a watchword of British foreign policy in the decades after 1830. Ministers at Westminster, when they were not distracted by domestic events like the passing of the Reform Bill or the accession of Queen Victoria, were intent on a bellicose disposition overseas. Wars were fought in India and Afghanistan, China and Africa, but today the only relic of British rule in these areas is the Colony of Hong Kong. With the return of the island to the Chinese Government, the question is how did we ever come to assume power there?

On 5 April 1843 the Privy Council issued Letters Patent under the Great Seal declaring the settlement on the island of Hong Kong to be a Crown colony by Charter, together with a Royal Warrant appointing Sir Henry Pottinger as Governor and Commander-in-Chief of the Colony and its dependencies.

From the start, the focus is on Henry Pottinger. It is a quirk that if he had not been selected as Plenipotentiary to China in 1841, with a remit to end the Opium War, it is most unlikely that the island would have been brought under the Crown. History chooses its man. No stranger to foreign campaigns, Pottinger had fought in India at Kikri during the Mahratta War and had been Resident at Sind. After Hong Kong he undertook further Imperial tasks in the Cape of Good Hope and at Madras. In all these theatres his role was important, but in Hong Kong it was decisive. His proconsular career can be seen as a rehearsal for his time as Governor – with a free hand that was sometimes manicured by Westminster. This book looks at the acquisition of Hong Kong, seen through his 'odyssey of battle', his moods, and sometimes his wrath.

The island of Hong Kong, from which the colony gets its name, measures thirty-two square miles. Later additions on the mainland opposite which came under British rule were Kowloon, acquired in 1860 along with Stonecutters Island, and the area called the New Territories, leased for ninety-nine years in 1898. Kowloon is about a tenth of the island in size, which is in turn a tenth of the New Territories. Hong Kong lies in the typhoon zone. It has a monsoon climate, subject to great heat and humidity in summer, and during the last century fever epidemics were frequent and lethal. The bare hills show the effects of prolonged soil erosion, and land that can be cultivated is found only in small valleys and crannies. For the British, Hong Kong's attraction lay in its harbour, and it was there that its activities were centred.

Archaeologists have discovered little evidence of early settlers, though Hong Kong's location at the mouth of the Pearl River suggests that they would have been fishermen. There is a theory that migrants from Canton known as Puntis, and Hakkas or 'guest people', occupied the island in the fifteenth century. Near the end of the Ming dynasty another group, the fierce Hoklos who were notorious for piracy, made use of the anchorage. Ming troops were driven to Hong Kong when their dynasty was overthrown by the Ch'ing dynasty of the Manchus, but as G.B. Endacott concludes, the area had little part in the main stream of Chinese chronology and its history really begins with the coming of the British in 1841.[1]

The earliest Europeans to trade with China had been the Portuguese, who settled at Macao in 1557, to be followed by Spaniards, Dutch, and English, as well as French merchants. The first British ship to establish successful commercial contacts was the *Macclesfield*, which put in at Canton in 1699. In the eighteenth century the British became more prominent, exporting goods from India and purchasing tea, which had become an addiction at home. The East India Company had a trading monopoly, and, for the Chinese, Canton obtained restrictive rights on western trade in 1757. Conditions for Europeans at Canton, as will become apparent, were never satisfactory. In 1833 the East India Company's monopoly was abolished and the following year the British Government sent out Lord Napier to fill the new post of Superintendent of Trade. Napier tried to establish better relations with the Cantonese authorities, but was severely snubbed.

British merchants with factories at Canton then enlisted some support at home. In December 1834 they petitioned the Government, itemizing their grievances and asking for the despatch of a Plenipotentiary supported by a force sufficient to teach the Chinese a lesson. In this limbo-like situation the advantages of securing an island off the Chinese coast attracted more interest. Captain Henry Ellis, who accompanied Lord Amherst's failed embassy to China in 1816, was impressed by the 'picturesque nature of the watering place' when their ship anchored briefly offshore.[2] Napier thought it would be desirable to occupy the island, and the arguments in favour of this course, both commercial and strategic, became more vocal. Trading at Canton was always going to be precarious and it would be much better to establish an outpost under direct British control. If, as seemed most likely, the Chinese would not liberalize trade until they were forced to do so, the prospect of naval action appeared on the horizon, and the navy would be much happier with their own island base. Lastly, there was the long-term view that a British-owned trading station, where law and order could be guaranteed, would rapidly develop as a commercial centre for import and export, for collection and distribution. Pottinger, with the precedent of Bombay in mind, was firmly of this opinion from the first time he landed on the island.

From 1834 onwards friction with the Chinese at Canton got steadily worse: there was a gradual drift into open hostilities, the basic cause being the traffic in opium. Most of it came from India, whence sales formed an important source of Government revenue. In 1800 the Chinese, after various decrees against the drug, completely banned imports, but in the absence of any machinery for enforcement, the prohibition was ineffective. Lintin Island in the Pearl River was the main clearing-house. As the volume of smuggling continued to grow, the effect on the Chinese economy was drastic. The British paid in silver for the Chinese commodities of tea and silk, but these payments were immediately reversed by the Chinese payment for opium, supplied by the British.

On opium, Westminster adopted a 'Pontius Pilate' posture. It was for the Chinese to see that their ban was carried out: there was nothing in British law to prevent trading in opium, and there was no obligation to assist the Imperial Court which had humiliated the Superintendent of Trade. The

British would not protect shippers who were caught carrying the illegal substance, but, on the other hand, they would not interfere. (Pottinger later urged the Chinese, without success, to make the traffic legal, so that it could be controlled.) In England there was some moral distaste for dealing in opium – this was the Reform Age which saw the abolition of slavery – but indignation was modified by reports of the outrages which Christian missions to China had suffered.

At Canton, the arrival of a new Imperial Commissioner bearing a mandate to suppress the opium trade did not improve relations with the merchants. On 18 March 1839 he demanded the surrender of all opium stocks, impounded the Europeans in their factories, and insisted on hostages. This was an affront, made worse when 20,000 chests of opium were handed over. Captain Charles Elliot, the Superintendent, brought the British contingent back to Macao and appealed to London for military assistance. Elliot and his cousin Rear-Admiral George Elliot were appointed Plenipotentiaries and put in charge of an expedition with orders to occupy the islands of Chusan and sail to the mouth of the Peiho. There they were to present British demands for restitution to be transmitted to the Emperor. Elliot reached the Peiho, but agreed to continue discussions at Canton, though they soon broke down. Elliot, who was no wizard at negotiation, seized the Bogue forts and prematurely announced a 'Convention' which would ransom the opium seized – and cede Hong Kong. The Chinese disavowed the convention and hostilities were resumed on the Pearl River. The Imperial Commissioner, now fearing the fall of Canton, asked for a truce and offered an inadequate payment for the opium. As a result Palmerston, thoroughly dissatisfied, recalled Elliot.

It was Henry Pottinger who was sent out to replace him and to bring the war to a conclusion. The fracas at Canton had been the main, and immediate, *casus belli*, but Palmerston was also incensed that the Chinese, occlusively self-sufficient, refused to treat with the British on anything approaching equal terms. Pottinger was expected to make progress on this matter. He was to obtain consent to the opening up of 'four or five principal towns', i.e. ports, to British trade. Alternatively, Hong Kong, or an island 'better adapted' should be ceded. Palmerston was not impressed by the potential of Hong Kong as an entrepôt, and did not believe that the Emperor would agree to give it up. Pottinger's instructions on Hong Kong were usually ambivalent and often contradictory, but he was always determined to retain it.

No oriental whirlwind could have been quicker than the new Plenipotentiary when he arrived at Macao; he made a hurried inspection of Hong Kong and set sail for the north. With his two commanders – Admiral Parker and General Gough – Pottinger pursued the campaign most vigorously. Chinese fortresses fell in quick succession before Ningpo was occupied as winter quarters. In October, Pottinger went back to Hong Kong to supervise activities there, and when he rejoined the expedition in June, nothing had changed his mind about the desirability of the island as a permanent base.

In a series of spectacular amphibious operations the British seized Chinkiang, blockaded the Grand Canal, and in August anchored off Nanking. (In the 1980s the same hazards of a long sea voyage, fragile communications, and uncertainty about the terrain and the enemy strength, were met by the British expedition which embarked on the journey to the Falklands in order to face the Argentine invaders.) The Chinese, looking down the muzzles of the British men-of-war, capitulated and agreed to Pottinger's terms – which included the cession of Hong Kong. The home Government accepted the *fait accompli* and made him the island's first Governor.

Pottinger created the structure of Hong Kong's administration. During his tenure he had more trouble with European merchants who wanted a free-for-all to trade at large, and with pinpricks from Whitehall, than from the Chinese themselves. If he did not increase 'the public stock of harmless pleasure', he stuck to the articles of the Nanking Treaty and got on remarkably well with the Imperial Commissioner at Canton. In England, Parliament acclaimed him and he was greeted as a hero, especially by those who saw a limitless market in the Far East. Exotic goods such as pianos from London and cutlery from Sheffield were shipped out to China, though an economy drained by the purchase of opium had little surplus cash. The cadre which Pottinger had left at Hong Kong grew in numbers and authority, but he was soon on his way to another warlike assignment.

Under the agreement reached at Nanking, the British have ruled at Hong Kong for the last 150 years; the wider effects of this Treaty are more difficult to evaluate. In 1842 the Chinese admitted, however reluctantly, that there were nations outside their Empire with whom they would have to treat. Their negotiators, seeing the presence of the formidable British force which controlled the Yangtse before the walls of the city, and the impressive demeanour of the Plenipotentiary, were compelled to accept the demands presented by Pottinger. Outside Nanking, however, there was little evidence of Imperial defeat to Chinese eyes. The élite Tartar garrisons had been crushed, but this was not widely known throughout the country. Though the Manchu officials who parleyed with Pottinger were realistic, their peers remained implacably hostile. Canton, where the trouble started, had not been pillaged. The Empire, exemplifying the oriental tendency not to regard any decision as final, still claimed a heaven-born right to override the restrictions of unjust treaties.

Since 1842, Hong Kong has changed both physically, in the mass of construction that covers its face, and in the attitude of its inhabitants. Even in today's post-colonial atmosphere, however, it is still possible to see that it was never like other colonies. As Lord Stanley, the Secretary of State, emphasized, it was founded 'not with a view to colonization, but for diplomatic, commercial, and military purposes'. Its unique nature was also reflected in the wide powers conferred on the first Governor. Pottinger was told that 'methods of proceeding unknown in other British colonies must be followed in Hong Kong'.[3] Applying a British system of government to an overwhelmingly Chinese population was in itself a novel feature. Hong Kong was not a colony in the sense of attracting regular migration by British settlers who would make their homes there. The Europeans were nomadic, remaining only for the financial rewards. If Hong Kong did not attain the dominant commercial position in the Far East that had been expected – particularly with the unforeseen growth of Shanghai – it was soon the headquarters of the leading firms to emerge from those that had operated the original Canton 'factories', and it has, of course, become an international financial centre. The credit for acquiring the island for the Crown, and for the structure of its administration, belongs to the first Governor, Sir Henry Pottinger, whose career will now be examined.

CHAPTER ONE

Three Pelicans in their Piety

In the days before the advent of the 'competition wallahs' fresh from their rigorous examination, the Honourable East India Company had a very random recruitment policy for service in India. Prospective cadets had first to obtain a nomination from someone with influence at the Company's headquarters in Leadenhall Street. They might attend the seminary for civilian officers at the East India College opened in Hertford Castle in 1806 and moved to Haileybury in 1809. They might be included among the Company's nominees (usually ten) to the Royal Military Academy; after 1809 they could attend the new establishment for Indian officers at Addiscombe – the 'great nursery of Indian captains' – where, according to Sir John Kaye, they would absorb the 'moral odour of Indian heroism'.[1] Others might even be commissioned direct into one of the Company regiments when they went out from England. Although the hierarchy was rigid and precise in the higher echelons, the arrangements for entering John Company's service were surprisingly flexible.

One feature that emerged from this haphazard admission system was the presence in India of whole families devoted to the interests of the Company – the Lawrences, the Conollys, the Broadfoots and the Pottingers, to say nothing of other related groups. The Lawrences, George, Henry and John, all had celebrated careers. The First Afghan War, however, took a heavy toll on the rest. The Conolly family lost three sons – Edward killed in the Kohistan, Arthur executed at Bokhara, and John who died in captivity at Kabul. It was no different for the Broadfoots. One fell at the battle of Purwundurrah in 1840; a second was killed a year later in the attack on the Kabul Residency; and George, who had performed heroically in the defence of Jalalabad, was a casualty at Ferozeshah in the Sikh War. Among the Pottingers, seven of whom served over two generations in India, Tom, a subaltern in the 54th Native Indian Regiment, died on the retreat from Kabul, and Henry's favourite nephew Eldred – of whom more will be heard – endured extraordinary hardships but did not long outlast the Afghan War. Henry Pottinger, the subject of this book, was lucky to be engaged only in the early, speciously successful, stages of this disastrous campaign, but he had already shown himself to have one of the essential gifts for proconsular advancement; he was a survivor.

The fifth son of Eldred-Curwen Pottinger and his wife Anne, the daughter of Robert Gordon, a minor landowner of Florida Manor, Co. Down, Henry Pottinger was born on Christmas Day 1789 at Mountpottinger, also in the county.

The origins of the Pottingers are, like those of many families claiming ancient tribal connections, lost in the fog of war and the mists of time, and have been described as being, at best, crepuscular. An article in the *Philadelphia Inquirer* of 1897, which attempted to trace the history of the Pottingers who crossed the Atlantic, boldly asserts that they show 'direct descent from Egbert, the first Saxon King of England, and the grandfather of Alfred the Great'. No trace of this royal connection has been found in contemporary Anglo-Saxon manuscripts, and the Philadelphia claim must be regarded as an exuberant *fantasia*. More certainly, the Ulster branch have on their coat of arms the device of 'Three Pelicans in their Piety', later matriculated by Henry in his own right. This is the same as that adopted by the early Orkney Pottingers, which is still visible on a tombstone (1632) in St Magnus Cathedral, Kirkwall. Both sides may have shared a Norse ancestry, a view supported by the derivation from the Norse 'potting jar', or apothecary.

English Pottingers settled in Berkshire and at the Hoo, Hertfordshire. Suggestions that their residence there dates from the Norman Conquest can safely be discounted, but their name appears among Members of Parliament for Reading during the seventeenth century. Warrior heroes, of course, have to be identified in the gallery. The most notable fell by the side of his patron and relative by marriage Richard Neville, Earl of Warwick, at the battle of Barnet in 1471. Family legend has it that Pottinger commanded a chosen body of horse and met his end leading a last desperate charge. However that may be, Edward IV's army disposed of both King-maker Warwick and his aide on the battlefield.

The connection with Ulster is first exemplified by a Pottinger grave in Belfast, which is credibly dated 1602. These Belfast Pottingers were merchants and a narrow alley still called 'Pottinger's Entry' was their place of business. One of them, not satisfied with a mercantile existence, made a name for himself as a mercenary leading a troop in the wars of the north of Ireland during Elizabeth's reign. Thomas, his descendant, was the first Sovereign (i.e. Mayor) of Belfast and is named in the city's grant of a corporate charter in 1613. By this time the Pottingers were prospering and the evidence is better documented.

His first son, Edward was a captain in the Navy and did his loyal duty when he conveyed King William to Ireland. Sadly, sailing the next day to intercept a French flotilla carrying supplies for James II, he was drowned when his man-of-war, the *Dartmouth*, sank with all hands on the night of 8 October 1690.

His second son, also called Thomas, was likewise Sovereign of Belfast and High Sheriff of the County. After King William landed in that part of Ireland Thomas sold part of his estate to raise money for his monarch; Protestant loyalty exacted a price. By his marriage to Miss Eccles of Feintonah he had an elder son Joseph, also in the Navy. Joseph married Mary, daughter of Lady Mary Dunlop who was the sister of the sixth Earl of Dundonald and thus related to the second Marquis of Montrose. (A slight tincture of blue blood was thus injected.) Joseph's son, Thomas was the first to be grand enough to affect the territorial designation of 'Mountpottinger' after his name. He married Frances, daughter of Edward Curwen of Sella Park and Workington Hall, Cumberland, who served as MP for Cockermouth from 1738 to 1741. The first child of this marriage was the Edward-Curwen Pottinger already identified as the father of Henry, the future Governor of Hong Kong. Edward-Curwen had a distinctly radical strain in his makeup. During the wave of patriotic fervour in 1779 he formed the 'Mountpottinger Volunteers' and was in the chair when the company, having resolved to pledge their 'might in arms against the foreign invader', added a significant rider.

> We do not fear to speak of political liberty for the people of Ireland as voluntary soldiers of this nation. We believe that Ireland should be a nation, independent and free, without impolitic restrictions on our commerce under which we groan.

A writer to the Irish News has identified this as one of the first Volunteer resolutions to speak of Ireland as a nation and call for political reform.[2] Throughout his life Edward-Curwen remained a reformer, and he was secretary of the freeholders' meeting at Ballynahinch in 1797 which called for 'a full, fair and adequate representation of the people of Ireland in Parliament, without regard to differences of religious opinions'. His son Henry never took part in Irish politics. In his various proconsular offices he was seen as a doer, a man for a crisis, rather than a thinker, but he retained something of his father's sense of what was fair, as in his protest against the British annexation of Sind. Unlike Edward-Curwen, despite his intractable reputation, he came to realize that he could do more by manipulation than by confronting his masters.

To round up this sketch of Henry's ancestry, a martial aspect can be detected from his mother. She was related to the old warhorse Major-General Sir Robert Rollo Gillespie who fought in the West Indies and in India before being killed during the attack on Kalunga, Nepal, in 1812.[3]

In 1672 the Pottingers, their finances being now in better shape, acquired land at Ballymacarrett, together with the Lagan ferry and the fishery rights, from the Claneboye family for the sum of £300, with an annual rent of £30.[4] There, on a site bounded by the Connswater and Lagan rivers, they erected the mansion known as 'Mountpottinger'. Some erosion of their fortunes is evident, however, when, in 1750, the *Belfast News-Letter* offered the dwelling-house at Mountpottinger to let 'with office-houses and a very good garden, all in excellent order'. The notice added that 'some very good hay and potatoes, a very good chair mare, and two good milch cows' were for sale.[5] In 1782 all the land at Ballymacarrett, except for the house and sixty-five acres, was sold to Barry Yelverton, later Viscount Avonmore.[6] The house was sold in 1811 coming into the possession of Francis Ritchie, a building contractor, and was later destroyed. The area deteriorated to become one of the less salubrious parts of Belfast, but the name Mountpottinger survived as a constituency in the old Stormont Parliament.

The original family burial place, situated in Belfast since the seventeenth century, was eventually moved to Kilmore, near Crossgar in County Down. The inscription indicates that the removal to Kilmore, occasioned by the demolition of part of the original tomb in St George's during rebuilding, had been 'out of respect to the memory of Charlotte Pottinger, whose remains are in an adjoining grave'. Charlotte, who died in 1813, was the much-loved first wife of Henry's brother, Thomas, and the mother of his nephew, Eldred.

There was no patrimony large enough to keep the whole tribe of Pottinger in its native Ireland. It had to seek further fields and five of Eldred-Curwen's sons, including Henry, were shipped out to India, there to make their careers – and often to end their lives. Robert, a Lieutenant in the Bombay Army of the East India Company, died on 15 November 1807, and Edward-Curwen, also in the Company's service, outlived him by barely a month. Charles James Fox, a subaltern in the Bombay Native Infantry, was killed in action in 1834, and only William, who did his full regimental stint in India and at Aden, enjoyed the plenitude of retirement in Ireland.

Henry's relations with his family were generally amicable but he did not get on with his eldest brother, the feckless Thomas. A casual, irresponsible way of looking after his affairs was the hallmark of Thomas Pottinger's way of life. After quickly dissipating his second wife's dowry, he thought of trying to recoup his finances in India, where two of his sons were already making their way, but the young Pottingers gave him no encouragement. Tom, in Delhi with his regiment, was horrified. He wrote to Eldred in some alarm that their father had a wild scheme for coming to Bombay

> as an agent for the Asphalt Association, which is some damned speculation for covering roads with Asphalt, etc. . . . It is a most extraordinary thing that a man of such splendid talent and excellent sense should be so easily gulled by every fool or knave he comes across.[7]

Tom intended to advise his father not to touch this kind of enterprise, but doubted if he would heed a warning. Eldred was just as emphatic when he wrote to his father on 3 December 1840.

> I cannot see any advantages in your coming out to this country, even in a high situation, but to do so in a mercantile situation will, I must honestly confess, grieve me much . . . and, as you have so often already done, I have not the least doubt you will throw up your appointment.

The letter ends with his 'petition that you will leave the pushing on in the world to your children and will yourself sit down quietly'.[8]

Thomas had also, much to Eldred's annoyance, tried to touch his brother Henry for an advance. Henry would have none of it, and, as he told Eldred, 'On one point I must warn you. That is not to advance a rupee to your father, or any of your relations. To him it will do no good.'[9]

Henry's niece Anne, who went out to India in 1839, was clearly aware of the domestic tension when she wrote to her mother from Bhooj in Sind.

> I do hope that Papa will not ask Uncle Henry to do anything to serve him, for I know that my Uncle has gone home with the idea that all his relations have only written to him and pretended to be friends in the hope of getting from him . . .[10]

Thomas reluctantly stayed at home. This correspondence is quoted, not to depict him as a spendthrift nor to stigmatize Henry as a skinflint, but to note that, for all their careful husbandry, there was a tendency towards improvidence in the Pottingers which was to emerge in notorious form in Henry's own son.

With his nephews, particularly Eldred, Henry was always at ease. Neither of them was outgoing, and it seems that they shared the same taciturnity, that impassive demeanour which Henry Lawrence saw in Eldred – after he had been acclaimed as the Hero of Herat for his exploits – noting that 'You might have sat for weeks beside him at table and never discovered that he had seen a shot fired'. Sir John Kaye records a more youthful episode in Eldred's career, when, still a subaltern, he was posted to be his uncle's assistant at Cutch.

> One day Eldred appeared before his uncle in a great state of excitement, declaring he had been grossly insulted by a native – a horsekeeper, or some other inferior person – on which Henry Pottinger, amused by his young relative's earnestness, said, smilingly "So, I suppose you killed him, Eldred?" "No" replied the young subaltern, "but I will, uncle." Thinking that this was an instruction from higher authority, he was quite earnest in his declaration. It need not be added that the joke exploded, and that the retributive hand was restrained.[11]

Henry's education was no more than rudimentary, though judging from his later despatches he received a good grounding. He was, like his brothers, entered at Belfast Academy, then ruled by the highly esteemed Dr Bruce. Henry was not an exceptional scholar, but he has an honoured place among the academy's Old Boys who earned distinction in wider fields. At first he was keen to follow some of his ancestors into the Navy, and in 1801 he completed a short voyage as a very young midshipman. (His young brother, John, died in 1807, while still a midshipman.) In 1803 he took leave of his family and embarked for India.

On arrival at Bombay, Henry had reached a domain for which no amount of briefing, or sailors' tales, could have prepared him. He was entering a kingdom within a kingdom. In John Company's territory, the Presidency of Bombay had never been happy that, since the Regulating Act of 1773 was passed, it, like the other Presidency of Madras, had been brought within the ambit of the Governor of Bengal in his new, additional, role as Governor-General of India. This was a situation which, on the face of it, was bound to provoke animosity, but the Governor of Bombay and his advisers had found various oriental ways of going about their business without paying too much heed to Calcutta. The constitution of the Government of India is outside the scope of this book, as is the relationship between the Company and the native population, more distant since the memsahibs had been fetched out to join their spouses, and since the Christianizing activities of the missionaries became more insistent. What cannot be ignored, however, is the effect of the climate. As the melancholy evidence of crowded graveyards demonstrates, cholera, dysentery, and chronic hepatitis found many victims. Summer temperatures were higher than a European could imagine, worse in Sind than anywhere else in India, and heat stroke could fell the Englishman without warning.

Despite the frequent thinning of their ranks, the Company officers went merrily on their way, impervious to the fragile nature of their authority, which was not regarded as an issue in the early 1800s. Native forces, had they combined, could at any time have expelled John Company, but rivalries among princes, the hard struggle to win a living from the land, a fatalist religion, and a generally debilitating atmosphere, resulted in acceptance of, or at least acquiescence in, British rule.

Life in the outposts might have its hazards, but in Bombay, with no telegraph to annoy by transmitting daily orders from the central government, the British were absorbed in creating their own oasis, with an ambience in imitation of a remotely remembered home country. It would be some time before young Pottinger became aware of these social preoccupations. He might have noted the peculiar swagger of the clerks who had come down to the quayside to meet the ship but was just as likely to observe the motes of dust which sparkled in the sunshine and seemed to swarm like the flies that would soon irritate him.

Thanks to the good offices of his fellow-Ulsterman Lord Castlereagh, Henry had been intended for the Naval service. Soon after he disembarked, however, friends to whom he had an introduction decided he was really a landlubber, and an application was sent home asking his sponsor to transfer his posting to the East India Company's army. (Castlereagh could be appealed to as a former Member for County Down in the Irish Parliament. More to the point, he had been President of the Board of Control, and a nod from him would be sufficient at Leadenhall Street.) This was the only occasion in his career when Henry benefited from patronage.

Meanwhile he was enrolled at the Company's college in Bombay where native languages were taught. Either because he worked exceptionally hard, or because he had a natural linguistic gift, he rapidly became proficient enough to be employed as an assistant teacher. Confirmation of his cadetship came from London in 1805, and on 18 September 1806 he was made an ensign. The commission signed by Governor Duncan promoting 'Henry Pottinger, Gentleman, to be a Lieutenant of Infantry under the Presidency of Bombay' was dated to take effect from 16 July 1809.[12]

CHAPTER TWO

Sind Ho!

The bare land of Sind, where Henry Pottinger was first put through his paces in the East India Company's service, extends to Shikarpore and Bahawulpore on the north. To the east lies the Indian desert, while the mountains and hills of Baluchistan offer a barrier to the west. Cutch to the south-east and the sea to the south complete the perimeter. The main geographical feature is the river Indus, which divides the country into two. There is a surface resemblance between Sind and Egypt. Each consists of a smooth and fertile plain bounded on one side by mountains and on the other by the wasteland of a desert, and each is bifurcated by a large river which takes the form of a delta as it flows near to the sea. Throughout the last century the fate of the inhabitants of both countries was much the same – a submissive people was ruled by a barbarous tribe which submitted reluctantly to a distant monarch, in the case of Sind the King of Afghanistan. Egypt benefited from trade with Europe but Sind, because of its isolation, did not share in much commercial activity.

The rich lands on the Indus were allowed to remain sterile, and as Mountstuart Elphinstone noted,

> The evils of this neglect of agriculture are heightened by the barbarous luxury of the chiefs, who appropriate vast tracts of the land best fitted for tillage to maintain those wild beasts and birds which afford them the pleasures of the chase.[1]

British policy towards Sind tended to veer in reaction to events, real or imagined, outside India. It had not always been so. The East India Company had operated factories (really trading stations) in Sind from 1635 to 1662 and again from 1758 to 1775, when they were closed down because of tribal warfare and a decline in textile manufacture. But after the India Act of 1784 brought the Company under the direct control of the Crown, British relations with Sind became an integral part of the foreign policy jigsaw.

From 1784 onwards there were fears in both London and Calcutta that a rival power – the French and later the Russians – would swoop down on Hindustan, and history testified to Sind's popularity as an invasion route. Alexander the Great had traversed Sind; Mahmoud of Ghuznee captured it in 1026; and Akbar added it to the Moghul empire in 1529. In the same century, the Baluchi came from the west to establish themselves as rulers. In 1783 a Baluchi tribe, the Talpurs, assumed control and it was with them that the British had their tortuous dealings. Mir Fatehali Khan ruled lower Sind from the capital, Hyderabad, along with his three brothers – an unusual example of fraternal amity. A cousin, Mir Sohrab Khan, founded his own dynasty in Upper Sind at Khairpur, while another Talpur, Mir Tharo, ruled Mirpur in the south-east of the territory.

The supposed threat of a French incursion was most acute in the last years of the eighteenth century, though the sheer geographic and logistic problems that would face an expeditionary force were almost completely discounted. Sind was strategically significant. It was vulnerable not only to the French – if they were ever to appear – but also to the intrigues of the Marathas. To add to the witches' brew, Zemaun Shah, the Afghan ruler, was pondering an invasion through Sind, which had nominally recognized Afghan overlordship since 1757. (The Sind Amirs, though ruling in the name of the King of Kabul, owed their power to force rather than to the favour of the Afghan dynasty. They were 'heartily disaffected' with the Afghans and always tried to defer or withhold the annual tribute.)[2] It was time to test current rumours, and in 1799 Jonathan Duncan, the Governor of Bombay, prompted by Governor-General Wellesley, sent a mission to Hyderabad with the aim of restoring friendly relations.[3] Mir Fatehali Khan was favourably disposed, not from affection for the British but because he wanted their help against a rival from the Kalhora tribe and against his Afghan overlord. In these and later negotiations, the Sind Amirs seldom failed to stipulate military aid, or a guarantee, as a prerequisite to a commercial agreement.

Wellesley now ordered Duncan to set up a factory in Sind 'not so much with a view to commercial as to political advantages',[4] the real objective being to keep a vigilant eye on the behaviour of Zemaun Shah. Minor concessions might be offered, but there was to be no military commitment.

Nathan Crow, despatched to Hyderabad in the spring of 1800, had to disarm the Amirs' suspicions that the British had designs on annexing Sind. (This was another permanent feature of parleys with them.) He was eloquent enough to obtain rights for the Company at Karachi and Tatta, and he wrote enthusiastically to Duncan that the Amirs' suspicions had been allayed,[5] itemizing the benefits of a foothold in Sind. It would strengthen the British hand against any hostile action by Zemaun Shah; it would keep out the French, or the Marathas; and, almost prophetically, it would be a good base for espionage in Afghanistan. Only as an afterthought at the end of the letter did he mention commercial matters.

Crow had been too optimistic. Fatehali's brothers urged him to get rid of the British, and on 28 October 1800 he ordered Crow and all the company's men to quit Sind at once. So ended the first British bout with the Amirs. These events were the backcloth to Henry Pottinger's later arrival on the Anglo-Sindian stage.

The collapse in Europe of the short-lived Peace of Amiens in 1803 renewed fears in India about the French menace. Lord Minto,[6] Governor-General since 1807, had no appetite for further British acquisitions, but he began once more to think of Sind as a buffer. He stated in the jargon of the time that:

> I do not allude at present to any expedition or any actual invasion of the British territories in India by a French army; but many considerations denote conclusively to the extension of the enemy's views to this country.[7]

There were also doubts regarding French diplomacy in Persia. At the turn of the century Captain John Malcolm was sent to Teheran to obtain (i.e. to purchase by bribes) a concordat with the Persians. In November 1800, Malcolm's largesse secured a treaty providing for mutual cooperation and prohibiting all Frenchmen from residence in Persia. The embargo on the French was ineffective. The Persians soon saw that the Russians were the real menace and, failing to enlist British support, they applied to Napoleon. The French General Gardenne appeared in Teheran, and alarm was compounded in July 1807 when Napoleon met Tsar Alexander on the celebrated raft on the River Nieman and signed the Treaty of Tilsit. Under the, temporarily secret, clauses Alexander was committed to war against England. Although India was not mentioned, official circles in Calcutta believed that an invasion was imminent.

In March 1808, the Governor-General was instructed to prepare to resist any hostile army attempting to cross the Indus, and to cultivate 'the favourable opinion and cooperation' of neighbouring states.[8] Malcolm was ordered back to Teheran but returned without having reached the Persian Court, and Minto was furious to learn that London had also sent its own emissary, Harford Jones, from Baghdad to Teheran. Luckily, the Persians were now disenchanted with the French, and the choleric Jones secured his treaty on 12 March 1809.[9] In short, British diplomacy in Persia, ignoring the ludicrous aspect of two emissaries simultaneously making overtures, had won a Pyrrhic victory at the expense of disregarding the Governor-General. But what of Sind?

Agents from Sind were reported to have reached Teheran, and a French mission was expected in Hyderabad. Minto felt that the sooner a British presence was established in Sind, the better, and Duncan in Bombay chose Captain David Seton, the Resident at Muscat, to lead the next, and, as it proved, unhappy, mission to the Amirs. (Pottinger was to go on the subsequent mission.)

Seton left Bombay in April 1808 with a strong escort but, lingering for six weeks at Mandavi in Cutch, he was beaten to Hyderabad by the French emissary who offered all kinds of wonderful things in return for the use of Sind ports. Seton had to outbid him. The Amirs now proposed a treaty highly favourable to them in return for allowing factories to be opened at Tatta and Hyderabad. Seton, thinking he would not get better terms, agreed to a treaty which included mutual assistance clauses. Minto, and Duncan at Bombay, were dismayed at the promise of military aid, but how could this be revoked without losing face? Minto resorted to a devious expedient; the Amirs were to be told that Seton was only the agent of the Bombay Presidency, that the treaty had not been confirmed by the Governor-General, and that Minto was now sending his own envoy to Sind. Raising the status of the emissary would appeal to the Amirs' sense of their own importance, and Minto's letter assured them that permanent friendship would be established 'by removing the veil of intermediate authority and opening a direct communication between the Supreme Government and the State of Scind'.[10] No one worried that Seton had been dropped in the Indus mud.

Nicholas Hankey Smith was to be fetched from his post at Bushire to be the Governor-General's representative, to be accompanied by a civil servant, Henry Ellis, and by Lieutenants Robert Taylor and Henry Pottinger from the Bombay Native Infantry. Captain Charles Christie, from the same regiment, was in charge of the escort. The complement was made up by William Hall, a surgeon, and Captain William Maxfield of the Bombay Marines as surveyor. Smith's orders, sent to him on 28 November 1808, required him to come to an agreement with the Amirs which would supersede Seton's treaty. There was to be no commitment to military aid against Afghanistan, to whom a friendly mission was being sent. The Sind territory should be surveyed as far as practicable. A detailed survey of the navigational possibilities of the Indus was already, and was to remain, a primary British objective.

Pottinger included a lively account of the mission's progress in the journal of his later personal exploration, published in 1816 as *Travels in Beloochistan and Sinde.*

Smith and his team embarked on the *Maria* at Bombay on 2 April 1809, and, escorted by the Company's cruiser *Prince of Wales*, reached Karachi on 9 May. It was a week before they obtained permission to land, and even then they were forbidden to approach the Manora Fort. As always, Sind officials were pathologically suspicious of the British. Had the *feringhees* not come to spy out the land for an invading force? As specious arguments continued, Smith, seeing that he had made no progress, decided to re-embark 'all the valuable part of the public property', i.e. the stores and gifts he had brought from Bombay.[11] This was partly bluff. The Amirs sent an arrogant reply to his representations after which he took a chance and broke camp. Pottinger observed that the price of horses had mysteriously risen overnight as the Sindees saw demand exceeding supply.

Smith reached Tatta, once the capital of Sind but now largely in ruins, on 16 June. (All British missions passing through Tatta greatly enjoyed the partridge shooting.) The Amirs tried to restrict Smith's movements by sending a boat to convey him to Hyderabad. Luckily it was too small for the whole party, which split into two in order to carry out a double reconnaissance. Pottinger, Ellis and Maxfield travelled on board, Smith and the remainder by land. On arrival at Hyderabad they encamped on the river bank till they had settled the dispute over whether the Amirs' messengers were of the right rank to receive the Envoy. Recognition of status was vital to the success of the mission, and Smith was very clear about the procedure he thought should be followed when he and his staff approached the Amirs before the *Musnud*. Pottinger noted that it was essential that all pretences about protocol should be crushed 'by the most explicit and immoveable measures'.[12] Otherwise, 'litigious etiquette' as he put it, would be interminable and cramp all negotiations. It is relevant that in all diplomatic exchanges throughout his career Pottinger was not a believer in 'the soft answer that turneth away wrath'.

Eventually the British party was received by the Amirs, richly dressed 'corpulent middle-sized men' who, as Smith had insisted, stood on his arrival. The half-hour durbar was taken up, as custom required, with flowery greetings and replies. Then the British were nearly overwhelmed by a throng of attendants and matchlockmen crowding round them. This, Pottinger suspected, was done by design to intimidate them.[13] The next day presents of pistols, mirrors and all the usual paraphernalia were handed over, but the Amirs' men threatened to return some chintzes which did not seem sufficiently costly. Smith said they were not just gifts but specimens of English manufacture, and offered to take the whole lot back. He knew that the Amirs' avarice would not let him do this and that they would accept, which proved true. The British were given some horses and oriental trifles in exchange.

According to Pottinger the principal objectives of the mission – the annulment of Seton's treaty, the Amirs' undertaking not to 'allow the establishment of the tribe of the French in Sind', and the re-establishment of the relative ranks of the two governments – had all been achieved.[14] But that is an over-simplified, young man's judgment. In fact, it had been more difficult. In Smith's words, the Amirs were 'capricious and ignorant' and wanted 'some advantage of equal value and importance' before they would admit a Company factory.[15] Ghulamali Khan, the senior Amir, was being urged by the Maharaja of Jodhpur and Bahawal Khan to expel the British officers who were nothing more than spies. The Amirs were showing signs of yielding to this argument when Smith, keeping his nerve, asked leave to depart from Hyderabad.

Ghulamali was shrewd enough not to push his luck too far and suddenly became more amenable. He would write to the Governor-General; he would not accept French overtures, and meanwhile there could be an annual exchange of missions, with an Indian representing British interests in Hyderabad. Smith knew he would get no more, and a treaty was signed; he had at least kept the French out.[16] The Amirs, for their part, went back to their feudal isolation, slaughtering game and oppressing their subjects. The mission left Hyderabad on 25 August and made for the port of Mandavi where the Company ships *Benares* and *Teignmouth* were waiting to take Smith and his colleagues back to Bombay.

Pottinger had obtained some insight into the pattern of negotiations with the Amirs – a form that often recurred later in his career. His first verdict on the Sind tribesmen was that they were 'avaricious, full of deceit, cruel, ungrateful and strangers to veracity'.[17] In extenuation they had grown up under a government of capricious Amirs, unequalled for extortion and tyranny. Their qualities were entirely physical, making them good mercenary soldiers. He adds wistfully that their dancing girls were distinguished by loveliness of face and symmetry of figure. Mountstuart Elphinstone, who had doubtless talked to Pottinger as his assistant at Poona, and whose help Pottinger acknowledges in a footnote to his book, takes a similar, but utterly unromantic, view of the inhabitants of Sind.

> There is little to praise in their character, which is debased and degraded by the oppression of their government. The only thing that struck me in the Sindees with whom I have conversed is their deficiency of intelligence. Those who know them well, however, add that they have all the vices of an enslaved people. The chiefs appear to be barbarians of the rudest stamp, without any of the barbarous virtues.[18]

This may have been so, but the Amirs were to prove obstinately intractable and caused mounting irritation to successive Governors-General over the next three decades.

CHAPTER THREE

Baluchistan

Soon after returning to Bombay Henry Pottinger took off on another, more dangerous, anabasis with his friend Charles Christie. Mountstuart Elphinstone describes their remit. They were

> to explore the Baluchi country and the east of Persia, tracts at that time wholly unknown to Europeans. They performed this enterprising and important journey with complete success, and joined Sir John Malcolm at Maraugha, almost on the borders of the Ottoman empire. The hardships, fatigues, and adventures of such an undertaking, may well be imagined.[1]

Malcolm had originally intended to make a detailed study of the terrain between India and Teheran, particularly the route that might be taken by an invading army. When his embassy to the Shah's court, which would have provided a pretext, was postponed, Pottinger and Christie volunteered to explore the territory by themselves.

The practice of sending young officers, either alone or with a minimal escort, to reconnoître vast areas of unmapped, often hostile, territory is a recurring feature in the annals of the East India Company. If today this seems an amateur, John Buchan-like way of proceeding, there were good reasons for it at the time. First, the Governor-General and his advisers at Calcutta knew very little about the geography, politics, or the rulers of much of south-east Asia, and they had a pressing interest in those countries that lay nearest to the boundaries of Hindustan. Exploration, espionage if need be, was required. The second restraint arose from the Company's shortage of manpower and financial resources to mount elaborate expeditions, which would probably have been denied admission to the domains of suspicious khans and amirs. Finally, in the army cantonments or in the entourage of the residencies, young men who were anxious to escape from the boredom of routine and seize a chance to make their mark could always be found.

Among the most memorable of these journeys were those undertaken by

William Moorcroft, a veterinary surgeon to the Bengal Army, who examined the sources of the Sutlej and the Indus, explored Lahore and Cashmere, and later visited Bokhara in 1825, before dying in mysterious circumstances at Balkh. The much-travelled Alexander Burnes, who served some time as Pottinger's assistant at Cutch, undertook three expeditions up the Indus, though only one of them came within the solitary, unofficial category. Eldred Pottinger, Henry's nephew, ended his journey in most spectacular fashion by directing the defence of Herat against the Persian army. Meanwhile, Henry Pottinger and Charles Christie had no mentor or precedent when they sailed from Bombay on 2 January 1810. Their immediate destination was Sonmeanee – historically the rendezvous of the fleet of Nearchus who named it the Port of Alexander – from which they proceeded to the town of Bela.

Baluchistan, the territory of their exploration, is bounded to the north by Afghanistan and Seestan, and to the south by the Indian Ocean. It has Sind to the east and Persia to the west. Lonely British travellers had an obstinate habit of adopting a native disguise. D'Arcy Todd, however, when he was ordered to take despatches from Herat through highly dangerous country to Simla in 1838, scorned this practice.[2] He said he would travel as an Englishman, adding tartly that 'all the difficulties that Europeans have encountered in these countries have arisen from their foolishly endeavouring to personate natives'. He considered that their success had been as great as Chinamen would meet in trying to carry themselves off as Englishmen on the strength of a pair of tight breeches. Todd had a point, but the young officers whose disguise as merchants, horse-dealers, holy men or pilgrims often aroused disbelief, or even open accusation, still survived unharmed. Why their deception should have been condoned by tribesmen usually hostile to the *feringhees* remains unexplained.

For their new identity Pottinger and Christie had their heads shaved and claimed to be agents of a Hindu contractor who supplied cavalry horses to the Bombay Government. They carried letters purporting to explain that they were on their way to Khelat to purchase mounts. To add credibility, a Hindu agent called Peetumberdass would travel with them as far as Khelat. Two more natives were sworn in, and they carried cash 'in gold Venetians, intended to use as a dernier resort'.[3]

Map 1. *Map from Lt. Henry Pottinger's Travels in Beloochistan and Sinde, 1816*

Pottinger's account contains a good military appreciation of the terrain covered. He considers the effect of the climate, the extent to which roads might be passable for guns, and the likely disposition of the tribes. His journal was written up later and published four years after the expedition. It includes a wealth of geographical and statistical material, and he acknowledged his debt to work that had been done by John Macdonald Kinneir.[4] From the start however, the journal is studded with vivid pictures of events and reflections on the local inhabitants. Attempting to leave Bela on 20 January they met a problem that would be repeated again and again – the tribesmen's procrastination. On this occasion Pottinger and Christie were called back by a self-important Baluchi chief, Ruhmut Khan, because it was up to him to arrange their escort. They had been warned about the Bezunjas, a sect 'who care not for the king, the khan, God, or the prophet', and who caused terror by their murderous rapacity. Pottinger describes them in relaxation, up to a point. Seizing their three-stringed sitars, they would sing

> in 'descant wild', their favourite airs, gradually working themselves by ridiculous and violent action, into a state of absolute frenzy; the din then became universal and quite stunning, and the auditory continued to applaud and join in the chorus with the singers till they were so completely exhausted that they could exert themselves no longer; the instruments were then laid hold of by others, and thus they were regularly passed round the circle.[5]

At Khelat, the next objective, their disguise was penetrated by one Fyz Mohummud, not surprisingly since he had seen them both in the company of Hankey Smith on the Sind mission. But he evinced no hostility.

Khelat, the capital of Baluchistan, was long the cause of a great deal of anxiety to the British. Later, during the ill-starred British foray into Afghanistan, its importance was enhanced because of its strategic position on the route from the Indus to Kandahar. It was essential that the Khan of Khelat should be well disposed, but the trouble was that no one had any clear idea of the extent of his power. Was he a puissant ruler, or was he no more than *primus inter pares* among a gaggle of warring chiefs? Pottinger was aware of the ambiguity surrounding the chief's authority. In his journal he wrote that the Khan could declare war or make treaties, and that if he did the tribal sirdars were bound to assist him. 'But if the common weal demanded a sacrifice of that nature from any particular community, the Khan of Khelat was expected to make an equivalent compensation.'[6] So the ambivalence remained. In 1839, when the Army of the Indus wound its weary way through Baluchistan on its way to Kabul, Mehrab Khan, then the Khelat ruler, was blamed for failing to supply the troops with provisions, though he had little to offer, and for his inability to restrain his marauding Baluchis from harassing the British column. Later, Macnaghten, the Envoy at Kabul, took a terrible revenge. General Willshire was ordered to storm Khelat, and Mehrab Khan and eight of his sirdars were slain.[7] Khelat was the scene of more bloodshed in the Afghan War, but that was still thirty years ahead. For the time being Pottinger was aware of sinister undertones, but he himself was not molested.

He made a careful record of the subdivisions of the various tribes, and their enthusiasm for going on *chupaos*, or plundering sorties. The Baluchi owned many slaves, captured on these raids.

> They were blindfolded and tied on camels, and in that manner transported, to prevent the possibility of their knowing how to return. The women's hair, and the men's beards are also shaved off, and the roots entirely destroyed by a preparation of quicklime, to deter them from any wish to revisit their native soil.[8]

The Baluchis claimed that their miserable captives, soon reconciled to their fate, became faithful servants.

At Khelat, Pottinger was given a present of a bag of snow. This, the first he had seen for nearly seven years, provoked some nostalgia for his 'native green isle', a sentiment to which he was normally immune. Leaving the city on 6 March, they were soon greatly affected by the severe cold, the water in their leather bags turning to ice. As they emerged from a deep ravine with sides of perpendicular black rock they were dazzled by what appeared to be a vast ocean before them. It was the desert, bearing the reflection of the sun on the sand.

At Nooshky the friends parted company, Christie making off north, on his way to Herat, while Pottinger continued westwards to Kirman and Sheeraz. On 25 March he left Nooshky in a hurry when he heard a rumour that a detachment sent by the suspicious Sind amirs was on its way to carry him off to Hyderabad. In the desert he was glad to survive the pestilential wind known as the Badé Sumoon, or Julot, 'the flame'. It was said to kill camels or other hardy animals, and as for its effect on humans,

> the muscles of the unhappy sufferer become rigid and contracted; the skin shrivels; an agonising sensation, as if the flesh were on fire, pervades the whole frame, and in the last stage it cracks into deep gashes, producing haemorrhage that quickly ends his misery.[9]

By the time he reached the Dizuk district Pottinger had changed his identity. The fiction of posing as a horse-dealer had worn pretty thin, so he declared himself to be a *Peerzaduh* (a religious devotee) en route to the sacred city of Mushed. This proved to be a mistake, as he was soon called to repeat a prayer of thanksgiving, but with a few of the relevant phrases he managed to stumble through, and later took part in an argument about the meaning of the Koran. Even this improvisation was not enough when a tribesman spotted a resemblance to a *feringhee*, later identified as a Captain Grant, whom he had met. Realizing that Grant had made a favourable impression, Pottinger shrewdly said he was a relation.

Moving on to Regan, he witnessed the alarming Jureed Bazee, or spear play in which a horseman threw a spear with a twelve-foot shaft at another rider galloping towards him who had to catch the weapon in flight and throw it back. Mistakes were lethal.

Making progress, Pottinger reached Kirman, where he was horrified at the macabre sight of a pyramid of skulls. It had been built by the ingenious chief Aga Mohummud Khan to commemorate the downfall of the Zund dynasty. He first had 600 prisoners decapitated, and then made a further 300 each carry two of their comrades' skulls to Bumm. On arrival, to complete the awful symmetry, they too were beheaded, and the pyramid was still on display to offer 'a horrid evidence of the conqueror's implacable and bloodthirsty deposition'.[10]

A minor incident at Kirman gives a hint of the intractable nature of Pottinger's character, even as a young man. While he was resting, he received a message from the personal emissary of the local ruler. The messenger had the impertinence, as recorded in the journal, to request the *feringhee* to rise to receive him. Pottinger would have none of it. He called his Brahoo attendant 'to show the man of rank the door, and the fellow sneaked off'. Preservation of status, however dubious, and saving face, was essential; as he observed in the same paragraph, his action was soon widely reported throughout the town.

As he neared Sheeraz he had travelled upward of 1,500 miles, traversing country of which nothing had been discovered since Alexander the Great passed through on his return from India. As a sign of the implacable aridity of the country, he noted in his journal that this was the first place where he had seen a running stream 'sufficiently deep to have taken a horse above the knee'. At Sheeraz he was overjoyed to be reunited with Christie, who had come by the Herat route. Neither – Christie tanned by exposure to the elements, and Pottinger now affecting Persian dress – at first recognized the other. The rest of Pottinger's expedition was less eventful. He joined Malcolm at Maraugha, to the south-west of Tabriz, and returned by way of Baghdad and Bussorah to land at Bombay on 6 February 1811, after an absence of over thirteen months. Poor Christie, who had been left in Persia on assignment to train the Shah's troops, was killed in a Russian attack on the Persian camp on 31 October.

Pottinger's journal contains many engaging asides which he jotted down when not recording strategic information. All Asiatics, he noted, 'attach the idea of rank to fairness of skin', probably because potential rulers were brought up in conditions sheltered from the ravages of the climate. For his part, however hard he tried, he could not bring his feet to the same weather-beaten colour as his hands and face, and once he was mistaken for a prince travelling in disguise. Greyhounds were greatly cherished by the Baluchis, who valued one as being worth two or three camels. Although camels were only 'serviceable for burthen', the dromedary, which could travel fast and go without food or water for many days, was especially useful for *chupaos*. Melons grown at Khelat, he observed with astonishment, were so big that a man could scarcely lift one. In Seestan the Asafoetida plant, stewed in rancid butter, was deemed a delicacy, but its ammoniacal stench was utterly nauseating.

At Mukran the most popular drink was a strong brew made of fermented dates 'which must be exceedingly pernicious in its effects'. The women of Mukran compared most unfavourably with the Sindees whom he had seen on the Hankey Smith mission. They were usually ugly, and proverbially unfaithful, they set no bounds to the gratification of their passions, and in consequence, at an early period of their lives they are tottering under decrepitude and premature old age.

The Mukranees paid so little regard to infidelity that, in case of discovery, a sheep or two was looked upon as 'an ample offering to appease the husband's wrath'.[11]

In his travels Pottinger showed signs of the resolution and resilience that marked his later career. Already he did not lack a critical eye, and the Persians he had met came in for his severest strictures. 'Falsehood they look upon, in all cases where it facilitates their ends, not only as justifiable but highly commendable, and good faith, generosity and gratitude are alike unknown to them.'[12]

This could be dismissed as a young officer's superficial, supercilious judgment, but later activities of the King of Kings and his advisers at Teheran were to give some contemporary substance.

CHAPTER FOUR

Poona and the Pindaris

On his return from Baluchistan, Pottinger was attached to the personal staff of Sir Evan Nepean, who had recently arrived to succeed Jonathan Duncan as Governor of Bombay. The worthy Nepean's career – secretary of the Admiralty, with a brief spell as Chief Secretary for Ireland – had been an unusual precursor to the Bombay Presidency. From Nepean, young Pottinger might have learned something of the wiles of politicians, but he was soon sent to a more arduous and significant post, in terms of his own prospects. He was to be assistant to Mountstuart Elphinstone, the Resident at Poona; in other words, an ADC to the Mission at the court of the Peshwa, the chief who had been an ally of the British since the Treaty of Bassein in 1802 dissolved the confederacy of the Maratha States.

Pottinger was fortunate in his assignment, for no one among John Company's servants pursued a more liberal and progressive policy, none enjoyed more respect and admiration, and none was more farsighted than Mountstuart Elphinstone. (He predicted with remarkable accuracy the end of British rule.) Born in 1779, he landed at Calcutta and was first employed at Mirzapore and Benares. In 1802 he was made assistant to Barry Close at Poona, but the routine of work at Court was soon disturbed by the conflict between the Peshwa and his rival chief Holkar which led to the Second Maratha War. Elphinstone, temporarily secretary to Arthur Wellesley, was present at the battle of Assaye, riding alongside the General. From 1804 to 1808 he was Resident at Nagpore, whence he was despatched on the fruitless mission to Shah Soojah in 1809. This earned no diplomatic triumph, but his *Account of the Kingdom of Caubule* was long regarded as prescribed reading for all concerned with affairs beyond the immediate frontier. In February 1811, after the Afghan mission, he was appointed to the Residency at Poona and held this post for eight years.

Pottinger's first months at Poona, more peaceful than those to come, were largely concerned with the Peshwa's attempt to force his refractory feudatories, the southern Jagirdars, into complete subjection. Elphinstone vetoed the Peshwa's aggressive plans and extended British protection to the Jagirdars under the Treaty of Pandharpore in 1812. This was the first serious breach between the Peshwa and the British.

Any appearance of tranquillity throughout Maharashtra was, however, no more than that. All the Maratha rulers, except possibly the Gaekwar of Baroda, were secretly hostile. Taking a wide view, Metcalfe describes the complicated situation of Maratha politics in 1816.

> There is Runjeet Singh looking eagerly from the north-west. There is Meer Khan within a few marches of the Agra and Delhi frontiers. There are Scindiah and the Raja of Berar settling whether they shall attack us or not; and thus virtually menacing our frontier from Agra down to Cuttack. There are the Pindarees ready to pour themselves into every defenceless country.[1]

The Pindaris were savage freebooters grouped in formidable bands; they were sometimes employed, or their activities condoned, by the Maratha chiefs. When they could not support themselves from plundering central India alone, they began to raid the territories of the East India Company and its allies. Metcalfe first said it would be necessary to attack the Pindaris in their own strongholds in 1814, and in time, with the campaign in Nepal reaching a successful outcome, plans were laid to extirpate them. It was always realized that this expedition would probably lead to a war with the substantive Maratha states, and their chiefs believed that this was the ultimate aim of the British. Elphinstone thought that action against Scindiah was probably inevitable, 'and even if we avoid that, we must one day have a Pindaree hunt, which is the same thing'.[2]

War there was to be, but its form remained uncertain. Official policy had, since 1802, supported the Peshwa against the other Maratha chiefs, but Baji Rao II, the ruler at Poona, was a degenerate, relying too much on his vicious Minister, Trimbakji. Currying favour came naturally to Trimbakji, who had worked his way up from being a despatch runner, but he went too far when he had the envoy from the Gaekwar of Baroda, Gangadhar Shastri, assassinated because he was said to have offended the Peshwa. (Shastri had rejected a devious offer to change sides and accept a marriage between his son and Baji Rao's sister-in-law.) It fell to Pottinger, acting Resident in Elphinstone's absence, to report the murder.[3] Shastri was a Brahman, and this was a religious as well as a political offence. Elphinstone, on his return to Poona, demanded the arrest of the culpable Minister. Baji Rao reluctantly assented, and Trimbakji was imprisoned in the fortress of Thana, on the island of Salsette, near Bombay. But on 12 September 1816 he escaped and was soon said to be raising an armed force, ready for insurrection. Baji Rao denied that anything untoward had happened.

The pace quickened in May 1817, when Baji Rao, still evasive about Trimbakji, was told to hand him over, and as proof of good faith, to give up three of his forts. He was also made to revise the Treaty of Bassein, to renounce all claims to headship of the Maratha confederacy, and to cede to the Company the fort of Ahmednagar. (Tact had thus been replaced by a tightening of the screw.) Baji Rao, under protest, signed a new Treaty in June 1817. Before the Governor-General launched his campaign against the Pindaris, John Malcolm went round the native courts on a roving commission, including Poona. The Peshwa, of course, protested his innocence of Shastri's murder and swore that he was the loyal friend of the British. Malcolm was impressed, but Elphinstone and Pottinger remained sceptical.

For the Pindari hunt – there was never any real doubt that it would have to take place – Governor-General Hastings could field a total of 120,000 men and 300 guns. The force was divided into two armies, the northern under Hastings's personal command, and the southern under Sir Thomas Hislop, the Commander-in-Chief in Madras, with Malcolm as his principal lieutenant. The strategic plan was to surround the Pindaris in a great enveloping movement, a giant circle centred on the Allahabad district, with a diameter stretching to 700 miles.

On 17 October 1817 Elphinstone asked his friend Richard Jenkins at Nagpore whether his Maratha Ministers were 'as intriguing, prevaricating, shuffling, lying, cavilling, grumbling, irritating a set of rascals as mine are here?'.[4] Elphinstone was content to give the Peshwa enough rope to hang himself. From his own very efficient system of espionage, he knew that Baji Rao was preparing to come out against the British and so kept a careful watch on the Peshwa's intrigues with the Sepoys.

About the 27th October I found them going on with increasing boldness, and repeated offers were also made to several of our dependants to join against us, and a large sum of money, with a quantity of shawls, &c were sent into the camp at night.[5]

Pottinger noted, and stored up for future reference, the importance of securing up-to-date intelligence of the enemy's plans. Elphinstone also taught him to be perpetually vigilant.

On the eve of battle, however, he had to rely on a pure hunch to avoid being captured, or worse. The incident, a sharp reminder of the vulnerability of the British, occurred on his way back from Bombay. Briefly, he left Panwell at the head of Bombay harbour late at night, and passed a small party near the top of Bhore Ghaut, half way to Poona. In the darkness he did not ascertain who they were. On reaching the Travellers' Bungalow at Wargaon, twenty miles short of Poona, his horse-keeper told him that Maratha patrols were active in the neighbourhood, and that a British officer had been speared the day before, close to Poona city. He wrote a note for the travellers he had passed, emphasizing the danger and urging them to turn towards Bombay. Leaving it with the man in charge of the Bungalow, he made off across country on his famous horse Bandicoot, and, though pursued by Maratha horsemen, he reached the safety of the British lines. Only days later did he learn the identity and fate of those he had passed in the night. They were two brothers, Captain and Lieutenant Vaughan from the Madras army, on their way to join their regiment. The Marathas seized them, marched them four miles to Tulagaon, and hanged them from the same tree, one brother being forced to put the noose round the other's neck.[6]

The Peshwa's troops became more insolent, but Elphinstone did not panic. He knew the Bombay European Regiment was on the way to Poona, and he maintained an impassive front to avoid arousing any suspicions about what he meant to do. Then on 1 November he took the whole brigade out of the Residency cantonments to a much stronger position four miles to the north-west of the city. The Peshwa sent a bullying message demanding that the British force should be moved to whatever place he chose; that the strength of the native troops should be reduced and that the European regiment should be sent away.[7] Elphinstone refused, and the Peshwa moved in to attack. The Marathas were said to have mustered

26,000 men and the aged Colonel Burr was heavily outnumbered with 2,800.

Grant Duff, the historian, gives an eyewitness account of the sight on the plain at the battle of Kirki.

> A mass of cavalry covered nearly the whole extent of it, and towards the city endless streams of horsemen were pouring from every avenue. Those only who have witnessed the Bore in the Gulf of Cambay, and have seen in perfection the approach of that roaring tide, can form the exact idea presented to the author at the sight of the Peshwa's army.[8]

Elphinstone also found the rush of horses, the sound of the hooves, the waving of the flags, and the brandishing of spears grand beyond description, but eventually ineffectual. At his command, Colonel Burr took the battle to the enemy and withstood the counterattack. By sunset 'we found ourselves alone in the field', and the Peshwa's beaten army had retired behind Poona. British casualties were about ninety men, the enemy's five hundred.

Elphinstone and Pottinger were in the thick of the fighting – this was a time when political agents had to double up with the sword. The Resident received high praise for directing the operation, and Pottinger was also commended by the Governor-General.[9] The cantonments had been plundered and the Residency set on fire; but the Peshwa was a broken man. When the subsidiary force under General Smith attacked the Peshwa's camp four days after arriving at Poona on 13 November, it was routed and Baji Rao fled the field. After a long chase, he surrendered to John Malcolm on 3 June 1818 near Indore and was exiled, as a Company pensioner, to Cawnpore, where he died in 1851.

The issue of the Third Maratha War was not in doubt, and it is not described in detail here. The principal Pindari leader, Amir Khan, reached an understanding with the British and became respectable as the Nawab of Tonk. Among the Maratha chiefs, Scindiah of Gwalior signed a fresh treaty on the same day as the battle of Kirki, Holkar's army was destroyed at Mahidpore in the only big battle of the war, the Bhonsla was also defeated, and the Peshwa was no more than a fugitive, if an awkward, intriguing one, till he gave himself up. The Pindaris saw that they would get no succour from the chiefs and began to surrender in large numbers. The main objective, the rooting out of the Pindaris, had been achieved and the Maratha rulers saw their territory annexed.

In effect, Elphinstone now became the Peshwa. The Governor-General argued that it would be pointless to elevate another princeling at Poona, because, with this historic title, he would act as a focus for future subversion. The annexation of the Peshwa's territory fitted in with the Governor-General's strategic plan to control the whole of Central India, and Elphinstone was to be sole Commissioner, invested with authority over all civil and military functions.[10]

At the outset, he impressed on Pottinger and his other officers that his appointment was not a licence for exploitation. This was 'the first native Government of which we have annexed almost the whole territory at once'.[11] While any part of the old state was not taken over, there would be a retreat for those who were disaffected; but when it was all brought under British dominion, many had to remain angry at their own loss of profit, 'and disgusted with the novelty of our institutions and manners'. With this in mind, Elphinstone's policy was to let the Company's system gradually 'encroach' rather than have an exacerbating, overwhelming effect.

In January 1819 he was still writing to Jenkins that 'We are learning the late system of Justice, Police, and Revenue'.[12] As he began to shape his administration, he persuaded Governor-General Hastings to re-establish the Raja of Satara as a ruler over his own domain. The idea was that, though the Raja would be a Company vassal with a minute kingdom, and in no sense a Peshwa, this concession would help to soothe national Maratha sentiment. Pottinger, who was privy to Elphinstone's deliberations, took their substance to heart. When, years later, he had to start from scratch in Hong Kong and went out of his way to conciliate the Chinese, he was especially gratified to receive an approving letter from his former master, now in retirement. The lessons, at least some of them, had been instructive.

The two things dreaded by Elphinstone for their effect on the natives were the imposition of law courts on the English model and any attempt to spread Christianity. Instead, he wanted to run the country on existing principles, and had already decided to leave administration on the ground

to the Collectors, of whom Pottinger was to be one. As he explained to
Hastings:

> Their Mamlutdars [revenue officers] would collect the revenue from the
> villages through the Patails [village headmen], as is now usual. The Patails
> might settle village disputes by village Punchayets [arbitration]. Important
> cases and all appeals would come before 'The Collector' himself, assisted also
> by Punchayets and by Hindoo lawyers. Criminal justice would be conducted
> in the same manner. . .[13]

It all depended on the Collector, whose powers in Poona were confirmed
by the Governor-General in September 1818.[14] He was the head of the
district. Besides fiscal duties, which brought him into direct touch with the
cultivators, he superintended the police and held magisterial powers; he
also dealt summarily with land disputes.

Before he left to take Nepean's place as Governor of Bombay,
Elphinstone had set up the framework of the new regime in the ceded
territories. He had given instructions that the laws of evidence to be
applied should be as simple as possible, but knew that there would always
be some malcontents, and where their disaffection was proved, the
sentence was severe and immediate. When a Brahman plot to murder all
the Europeans at Poona was detected, he had the ringleaders blown from
guns, remarking grimly that this form of execution had the merit of being
painless to the criminal and terrible to the beholder.

Early in the nineteenth century, Elphinstone was not alone in thinking that
the British had an obligation to improve the lot of the natives and to
encourage them 'in all the arts of civil life'. Malcolm, Munro, and Metcalfe
all held similar views, though they did not support the missionaries' zeal to
achieve a wholesale conversion to Christianity. They were hard-headed,
pragmatic administrators. Metcalfe's warning is typical.

> Our dominion in India is by conquest; it is naturally disgusting to the
> inhabitants and can only be maintained by military force.
>   It is our duty to render them justice, to respect and protect their rights,
> and to study their happiness. By the performance of this duty we may allay
> and keep dormant their disaffection; but the expectation of purchasing their
> cordial attachment by gratuitous alienations of public revenue would be a
> vain delusion.

The problem that faced Pottinger when he took up duty as Collector at Ahmednagar was to apply high moral principles in daily routine. He began with enthusiasm; this was an exciting new appointment, and he always welcomed an active post. Given his head, he could stimulate those under him; he might perhaps bait his immediate superiors more than was wise, and, as time later showed, he was prepared to ignore or defy the highest authority, even the Government at Westminster.

That lay in the future. Meanwhile, armed with all powers except those of capital punishment, he was fully occupied. He had to spend much of his time trying cases as a magistrate, or turning a beady eye on revenue officers. Policemen who stitched up the accused, clerks who forged and embezzled for their families, and eyewitnesses who could not possibly have seen the events to which they testified, all came before him in daily procession. Revenue work was equally corrupt as officials regarded it as a way of life to discredit their colleagues in order to keep their jobs. It was a merry jamboree where everyone had their price.

An experienced officer, trying to uphold a semblance of law and order, and to protect the *ryots* from the worst forms of exploitation, knew that brawls over land or women were liable to lead to bloody vendettas, and that remote areas might be ravaged by dacoits. The Collector had to be wary of forming close relationships with Indians, for whom friendship carried an obligation to grant favours. He was one of a ridiculously small élite and if he was to survive would have to count on his subordinate staff remaining loyal and on local potentates being ready to cooperate. The chiefs, he knew, were often vindictive and violent; they had to be in order to suppress warring factions and outlast recurring feuds.

It is a fair supposition that, judging from a minatory letter that Elphinstone thought it necessary to send him, Pottinger was finding it hard to cope with his new responsibilities.

> You will conjecture that it concerns your temper, but in reality it is rather your manner to which it relates. Without being so forthright as many of your neighbours, you have got into a habit of talking angrily, which though a matter of no consequence to anyone who knows you, is really a serious thing as it regards the *ryots* of a new country. If you will allow yourself to be put out of temper by them, you will soon frighten them from your presence, and will be at the mercy of the people about you who know your real disposition, and

who will take pains to give false impressions of it to others. If you really had a
bad temper it would be needless to remonstrate, but it is a pity to sacrifice
the advantage of a good one to a habit of giving way to every provocation.[15]

Despite the studiously temperate nature of this warning, the message was
clear. In today's terms it would simply be 'Cool it!' Pottinger may have
taken this sound advice seriously, because he was soon coping better with
the demands made on him; as the revenue rose he earned respect, and
sometimes affection. He also took time off from his duties to acquire a wife,
and in 1820 he married Susanna Maria, the twenty-year-old daughter of a
fellow Irishman, Captain Richard Cooke, whose family came from
Cookesborough in Westmeath.

From Bombay, Elphinstone kept an eye on his protégé, and when
Susanna presented her husband with a son, he told Pottinger that he was
flattered to be godfather.[16] It was also due to Elphinstone that Pottinger got
his next move. In the course of a long-term, recurring complaint, civilian
officers of the East India Company represented that posts like the
important one at Ahmednagar, which rightly belonged to them, had been
usurped by army officers. One solution would be to transfer Pottinger to
another role, and this Elphinstone did. He appointed Pottinger to be
Resident at Cutch, where he arrived in May 1825.

CHAPTER FIVE

Up and Down the Indus

Cutch was never going to be a peaceful assignment for Pottinger. It was too near Sind, and the Raj's attitude to the whole area fluctuated from suspicion to irritation, and finally exasperation. An early source of annoyance was the Sind Amirs' recurring ambition to extend their dominion to their neighbour. Cutch had already come under notice as a base from which pirates and marauders interfered with British trade and harassed border stations. From Bombay, 500 miles away, Nepean contemplated some punitive action, but the Governor-General, Lord Moira (later elevated to Marquess of Hastings) advised restraint. In 1814 however, Colonel Holmes was despatched from Bombay to make a démarche, and treaties signed in 1816 and 1819 had the effect of making Cutch a British dependency.

Relations with Sind were soon exacerbated by disputes over raids on Cutch carried out by the Khosa tribe, and Elphinstone, now Governor of Bombay and normally the most sage of satraps, was in favour of a full-scale attack, even proposing a force of 10,000 infantry and 2,000 cavalry with artillery support. The Governor-General's secretary replied tersely that 'few things in His Lordship's judgment can be conceived to be more impolitic than war with Sind'[1] and that there should be an amicable settlement. Sind sent emissaries to Bombay, and a treaty was concluded on 9 November 1820. Optimistically, this provided for mutual friendship, the prohibition of Europeans from residing in Sind (a sop to the Amirs' ineradicable suspicions) and the exchange of envoys. Elphinstone still believed that the Amirs had agreed because they thought that war was imminent, but he sent Captain Saddler to Sind with orders to conduct his mission 'on the lowest scale consistent with respectability . . . as a proof that the advances of the Ameers had not been rejected'.[2]

With the first stages in the pavane completed, there were a few years of uneasy peace in Anglo-Sind relations. Meanwhile, at Cutch, Pottinger was

fully occupied with domestic administration and with getting the Regency –
the ruler, Rao Daisuljee was a minor – into shape. He also had to keep a
careful watch on the deposed prince, Rao Daisuljee's father, who had,
improvidently, been allowed to stay in Bhooj, the capital, near his son.

Sind's strategic importance was enhanced in the late 1820s with the
assembly of pieces on the chequer-board for the next moves in the 'Great
Game'. Persia, disillusioned by the British failure to adhere to the 1814
treaty, had signed a concordat with Russia. At the Board of Control in
London, Lord Ellenborough shared his Directors' fears stating that 'I feel
confident we shall have to fight the Russians on the Indus'.[3] He found little
comfort in Colonel De Lacey Evans' book *On the Designs of Russia*, which
attracted a great deal of interest in 1829. Evans argued very plausibly that
the Russians could invade India through Afghanistan.

Interest in Sind was whetted by a report by Dr James Burnes after a visit
to the country in 1827. Burnes had been sent to give medical attention to
the chief Amir, but was rather disconcerted when Murad Ali, whom he
called an 'Asiatic Tiberius or Philip the Second', promptly purloined his
entire stock of quinine for the use of his own family. Burnes was
extraordinarily sanguine about taking the field against the Amirs.

> It is scarcely possible to conceive a more easy, or as far as the people generally
> are concerned, a more willing conquest, were our victorious arms turned in that
> direction. . . . Then the River Indus might once more become the channel of
> communication and wealth between the interior of Asia and the Peninsula of
> India.[4]

The good doctor was not an expert surveyor. The Indus was a poor channel
of communication: it silted up and, full of shallows and sand bars, its course
frequently changed.

Ellenborough, however, seeing spectres of infiltration by Russian traders
and of invasion by Cossacks, decided that there must be a proper survey of
the river. Knowing that the Amirs would object, he made use of a curious
diplomatic ploy to achieve this. Runjeet Singh, the Sikh ruler, had sent a
present of cashmere shawls to King William to mark his coronation.
Reciprocity had to be observed, and, as is common when gifts are
exchanged between heads of state, it took an absurd form. Runjeet's

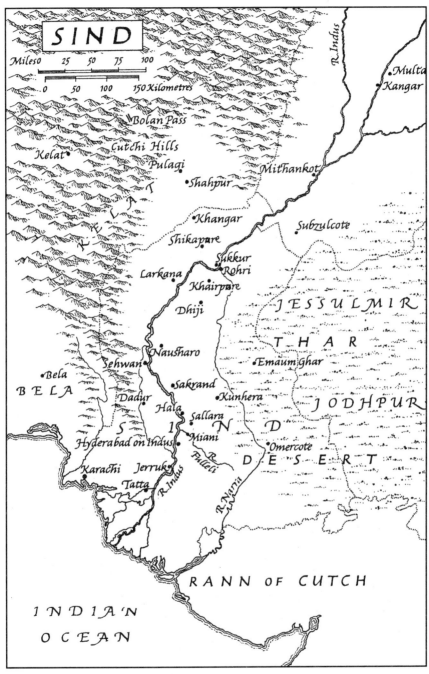

Map 2. *Sind*

inclinations were known to lean towards various forms of debauchery, but he also had a passion for horses. Lord Amherst, back in England after his stint as Governor-General, proposed that a few peculiarly English animals – as it turned out, five dray horses, a stallion and four mares – should be sent to Runjeet. With little sense of the ridiculous, Amherst's suggestion was approved and the hardy beasts, after six months at sea, reached Bombay at the end of 1830.

Now the subterfuge emerges. The Government of India had to get the horses to Lahore, 1,000 miles away. An overland journey was not practicable, so they would have to be ferried up the Indus by boat. In charge would be an emissary who would claim to be 'an Agent deputed solely for arranging the safe passage of the horses and of presenting them to Runjeet Singh'.[5] The small flotilla of five native boats sailed from Mandavi in Cutch on 21 January 1831. Only then were letters sent to the Amirs warning them of the expedition. The idea was that they would arrive 'too late to prevent the receipt of any answer having for its object the prevention of the mission, until the boats shall have advanced too far to admit of being stopped'.[6] As a final touch, a large, unwieldy carriage was included as a gift to Runjeet from the Governor of Bombay. This was done at the instance of Henry Pottinger, who pointed out that the size of the carriage would make it obvious that the mission could only proceed by water, and so mollify the Amirs.

The real purpose of the expedition was to survey the course of the Indus, to assess its navigability, and, in short, to find out as much as possible about the area. It was also intended to impress on the Sikh leader the commercial advantages – to Lahore as well as to the British – of opening up the river to traffic. One member of the Governor-General's Supreme Council, Charles Metcalfe, objected to the duplicity of the plan.

> It is a trick, in my opinion, unworthy of our government which cannot fail, when detected, as most probably it will be, to excite the jealousy and indignation of the powers on whom we play it. . . . It is not impossible that it will lead to war.[7]

Governor-General Bentinck appended Metcalfe's comments in his despatch to London, dated 7 November 1830, but it did not lead to a change in plan.

Pottinger's assistant at Cutch, Alexander Burnes, was to lead the equine escort. The brother of Dr James Burnes who had already been on a Sind mission, Alexander was only twenty-five but already had a high reputation as a linguist and was known for his interest in exploration. In 1829 he had volunteered to explore the deserts between India and the Indus and to follow the river down to the sea. At Calcutta, the Governor-General gave his approval after reading Pottinger's report that 'there was no officer of whatever rank or standing in the army, who was so particularly well qualified as Lieut. Burnes to give full effect to the plan'. But Burnes had got no further than Jeysulmeer when he was called back. The Governor-General, advised by Metcalfe, had changed his mind and cancelled the expedition lest it alarm the Amirs. The mission to Runjeet gave Burnes another chance.

Pottinger had at first thought highly of Burnes, but was later distinctly cool about the young man's judgment and conduct. Pottinger was sixteen years older than Burnes and no doubt he saw him as an upstart. In the service of the Raj, patronage and aristocratic connections still counted for much, but both men were promoted on their own ability. The difference between them was that Pottinger, stern and upright, with a high sense of responsibility, took his job, his orders, and himself, very seriously. He had many years of public service behind him when he eventually received real recognition. Burnes, for his part, had flair; he could charm and flatter and, something of a coxcomb, had no inbuilt respect for seniority. After his mission to Runjeet he made another, more spectacular, journey, getting as far as Bokhara. He published his account, and while home on leave, was lionized for this achievement.[8] Ellenborough, however, thought his wings needed clipping. On his return to India, Burnes, much to his chagrin, was to be sent once again to serve under Pottinger at Cutch. But that is looking ahead.

In January and February 1831 Burnes, now in charge of the horses for Runjeet, found the Amirs as obstinate as had been feared. Twice he even failed to land, while the Amirs argued that the presence of marauders in the area and the lack of water in the Indus made it essential for the convoy to go overland.[9] Pottinger broke the impasse. He forcibly reminded the Amirs how vulnerable they were *vis à vis* the Sikhs and the Afghans, and told them that they would do well to cooperate with the British.[10] On 20 March he reported that the Amirs had consented to let Burnes proceed. Burnes went on to Lahore, where the Sikhs were astonished at the size of the dray horses and their enormous hooves. Runjeet handed them over to his court grooms, and they eventually succumbed to overfeeding.

During Burnes's voyage upstream he met a syud who lamented, 'Alas! Sinde is now gone since the English have seen the river, which is the road to conquest.' It was to be a few years before this prophecy was realised. In his official report, Burnes was as sanguine as his brother had been about the river's potential, stating that 'There is an uninterrupted navigation from the sea to Lahore. . . . The Indus when joined by the Punjab river never shallows in the dry season to less than fifteen feet.'[11] Pottinger was aware that this was an exaggeration, and wrote succinctly to Bombay, 'I *do* differ from many of the facts and opinions stated by Lieutenant Burnes'.[12] (In his own published account, three years later, Burnes admitted that only flat-bottomed boats could traverse the river, and that no vessel with a keel could be safely navigated.)[13]

Meanwhile Ellenborough in London for commercial reasons, and Governor-General Bentinck at Calcutta for political ones, were equally determined to get access to the Indus. Ellenborough said it was essential 'for the disposal of produce and manufactures of the British dominions' – an argument that lacked specification. Bentinck, having studied Burnes's official report, was satisfied that the political advantages had not been overrated.[14] He told Lord Clare, now Governor of Bombay, that Pottinger was to persuade the Amirs to agree to the opening up of the river. His brief required him to negotiate a commercial treaty with the chief Amir, Murad Ali, and a separate one with Murad's cousin, the ruler of Khairpur. This provided an extra snag, because Murad claimed hegemony over Khairpur. The mission, including Henry's brother Lt. William Pottinger, embarked on the Company steamer *Hugh Lindsay* and landed at Mandavi on 4 December 1831.

On his way to Hyderabad, Pottinger was indignant to discover that the Hindus who had helped Burnes on his journey had been threatened with forced conversion to the Moslem faith. 'It is scarcely credible,' he wrote, 'that the rulers of any country pretending to the most remote degree of civilisation could be so backward as to promulgate such sentiments.'[15] But in camp on 30 December, he received a missive from Murad Ali agreeing to send an escort and giving an assurance that his letter was 'written by the scented pen of friendship'.[16] Pottinger had, in the meantime, told Lt. Del Hoste to carry out his survey, but not to use any heavy equipment that would arouse suspicion.

A routine offer of gifts preceded the negotiations, and Murad at first complained that the guns he had been given would not fire far enough. Pottinger, never lacking confidence, remarked that they were lethal up to 4,000 yards. Suddenly becoming more amenable, Murad then brought out a sword and asked Pottinger to have six copies made for him in London.[17]

Pottinger was intent on getting his treaties as fast as possible. Profiting by the more favourable atmosphere, he persuaded Rustum Khan of Khairpur to sign first, and after further argument, Murad Ali a fortnight later on 20 April. In discussion with Rustum he let slip how beneficial it would be to Khairpur to have a resident agent, but he met with a stony response.[18] Neither Murad Ali nor Rustum would admit British Residents. Pottinger did, however, obtain the promise of unimpeded traffic, with reasonable tolls, on the Indus. Murad Ali insisted that the river should not be used by armed vessels, or for the transport of military equipment, and that no Englishman should settle in Sind. One clause had its own inbuilt irony. 'The two contracting parties bind themselves never to look with the eye of covetousness upon the possessions of each other.' Eleven years later the British annexed Sind.

At the end of June 1832, Pottinger received back the treaties, which had now been formally ratified by Bentinck. He was to have charge of Sind affairs in addition to his duties as Resident in Cutch. He had opened up the Indus, but the immediate results were disappointing. A few experimental cargo ships were sent up river, and down from Lahore to Shikarpore, but there were still problems with navigation and the threat of attack by riparian tribesmen. Pottinger suspected the Amirs of levying heavy tolls in order to discourage traffic, and wanted a simple formula based on the size of the boat. He proposed to change tactic and 'assume a dictatorial tone'.[19] Bentinck agreed about the toll, and said that, while not interfering with internal trade, they should again try to get a British agent at the mouth of the Indus. (Clare at Bombay had foreseen endless difficulties without a man on the spot.)[20]

In October 1833 Murad Ali died, to be succeeded by his son Nur Mahomed. The new chief Amir was equally obdurate in refusing to admit a British Resident. Pottinger threatened that he would not draw up new treaties – the existing ones lapsed on the death of Murad Ali – but this was a weak card, as the Amirs were not, in any event, keen to sign a new concordat. Pottinger's temper was wearing thin and he began to contemplate a blockade of Sind ports. From Calcutta, William Macnaghten, the Governor-General's secretary, was inclined to agree, and Bentinck accepted his advice.

His letter to London took a much firmer line. Unless the Amirs acquiesced within a time to be fixed by Pottinger, and fulfilled the treaties to which they had already agreed (though there was no proof that they had done so), 'we should be compelled to adopt measures of coercion, as might be necessary to insure their compliance'.[21]

The Amirs, however, had reached the limit of their brinkmanship. Under the treaty they signed on 2 July 1834, they conceded a uniform toll, and the stationing of a native rather than a British agent at the mouth of the Indus to settle disputes. A British official could visit Sind to dispose of outstanding difficulties. Pottinger had earned a reputation as a hard negotiator: he had frightened the Amirs into giving away more than they intended but had not achieved the main objective of inserting a resident agent into Hyderabad. He could only fume in frustration at Cutch.

CHAPTER SIX

The Sind Whirligig

From 1834 onwards relations with the Amirs were punctuated by ever more imperious British demands for concessions by the Sind rulers that were met, in the nature of things, with obduracy and evasion. Pottinger, who came to believe that steadily mounting exactions were a mistake, still found that the Amirs were animated by hostility and proceeded by treachery.[1] Compared with neighbouring states, Sind was a backward, barbarous country, ruled by descendants of the Talpur princes who had taken possession sixty years before. Native inhabitants were cruelly oppressed by the Amirs who cared more for their game reserves, their *shikargahs* or hunting forests, than for their subjects. Arrears of taxes were collected by blinding or rectal assassination with a hot iron bar. Surplus female children were suffocated and domestic servants crucified as a deterrent to idleness. British actions in Sind can be questioned for their morality, and in fact were at the time, but it is difficult to sympathize with the corrupt Amirs. Mountstuart Elphinstone, now retired, writing from the distance of his seat in Albany, summed it up. 'Sindh' he said, 'was a sad scene of insolence and oppression.'[2]

The immediate British objectives after the signing of the 1834 treaty remained to carry out a scientific survey of the Indus, to encourage commercial traffic on the river, and to set up a Residency in Hyderabad. By 1838 all three had been achieved, largely thanks to the minatory activities of Runjeet Singh at Lahore.

In 1835 Runjeet's claim to Shikarpore frightened the Amirs into seeking an alliance with the British against the Sikhs. Given the British relationship with Runjeet, this was not a runner, but seizing the chance that the Amirs might be more amenable, Pottinger sent Burnes to Hyderabad. At the same time, on request, he despatched Dr Hathorn to attend to the illness of Nur Mahomed. What followed was an undoubted cock-up. As Resident in Cutch, Pottinger came under the Bombay Government, but was responsible to the Central Government at Calcutta for his actions in Sind.

The Bombay Government now sent their own doctor, J.F. Heddle, along with Lieutenant Carless, who was, of course, to survey the river surreptitiously. Pottinger was furious, and with his approval Burnes sent Carless back.[3] Nur Mahomed, somewhat bemused and content with Hathorn's treatment, ignored Heddle, who departed in disgust. A ludicrous correspondence between Bombay and the Governor-General ensued; Bombay claimed that the Amirs had acted from 'love or fear of Colonel Pottinger';[4] Nur Mahomed's gifts to Bombay were refused in pique, and then accepted; the Governor-General gave a Solomon-like decision against Bombay and the Amirs were finally mollified and agreed to the Indus survey. The report eventually produced by Lieutenants Carless and Wood, absorbing some comments by Heddle, confirmed that Indus prospects were not all they were cracked up to be.

Governors-General had a fixation about the capabilities of the Indus. Captain Eastwick, addressing a special court of the East India Company on 29 January 1844 was to discount it in this way:

> I believe there never was a greater fallacy than the expected advantages from what is called opening up the Indus. It is known fact that the delays in upward navigation are so great, that merchandise is transported on camels in preference, from Kurachee to the interior; but I am told we are to employ steam. I can only say I should be very sorry to embark my money in any such speculation.[5]

That was eight years later. Meanwhile Auckland, now Governor-General, did not agree with Carless's assessment. 'I am desired to acquaint you that the Governor-General in Council regrets the unfavourable accounts already received . . . it would be premature to record any opinion upon the question at present.'[6] Unpalatable advice was to be rejected.

There never was any doubt that Runjeet Singh wanted to bring the Sind Amirs to heel. In 1826 he demanded the tribute that they owed to Kabul on the grounds that he had now taken over most of the Afghan empire, palpably in disarray, but he did not press his claim at the time. In 1835 the Sikhs attacked the marauding Mazari, a tribe under the Amirs' jurisdiction, but their real objective was the trading centre of Shikarpore. Next year the Sikhs were on the move again and the Amirs asked for British help.

Macnaghten, writing on behalf of the Governor-General, returned to a familiar theme when he told Pottinger that, in return for protecting Sind from imminent danger, the Raj might justly expect some recompense. The price of permanent protection against the Sikhs was to be the admission of a British garrison to Hyderabad, and for help in the present crisis a British Resident had to be accepted in the capital.[7] The truth was that in strategic terms Sind was a weak link in the overall defence of Hindustan, and the recalcitrant Amirs had to be brought into line so as to provide a stronger bastion. Only Charles Metcalfe objected to stopping Runjeet's advance; to do this, he argued, was illegal under the British treaty with him of 1809: it would be foolish to risk a war with the Sikhs.[8] Auckland, in reply, cited Runjeet's restless ambition, the importance of the Indus, and the current danger posed by the Persian threat to Herat, the invasion route. By mid-November Runjeet had not made a move, thinking it better to stick to his old relationship with the Raj, even if it meant that he did not get Shikarpore. Auckland, though he had kept Runjeet out of Sind, still wanted him as an ally.

Pottinger, who had plenty on his hands trying to persuade the Amirs to see the light, had meanwhile quarrelled with Burnes. While he was absent from Cutch, Burnes had disposed of a local problem, trivial in itself, in a way that greatly displeased him, as Pottinger made known. Colvin, Auckland's private secretary, intervened, writing to Pottinger as 'an officer of long and distinguished public services', and to Burnes as 'an officer of distinguished promise' – a very precise bureaucratic difference – urging them not to let their private feelings impair their public conduct. Colvin ended with an impeccable exhortation: 'It is most essential that all British Agents should be seen to be animated by one common spirit in the execution of their instructions.'[9] By now it was apparent to Auckland and his staff, even at a vast distance, that the austere, resolute Pottinger and the cocky Burnes were always likely to be at odds, but for the time being they were too valuable to be replaced. As required, they patched up an uneasy truce, but their mutual resentment broke out again two years later.

Runjeet had not abandoned his claim to Shikarpore or the Mazari country he had overrun, and there were protracted discussions about the appointment of a mediator. In March 1837 Pottinger was faced with two problems. First, he suspected that Claude Wade, the agent at Ludhiana, was taking Runjeet's side, and a touch of temper was revealed in his letter to Macnaghten in which he advised that 'Runjeet should be distinctly warned off'. (He also objected to Mackeson, Wade's assistant, being the arbitrator.) His second difficulty was that Auckland was really trying to retain the cake and eat it. He approved of settling the Sikh/Sind dispute by arbitration, but it had to be informal, and Pottinger was sternly enjoined 'to avoid anything which can be construed as pledging the British Government to a formal and authoritative mediation between the two states'.[10]

Though he had been at Hyderabad since the previous November, Pottinger, bombarded with indecisive letters from Auckland, was having a hard time with the Amirs. As the Sikh menace seemed to decline, the Sind rulers became correspondingly more bloody-minded. When he reported that the Amirs were now disposed to ask for British protection in the treaty being negotiated, he got an unhelpful riposte from Macnaghten.

> It is not the policy of the Government by promises of general arbitration and an absolute guarantee of protection, to be implicated without reserve in the uncertain policy and conduct of Sinde, and in the maintenance of all its existing Frontiers variously acquired as they have been, and wild and ill-controlled as, in many parts, they are.[11]

This was the opinion of the Governor-General who had minuted on the previous Christmas Day that it was still 'a main object of our policy to bring the Government of the Ameers into a more avowed connection with us'.[12] Was it Auckland or the Sind rulers who were resorting to the most guileful oriental practices? Resigned as he was to receiving confused, conflicting, or totally impracticable instructions, Pottinger still kept the main objective in his sights. He had to get a British Residency established in Hyderabad.

It had seemed that the most xenophobic of the Amirs, Nur Mahomed's cousin Mir Sobdar Khan, would prevent any progress being made, but with a slight change in their attitude Pottinger penned and despatched a draft treaty. Much to his annoyance, Macnaghten thought that it went too far, especially in the offer of protection for Sind. It should have been enough to remind the Amirs of 'the friendly disposition which has already been pursued towards them'.[13] Pottinger sent a terse reply to this cold douche. He had told the Amirs that British mediation depended on Lahore and

Sind both concurring, and that even this could only happen when a British Minister had been stationed at Hyderabad.[14] Later, in June 1837, the Amirs came up with a draft which did equate British protection with agreement to a Residency. Pottinger believed he had done his bit. Auckland, however, was still swithering; it was too big a commitment, and on this score he would write directly to the Amirs.[15]

While the Amirs continued to slaughter game in their reserves, and to administer their perverted form of justice to their subjects, Pottinger was baffled. In this unpromising situation the whirligig suddenly took a perilous turn; the Sikhs and the Amirs began direct negotiations. Should they succeed, the need for arbitration, the lever to insinuate a British Resident, would lapse. Macnaghten alerted Wade to the implicit dangers, and to Pottinger he wrote in magisterial terms. He should tell the Amirs that it was all very well for them to talk to the Sikhs, but they should remember that any favourable agreement they might get would be due to the 'friendly interest' which the British had taken in the Sind state. Finally, he was to impress on them that:

> If they continue to manifest so great an aversion to form a closer alliance with the only power competent to render them efficient aid, the British Government must refrain on any future occasion to secure their independence.[16]

Either because of this warning, or, more likely, from mutual distrust, the Runjeet/Amirs talks broke down. Pottinger needed no reminder from Auckland that this was the time to turn the screw. The Amirs were to be told sharply that, without a Residency, they would get no help in persuading Runjeet to restore the Mazari territory, or to give up his demands for Shikarpore.[17]

It still took another two months, but in April 1838 Pottinger, wondering how many times he had marched through the Hyderabad court to the *musnud*, wore down the Amirs, Auckland happily told the Secret Committee of the Board of Control that the Amirs had yielded. A British Resident would at last take up post in Hyderabad, and the Governor-General would lean on Runjeet to stop his conflict with Sind.[18] To satisfy their *amour propre*, all four Amirs were given separate treaty documents, but Nur Mahomed and Nasir Khan were recognized as having primacy.

Auckland's view in June 1837 had been that 'I look for a clear connection with Sinde as of importance'.[19] Now, despite his hesitancy and muddle-headedness, it had come about, and the treaty had been signed. Who else but Colonel Pottinger was to become the first British Resident at Hyderabad? Captain Melville of the 7th Bombay Native Infantry was appointed as his assistant. There was little likelihood that his tenure would be without friction. For the Amirs, Pottinger was the embodiment of the Raj. He had made them agree to traffic on the river which they regarded as their private possession, and their feudal rule was now to be conducted under his eye as British Resident. But neither Pottinger nor the Amirs could have foreseen how soon the Governor-General's policy towards Afghanistan would add a new dimension to affairs in Sind.

CHAPTER SEVEN

Auckland's Promenade

A succession of Governors-General had held sway in Government House at Calcutta since young Pottinger landed in Bombay in 1803. First, the Marquess of Wellesley, appointed in 1798, held office till 1805, when his insatiable appetite for expensive building projects became too much for the Court of Directors in London and he was summoned home. The veteran Lord Cornwallis, who had been Governor-General from 1786–93, was brought out of retirement to institute economies, but he died a couple of months into his second term. Sir George Barlow, a civil servant, acted as interim till the Earl of Minto, who had been President of the Board of Control, went out in 1807, determined to pursue a policy of retrenchment. There were to be no campaigns on land, but Minto kept the armed services busy with expeditions against the French in Mauritius and the Dutch in Java.

An Irish peer, the Earl of Moira, who was notoriously hard up and needed the emoluments of office, was preferred in 1814, thanks to his friendship with the Prince Regent. Moira, whose style at Calcutta was as grand as Wellesley's had been, fought an unnecessary war against the Ghurkas, for which he was made Marquess of Hastings, and a more justifiable one against the Marathas, in which Pottinger took part. His successor, Lord Amherst (1823–8) left the flippant apothegm, 'The Emperor of China and I govern half the human race and yet we still find time for breakfast'. It was he who suggested sending the dray horses to Runjeet Singh (Chapter Five). Lord William Bentinck (1828–35) had a peaceful tenure, during which he carried out many humane reforms, abolishing *suttee*, recruiting Indians to official posts and organizing a comprehensive educational programme. (Bentinck did not, however, impress Calcutta society. He sometimes dispensed with his escort, and had even been seen on foot carrying an umbrella.)

After Bentinck there followed a game of Imperial musical chairs. The

Court of Directors wanted to confirm the acting Governor-General, Sir Charles Metcalfe, in office, but his insistent integrity could be embarrassing, and he was not popular in London for removing restrictions on the Indian press. So the Tory Lord Heytesbury was selected, but while he was being measured for his uniform, the Government fell, and the Whigs appointed George Eden, Lord Auckland. A bachelor aged fifty-one, Auckland came from a political family, being nephew of the Lord Minto who occupied the palace at Calcutta earlier in the century. He had been an unexceptionable minister at the Admiralty and at the Board of Trade. Diffident, upright, he went out to India full of good intentions and keen on liberal reforms, but he was not decisive, later described as being 'afloat on a sea of conjecture' as he wrestled with reports, often contradictory, from his agents. Pottinger received more orders from him than from any other Governor-General, and it was Auckland who started the First Afghan War.

The 'insane military enterprise' began in the autumn of 1838 when Auckland sent the Army of the Indus to invade Afghanistan. Kabul was occupied, but the Grand Military Promenade, which began amid great euphoria, with pennants unfurled and bands playing, was not the merry jaunt that had been expected. Torrid deserts, ambushes in mountain passes, and an improvident supply system, all eroded the Army's morale before it encamped at Kabul in August 1839. The British set up the totems of permanent occupation, but two years later the Afghans rebelled and drove them from the capital. During the retreat, the entire force, except for a handful of prisoners and hostages, was annihilated in the course of a week, and only one European reached the safety of Jalalabad. British honour had to be avenged, and in 1842 the Army of Retribution routed the Afghans and retook Kabul. The British destroyed the Grand Bazaar and a couple of mosques before marching back across the Indus. It had been a disastrous campaign, but the remarkable thing was that there had been no contact with the Russians, who were the real enemy.

Auckland was conveniently regarded as the scapegoat for the catastrophe, but in the light of events in Europe in the early nineteenth century and of Afghanistan's geographical situation, a war there would probably have been unavoidable. The British had long been pathologically suspicious that first the French, and then the Russians, planned to invade Hindustan, and this view was common to Calcutta and to Westminster. By the 1830s it was a current belief in diplomatic circles that British security in India would eventually require measures that would embrace both the Punjab and Sind. (Pottinger's despatches from Sind figured prominently in the Governor-General's deliberations.) Meanwhile, the Russians were edging towards Khiva and Bokhara, and Afghanistan, from its very location, lying between the Indus and the Oxus, exercised a magnetic attraction to both governments. From this it was easy to conclude that if Persia was amenable to Russian influence, it was essential that Afghanistan should be equally well disposed to the British. Auckland at Calcutta feared a Russian incursion: in London Palmerston, an obsessive Russophobe, determined to contain the Muscovites in Europe, was an enthusiastic supporter of the Afghan venture.

The immediate question was whether any Afghan ruler would be interested in welcoming the British, a problem further confused by the domestic situation in Afghanistan. The two claimants to the Afghan throne, coming from rival tribes, the Suddozyes and the Barukzyes, had been at each other's throats for the last fifty years. Shah Soojah, the Suddozye chief, had been driven out of Kabul by Dost Mahomed, the leader of the Barukzyes, and had been living on a small British pension at Ludhiana. But Herat, always thought to be strategically important, was ruled by Soojah's nephew, Shah Kamran, who was under threat from Persian ambitions. As the brick in the riddle, in 1834 the Sikh Maharaja, Runjeet Singh, infuriated Dost Mahomed by seizing Peshawar, for long an Afghan city. The Dost entertained a cordial hatred for Runjeet, but to compound Auckland's difficulties, the Sikhs could still point to an 1809 treaty with the British. A shrewd analysis and clear judgment were required. Sadly, the staff at Government House failed on both counts.

Auckland sent Alexander Burnes to Kabul on a mission originally described as commercial, but later transformed into a diplomatic embassy.[1] Burnes was well received by the Dost, whom he had met en route to Bokhara four years earlier, and from September 1837 till April 1838 he repeatedly recommended that Auckland should forge an alliance with him. Others took a different view, notably Claude Wade at Ludhiana, and at

Calcutta the Governor-General's closest advisers, the volatile Henry Torrens and the self-willed John Colvin, as well as William Macnaghten. After some heart-searching, Auckland decided that the Dost should be replaced by the overtly compliant Soojah. (The British alliance with Runjeet made it impossible to reach any concordat with the Dost.) Runjeet was induced to join the campaign: Macnaghten went the rounds to secure a tripartite treaty with him and Soojah; and Auckland had cleared the decks for war.

On 1 October Auckland issued his Simla Manifesto. This masterpiece of casuistry claimed that Dost Mahomed had made an unprovoked attack on the ancient British ally Runjeet Singh, had declined British mediation, and with foreign encouragement had persisted in plans for aggrandizement. Herat had been under siege by the Persians since November 1837, and the Dost's brothers, the Kandahar chiefs, were known to be in touch with them. In this crisis, 'the Governor-General felt the importance of taking immediate measures for arresting the rapid progress of foreign intrigue towards our own territories'.[2] His attention was 'naturally drawn at this conjecture to the position and claims of Shah Soojah-ool-Moolk . . . whose popularity throughout Afghanistan had been proved'. In short, Soojah was to be restored to the throne of Kabul; he would be supported by a British army and Runjeet would take part.

The threat to Herat had been cited as a reason for invading Afghanistan, but Herat held out, largely due to the fortuitous presence of Eldred Pottinger, Henry's nephew, who directed the defences, and the siege was lifted on 9 September 1838. The news, however, did not reach Auckland till after he had issued his Manifesto.[3] He was not to be deterred, and following a grand durbar at Ferozepore the Grand Military Promenade was under way.

The Simla Manifesto promised briefly that 'A guaranteed independence will upon favourable conditions be tendered to the Ameers of Sinde', but behind this cryptic announcement Auckland was quite clear about what he wanted from Sind. The Amirs had not been consulted about the Tripartite Treaty of June 1838, but article 16 blandly provided that Soojah would surrender his claims to tribute from Sind in return for a payment (expected to be more than twenty lakhs) to be settled by the British. In June, while his Afghan plan was taking shape, Auckland already had in mind that Soojah should get a lump sum from the Amirs. Most of this would be set against the cost of the force being mustered in Soojah's name, and the rest would be a sweetener for Runjeet. Colvin asked Pottinger how much the Amirs could afford, and what would be 'just compensation' for Soojah giving up his tribute. Pottinger put the Amirs' revenue at fifty lakhs, and the compensation was fixed at twenty. (Always fair, though as severe with the Amirs as events required, his last official act in Sind was to propose a reduction as he believed he had overestimated the revenue, but Calcutta found a counter-argument.)

Auckland at his most pompous had written to Pottinger in July, enclosing a copy of the Tripartite Treaty, telling him to soften up the Amirs with a warning that in this crisis, the real friends of the British should 'unequivocally manifest their attachments' to British interests, and that since 'powers to the Westward' were conspiring against them, the Governor-General had to enter into a 'counter-combination for the purpose of frustrating these objects'.[4] More explicit orders soon followed. Pottinger was to inform the Amirs that Bombay troops might have to occupy Shikarpore, and that the treaty ban on transporting military equipment up the Indus would have to be put into abeyance.[5]

The reason for these peremptory requests soon became clear; the Bengal Army under Sir Willoughby Cotton was to march down from Ferozepore to cross the Indus at Roree. Meanwhile another force of three brigades and one Sepoy corps commanded by Sir John Keane was to sail from Bombay, land at Karachi, and come upstream through the Amirs' domain. Both forces would then be joined by Soojah's contingent to advance from Shikarpore to Quetta, Kandahar and Kabul. This route was preferred to the easier one through the Khyber Pass, which would have left the entire force at the mercy of the Sikhs, allies though they were. Sir Henry Fane, Commander-in-Chief of British forces in India, had been designated overall commander, but with the relief of Herat the size of the army had been reduced, and Keane was to take charge when he joined Cotton.

Auckland needed a pretext for his high-handed behaviour towards Sind. Pottinger did his best to provide some, though they were not convincing.

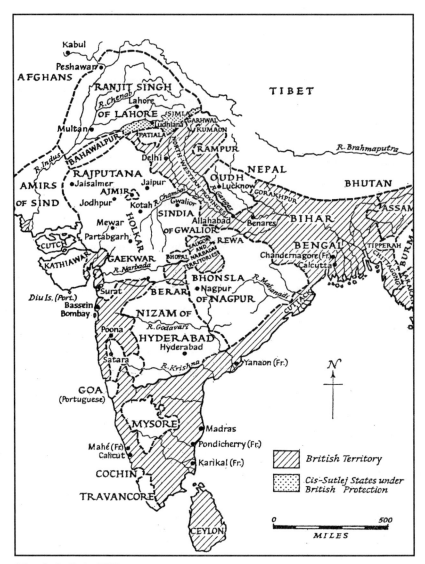

Map 3. *India in 1838*

On 13 August, Pottinger forwarded a translation of a letter from Nur
Mohamed, the chief Amir, to the Shah of Persia, adding that he himself did
not attach to it any great political significance. He did, however, intend to
'demand a categorical declaration of their intentions'.[6] A month later he
transmitted the substance of the Amirs' hostile reply to Soojah's requisition

for a passage for his army through Sind, and on 15 October he wrote that the Amirs had been detected in an intrigue with the Kandahar chiefs – though the report was later found to be incorrect. This was, however, enough for Auckland, who told Carnac that the Amirs were 'justifying any measures of vigour we may decide upon taking against them. Colonel Pottinger writes upon their conduct with extreme wrath, and he would not be hastily excited against them . . .'.[7] A classic case of Auckland believing what he wanted to believe.

Colvin had written privately to Pottinger, urging him to make the most of his golden opportunity. If he could manage to insert a subsidiary force into Sind without putting the Afghan expedition in jeopardy, 'you will, I need not say, have conferred a most essential benefit upon your country – such as would form a noble crowning triumph to your long and honourable career of service'.[8] Pottinger was apparently being given a free hand to step up the pressure. No feeling of remorse, no questioning about the propriety of the treatment of the Amirs, worried Auckland or his advisers. No one doubted the equity of trying to square the current negotiations with the 'guaranteed independence on favourable conditions' promised in the Simla Manifesto. British security in Sind was too important to allow any misgivings.

So far Pottinger had not made much progress with exacting the twenty lakhs to commute the tribute to Soojah. The Amirs claimed that they were no longer liable, and produced releases signed by Soojah in 1835 as recompense for help in his unsuccessful invasion of Afghanistan. When Pottinger felt obliged to point out that the papers were genuine, Auckland's response was a gem of sophistry. The documents 'would hardly appear to be applicable in present circumstances', and Soojah in signing them must certainly have obtained a 'counterpart agreement' which had not been fulfilled.[9] The releases were accordingly null and void.

Making all allowance for the wiles of oriental conduct, this was a disgraceful piece of chicanery which certainly made Pottinger's relations with the Amirs much more difficult. He was still expected to persuade them to agree to the stationing of a subsidiary force in Hyderabad, and to abolish all tolls for traffic on the Indus – a major source of revenue. The climax of his time in Sind was at hand.

CHAPTER EIGHT

The Amirs Coerced

Though his relations with the Amirs were becoming more testy day by day, Pottinger overcame the Amirs' objections to the passage of British troops through Sind. It then occurred to him that, applying the time-worn principle of *divide et impera*, it might be better to deal with each Amir as a chief in his own right, rather than face endless, combined intransigence. Auckland agreed, but meanwhile discussions on the remaining topics looked ominous.[1] On 1 January the Amirs disingenuously said they hoped that Keane's army had received all the carriage and supplies he needed. Pottinger replied that no services had been performed and that he was wearily accustomed to their promises not being fulfilled.

Changing tactics, Pottinger embodied the rest of his proposals in a draft treaty, and deputed Lieutenant Edward Eastwick, accompanied by Lieutenant James Outram, Keane's ADC, to take it to the Amirs. He authorized Eastwick to say that 'the smallest act of hostility would plunge matters beyond recall'.[2]

Eastwick was greeted with professions of friendship but Nur Mohamed brought out a box containing all the past treaties they had signed. Throwing them down, he complained vociferously that the British were never satisfied. He could refer to the 1809 treaty, article II, 'Enmity shall never appear between the two States', or 1832 (which mentions Lt. Col. Pottinger in article I) article II, 'The two contracting parties bind themselves never to look with the eye of covetousness on the possessions of each other'.[3] The awkward thing was that, from the Sind point of view, Nur Mohamed was right.

As the Amirs objected to the autonomy proposed for each chief, which they readily saw would weaken their bargaining power, Outram was convinced that they were playing for time. He saw hostile Baluchi thronging into Hyderabad, and noted that 'orders have been issued within the last twenty-four hours urging the immediate assembly of all fighting men at the capital'.[4] Eastwick asked for a reply to the British proposals, but got none. He and Outram stood to all night.

> A party of armed Belochees intoxicated with spirits and bang, came down from the town at midnight: they occupied the village, and made no secret of their intention to attack our camp, when reinforced.

At daybreak Eastwick and Outram withdrew down the Indus. On hearing their report Keane, who had advanced as far as Jerruck, half way from Tatta, declared that the time for talking was over. This was a military matter. There would be a combined assault on Hyderabad by his force and Cotton's army.

Since there was to be war with the Amirs as well as with the Afghans, Pottinger sent a signal to Bombay asking for the despatch of the Reserve force, HM's 40th Foot, the 2nd Bombay Grenadiers, the 26th Native Infantry, and supporting arms.[5] The Reserve did not reach Sind in time to affect the immediate issue with the Amirs, but its seizure of Karachi had long-term consequences. It also cast an interesting light on Pottinger's character.

Rear-Admiral Maitland, transporting the Reserve on board the *Wellesley* and a smaller accompanying vessel, claimed that as he approached Karachi a shot was fired from the fort at Manora Head. He promptly brought his seventy-four guns to bear on the fort, and the landing party was not opposed. Pottinger later reported that the whole business was quite unnecessary; the shot fired had been the normal courtesy salute when a square-rigged vessel came in sight. 'This I had myself witnessed when I came to the port in 1809 with the mission under Mr Smith, and I likewise know it was done when His Majesty's frigate *Challenger* anchored off it in 1830.'[6] It was also the usual practice at the Bombay lighthouse. The Amirs swore to Pottinger that there had been no shot in the cannon which fired. He confirmed that the fort only had six pounds of gunpowder, kept in an earthen pot, and that the garrison – all of sixteen men – had been admiring the *Wellesley* from the rampart when the firing started. The Governor of Karachi assured Pottinger that he had explicit orders to cooperate with the British. But Brigadier Valiant, the Reserve commander, maintained that 'no attention was paid'[7] to his pacific overtures before he felt compelled to resort to force. It does, however, seem most likely that Maitland wanted an excuse to open fire.

Auckland took this unexpected acquisition very seriously, reporting to London that he had told Pottinger that to retain the port was a matter for 'our own discretion', and that 'meanwhile it must be considered indispensible'. Pottinger took strong exception to occupying Karachi. The British should, he argued, have free access to the port, but it should be handed back to the Amirs, its lawful owners. Though he had more cause than most to dislike the Sind rulers, it may be argued that the course he proposed was the honest one. But Auckland prevailed, and in their 'discretion' the British held on to Karachi till 1947.

Upstream, the Bengal army had reached Roree when Cotton learned that the Amirs were still being obdurate. Like Keane, he was quick to decide that they would have to be attacked in their stronghold.[8] There was, admittedly, a military justification: the lines of communication to Kabul were going to be lengthy and fragile; the rear areas had to be secured. But there is little doubt that both Keane and Cotton – and certainly their troops – were attracted by the prospect of pillaging the treasure house of Hyderabad. So, with dreams of loot, both armies were converging on the city. Auckland, as he told Cotton, was not pleased with this diversion,[9] and Macnaghten wrote in intemperate terms about this 'wild goose chase'. But the Amirs at last saw that resistance would be futile, and the irascible General Nott, who was leading Cotton's advance force, could not hide his chagrin. 'Thus I have lost two or three lacs of rupees by the timely wisdom of these violent Ameers.'[10] The Sind rulers had capitulated, and when Keane's column reached Kotree opposite Hyderabad on 4 February, the native levies which had alarmed Eastwick had all been dispersed.

The Amirs yielded on 1 February; they signed Pottinger's draft treaty two days later, and they had paid half their tribute of twenty lakhs by 7 February. This was a collapse. Why had they given in so suddenly and so completely? They knew by now that Pottinger meant what he said, and he had told them that the British were ready 'simultaneously to overwhelm all opposition, and to come from all quarters "like the inundation of the

Indus"'. Outram thought their quick, if belated, surrender was due to the approach of the Bengal army.

> They know that our power at present is irresistible, but they hope when once in Afghanistan we shall be so long and fully occupied that they may take measures to prevent our return through their country: expelling in the meantime the weak reserve we leave behind: for it is difficult to believe that they have any intention of faithfully fulfilling the terms of the treaty.[11]

Auckland sent Pottinger his cordial thanks for his patient work with the Amirs, and for obtaining the promise of a permanent foothold on the banks of the Indus. He offered him six months' leave in Bombay, but also admonished him for pursuing his quarrel with Burnes to the point of threatening to resign.[12] Though Pottinger could be prickly in his personal relations, it is a moot question why he should have taken such offence at a time when he was riding high. As with many affronts, there are clues, but no convincing explanation.

Pottinger may have been annoyed not to get the plum political job in the Afghan campaign, and Burnes was certainly disappointed that he was overlooked. The irony is that when Auckland was considering who should be the British Envoy at Kabul, Macnaghten had recommended Pottinger, and as he was the Governor-General's senior adviser, his views carried weight. But Auckland knew that Pottinger was not noted for his tact, and besides, he was the key man in Sind, far too important to be moved. So Macnaghten himself was appointed, which gives rise to one of the more irritating 'ifs' of history. Macnaghten, a distinguished oriental scholar, was not the man to deal with the tribesmen who conspired to throw the British out of Kabul. He believed that 'all was tranquillity', and ignored reports that rebellion was imminent. Trusting the Afghans, he was shot with the very pistol he had presented as a gift to their leader, Akbar Khan. It is hard to imagine that the pragmatic Henry Pottinger would not have been more resolute with the rebels, or that he would not have fortified Elphinstone, the enfeebled military commander, to take more decisive action.[13] It is arguable that the disastrous retreat, in which the British force was wiped out, need never have happened.

Alexander Burnes was very bitter not to get the post of Envoy. He had just been knighted for his services on the mission to Dost Mahomed –

Colvin, in offering his congratulations warned him to 'drop all appearance of controversy' in his relationship with Pottinger – but he had to be content with appointment as Resident, in fact as Macnaghten's number two. As such he was sent ahead of the Bengal column to Upper Sind to arrange for the passage of troops through Khairpur. This meant getting the consent of the ruler, Rustum Khan, who was being urged by Nur Mohamed from Hyderabad not to cooperate. Rustum had said he would not yield to Nur Mohamed's blandishments, but Burnes had taken a tough line. As he wrote to Pottinger, 'I could only tell him that if a shot was fired in the country against the English, Sinde would become a province of British India'.[14] Pottinger thought this 'rash and embarrassing', and altogether too extreme. He was already dismayed, as were many others, that Burnes had got a knighthood, while his nephew Eldred, who had been acclaimed as a hero for his defence of Herat, had only been made a Companion of the Bath. Now here was Burnes, a known insider in the Governor-General's circle, popping up again to flaunt his accolade in Pottinger's bailiwick.

But Burnes obtained his treaty, under which Khairpur accepted British protection. The aged Rustum was easier to deal with than Nur Mohamed, but Burnes had done well. For the British it was a good agreement, which enabled them to use the midstream fortress of Bukkur, vital for crossing the Indus.[15] It was signed on 28 December 1838, and Pottinger, still struggling with the Amirs, felt upstaged by the impertinent Burnes.

There seems, however, to have been more to it. Auckland wrote to Macnaghten, now with the Army of the Indus, that he thought highly of Burnes's merits, but that his failings were 'to say the least of them, sometimes exceedingly provoking',[16] and that Pottinger had complained bitterly 'in some respects with reason and in others without reason', but had certainly not made a case for resigning. Auckland added shortly afterwards that Burnes was often petulant in his approach, 'and petulance from him to such a man as Colonel Pottinger is to say the least of it exceedingly misplaced'.[17]

Auckland did not want to upset his Resident at Hyderabad because his advisers at Government House had convinced him that the treaty which Pottinger had proudly forwarded after his Herculean labours should be amended without, of course, altering its 'essential spirit and character'. The revised version, fourteen articles replacing Pottinger's twenty-three, was still harder on the Amirs, and confirmed the occupation of Karachi. In short, the Amirs had been persuaded, cajoled, or threatened into breaking up their confederacy, giving the British control of their foreign policy, abolishing the river tolls, and accepting both a Resident and a garrison at their expense. On 11 March 1839 Auckland approved the treaty, as altered, and sent it back to Pottinger for final ratification by the Amirs.

Writing to Hobhouse at the Board of Control, the Governor-General, impervious to any moral qualms, was cock-a-hoop.

> The Ameers have committed many a fault and many a blunder. They have neither been wise in their treachery or brave in their hostility, and they have yielded without dignity.

He went on in the same complacent vein to add that he hoped the Amirs had learned their lesson and would be prosperous and happy 'in separate independence under British protection'.[18] Pottinger, who had made it all possible, took a different view. In terms which recalled earlier representations by Charles Metcalfe, he protested:

> It would be better at once to take possession by force, than leave it nominally with the Ameers, and yet deal with it as our own. One line is explicit and dignified and cannot be misunderstood; the other I conceive to be unbecoming to our power, and it must lead to constant heartburnings and bickerings, if not to a rupture of all friendly relations.[19]

Events proved that he was right.

At the end of 1839 Pottinger, feeling that even his undoubted stamina was showing signs of many years spent in one of the hottest and most inhospitable parts of India, decided to take home leave. Auckland appointed Outram to be Political Agent at Hyderabad, but without Pottinger's rank of Resident.[20]

Subsequent sorry happenings in Sind can be summarized thus. In the aftermath of the Afghan war, on the pretext that the Amirs had been unfriendly during that affair, it was proposed to take permanent possession of Sukkur and Bukkur, as well as of Karachi. Before Outram could carry out negotiations he was arbitrarily removed by the new Governor-General,

Ellenborough, the former Chairman of the Board of Control, and Auckland's successor. The 'eccentric swashbuckler' Sir Charles Napier was given military and political control in Sind in September 1842. In his diary he wrote, 'We have no right to seize Sind, yet we shall do so, and a very advantageous useful, humane piece of rascality it will be.'[21] On the pretext that Sind troops had attacked the Residency, Napier defeated them at the battle of Miani in February 1843. The Amirs were exiled and Sind was annexed, the Mir of Khairpur alone escaping.

The British violation of previous treaties with the Amirs was denounced by liberal opinion at home. Edward Eastwick, Pottinger's sometime assistant and an old Sind hand, was among those who itemized the unscrupulous nature of British behaviour before a Court of Inquiry set up by the East India Company. Napier's brother, Sir William, was especially incensed that an anonymous letter in the press condemning Sir Charles's actions was said to have been written by Pottinger.

> Pottinger's letter is believed to be true and was designed to influence the debate: these Indian fellows are evidently liars by habit. . . . I hear Pottinger [now in China] is a strong plunderer, the Navy all say so, but old Gough keeps quiet because he is only not *so* bad.[22]

Why, he asked, should Pottinger now call it cruel and tyranical to annex Sind when he was on record as saying that this would be better than to pretend it was independent and yet 'deal with it as our own'? Charles Napier said he would challenge Pottinger when he passed through Bombay on his way back from China, but there is no evidence that he did so.[23]

Two postscripts may be added. First, Prime Minister Peel wrote to Ellenborough in Calcutta.

> I have heard that Sir Henry Pottinger declared when he was at Bombay, that he was resolved on his arrival in England to exert himself in favour of the Ameers, that he expressed very strong opinions on the subject of their deposition, and had an interview with Meer Roostum, whose cause in particular he espoused.

He and Lord Aberdeen, he goes on, each had an interview with Pottinger on his return. Sir Henry had spoken incidentally to Peel about his time in Sind, but had not alluded to the Amirs or to their treatment. Peel's final paragraph, however, reveals a measure of respect:

He did not mention the name of Meer Roostum. Still I am inclined to think that he feels strongly on the subject, and his opinions will probably not be concealed.[24]

The second postscript concerns a letter from Pottinger to a friend, which mysteriously found its way to the *Morning Chronicle,* and which said:

No explanation or reasoning can, in my opinion, remove the final stain it [the annexation] has left on our good faith and honour; and, as I know more than any other man living of previous events and measures connected with that devoted country, I feel that I have a full right to exercise my judgment and express my sentiments upon the subject.[25]

In a modern, decolonized, world, British behaviour in Sind could not be condoned, but it has to be judged against the philosophical and political background of the day. Neither Auckland nor even the imperious Ellenborough went out to India with the intention of extending the Raj's domain, but geography and events dictated otherwise, and there were arguments at the time which seemed to support the British attitude. First, there was security. If fears of French, and then Russian, invasion, as seen in Calcutta and Westminster did not materialize, that did not mean they were groundless, and by the time they declined there was a defensive commitment to push forward into new territory.

Commercial factors were also adduced, though the source of the promised traffic up the Indus was never clearly identified. More practically, action had to be taken when, as often happened, the frontiers were harassed by marauding tribes. Peel went as far as to claim that the peaceful occupation of one area led inevitably to the acquisition of its neighbour, if the first was subject to law and the second still subject to savagery. His view was that there was 'some great principle at work whenever civilisation and refinement come in contact with barbarism'. Put another way, the Raj, as in Sind, was rescuing the peasantry from oppression by cruel, corrupt rulers.

This theory may be regarded as too adventitious, but John Company still ruled British India through the three Presidencies, Bengal, Madras and Bombay, and Pottinger was its loyal servant. In Sind he endured more than his share of slings and arrows in the shape of peremptory demands emanating from the Governor-General, or the devious practices of the Amirs. Even when he protested at the policy of imposing restrictive treaties, he had little doubt that 'Nur Mohamed is still the intriguing faithless person he has ever been',[26] and that it was impossible to believe a syllable he had uttered. But he seldom voiced his exasperation, though he came to detest the flamboyant Alexander Burnes, soon to meet a dreadful end in his Residency at Kabul.

Taking stock, the question is whether Pottinger was recognized, and rewarded with a baronetcy, just for being on the spot at a critical time, or whether he did better than others might have done. He was reliable, a sound man with plenty of bottom in an emergency. His achievements in Sind were patent for all to see, but they did not match those of the greatest Indian administrators in the first half of the century – Elphinstone the humane scholar, Metcalfe the liberal realist, the high-spirited Malcolm, or the conscience-inspired Thomas Munro. They were more powerful, and they achieved more. Before long Pottinger was offered pastures new outside Hindustan.

CHAPTER NINE

The Fragrant Harbour

Ever since Hong Kong was occupied by the British it has been primarily a trading centre. The odd thing is that the original entrepreneurs who set up business there were engaged in purveying hallucinations. They offered their Chinese customers illusions, an escape from sordid reality, the fallacious feel-good factor induced by smoking opium. The profits, however, were not illusory, and merchants were seldom troubled by the ethics of dealing in the product of the poppy.

The British had long made a practice of absorbing new colonies, while at the same time denying that they had any territorial ambitions. The Treasury might cavil at the cost of defending each new acquisition, but their protests were overruled. As traders pushed further afield to find outlets for the products of industrial Britain, they needed protection from their competitors, or from native inhabitants; they wanted law and order, policing, stability to let them earn profits. In time, the decision to annex, even without the strategic argument seen in Sind, became inevitable. The occupation of Hong Kong, however, was not only subject to the usual disclaimers, but was also distinctly unwelcome at Westminster. Palmerston, as Foreign Secretary, wanted to bring hostilities with China to an end and to obtain trading rights at certain Chinese ports, but he was emphatic that it was 'utterly premature' to have annexed Hong Kong, which was nothing more than 'a barren island with hardly a house upon it'.

The merchants already trading in Canton, or more precisely from warehouses outside the town, on the banks of the Pearl River, thought otherwise. For years they had been engaged in a Chinese obstacle race. They were forbidden to build factories inside the city. They could not bring women with them, use sedan chairs, or carry firearms. A curfew might be imposed without warning, and worst of all, these restrictions, as well as port dues, were enforced or not at the whim of the Mandarins. Chinese officials had to be addressed by 'petition' (implying recognition of their superior status) to the Co-Hong, the local guild that exercised a monopoly over trade.

To make life even more difficult, foreigners were permitted to man their factories only during the trading season, and in the summer months they had to retire downstream to Macao, where the Portuguese were precariously established. Those brave enough to ply their trade further north were often insulted or imprisoned. Up and down the Pearl River the commercial community had little doubt that it would be a good thing to have a base at Hong Kong, the 'Fragrant Harbour', the 'Sweet-scented Bay', where there was a deep water anchorage, much better than the shallows of Macao, and where, under British protection, the scope for Chinese interference would be greatly reduced. There was, however, no sign that this idea found any response in the fertile minds of those who advised the Foreign Secretary.

Meanwhile the British, together with small contingents from other European countries and from America, kept their factories at Canton in operation, despite many concurrent hazards. Why did they do so? The climate was dreadful, living conditions were subject to restraint, and the Chinese officials, even in receipt of regular bribes, were often hostile. The answer lies in one exceptionally lucrative commodity – that of opium. Indian cotton and English woollens were also imported by China, but it was the trade in opium and the flow from the country of Chinese silver to meet the bill, that caused friction between the two nations.

Historically, the Chinese had been slow to develop a taste for opium, which for centuries was regarded only as a medicine. In the early seventeenth century the Dutch in Java started adding a pinch of the stuff to their pipe tobacco, and thereafter the habit of smoking opium spread rapidly throughout China. In 1729 the Chinese Emperor issued a decree restricting its import, but traffic continued unabated, with much official connivance. European merchants wanted tea and silk from China, but these markets were still sluggish compared with that for opium, which was in great popular demand. Despite an absolute ban imposed in 1800, the 4,000 chests traded in that year had risen to 39,000 by 1839.[1] It came from India and the East India Company, which controlled the supply, depended on it heavily as a source of revenue. The Company acknowledged that 'The great object of the Bengal opium agencies is to furnish an article suitable to the tastes of the population of China'.[2]

The Company purchased opium from the growers, chiefly in Patna or Benares, and sold it at auction to merchants who despatched it to ships, acting in effect as floating warehouses, lying off the small island of Lintin. There the smugglers, having paid for their cargo at the houses of agency in Canton, took possession and ferried it to China. The Company, the houses of agency, of which Jardine Matheson was the largest, and the Mandarins all knew what was happening. The trade was not illegal until it touched the shores of China, and never had so many blind eyes been turned. The British smothered any qualms with the conventional argument that China could not exist without opium; if they did not supply it, foreigners would. The cash flow in silver was vital to cover the cost of buying tea for sale in Britain, and by 1830 enough opium was being smuggled into China to cover the bill of $9m for tea. But in the era of the Reform Bill, monopoly in anything was subject to challenge, and in 1833 the Company's control of trade to China was abolished. The opium business was now in the hands of private merchants who exported more chests than ever before.

The Imperial Court at Peking believed with unalloyed arrogance that China was supreme in the universe, and that all other countries were inhabited by barbarians who, if they approached the Emperor's domain, could only do so in order to make obeisance and pay tribute. This attitude was a source of perpetual resentment to Britain as a great maritime power, but attempts to persuade His Imperial Majesty to receive an Ambassador – the abortive missions by Lord Macartney in 1793, and Lord Amherst in 1816 – ended in humiliating failures. After the abolition of the East India Company's monopoly, British interests at Canton were assigned to a new post of Chief Superintendent of Trade, who was to be responsible to the Foreign Office. In 1834 Palmerston appointed Lord Napier to be the first Chief Superintendent and told him to make his mark with the Chinese Viceroy at Canton, in practice the only port of entry for European merchants.[3] The Viceroy would not receive him as an equal, and Napier had to return to Macao, where he died shortly afterwards. Palmerston's remit had been carefully ambivalent on opium smuggling. Napier was not

Map 4. *The Opium War: the China Coast*

to approve of it overtly, but had to remember that he had no authority to intervene.[4] Palmerston was well aware that there were many in England who were uneasy about, or downright opposed to, the opium trade. But he also knew that reports from the Governor-General in India, whose jurisdiction included matters affecting China, reiterated how important opium income was to the Indian budget.

Attempts by the British to get nearer to parity in relations at Canton suffered a setback with the arrival in the city of the formidable Lin Tse-hsu. As Governor of Hu-Kuang he had cleared his province of opium addiction by confiscating pipes and supplies and promising to execute offenders. In memorials to the Emperor he suggested that the same course should be followed elsewhere, and at the end of 1838 he was appointed Imperial Commissioner at Canton, with the special task of dealing with the opium trade. Lin soon made it clear that he was a reformer. He announced that the merchants must give up all stocks of opium and that ships' masters were to sign a bond not to carry the drug. To show he meant business, he cut off food supplies, took away the merchants' servants, and penned crews in their ships. Captain Charles Elliot, the new Superintendent, thought it best to comply, and 20,000 chests were surrendered, to be publicly destroyed by mixing with lime and water. Elliot was reviled for conceding too much, and the pace hotted up when William Jardine, back in England, took the lead in urging the adoption of a more bellicose policy. Otherwise the Chinese would never agree to liberalize trade.

Palmerston's difficulty was that the high moral line – in public at least – was gaining support. (The abolition of slavery was one instance of this.) However, he was wily enough to get what he wanted. It was not to be a question of legalizing the opium trade which would be morally unjustifiable. Rather it was a matter of seeking amends for insolence afforded to British subjects in China. Despite Gladstone's eloquent intervention, Palmerston prevailed by nine votes in the Commons.[5] In the Lords, where the Tories had a majority, Wellington would not take a party line and declared that in fifty years of public service he had not seen such insults and injuries as Elliot had suffered at Canton.[6]

The time needed for the transmission of despatches between Macao, where Elliot was based, and London now became relevant. Even before the proceedings in Parliament, British frigates had defeated a fleet of war junks at the first battle of Chuenpi, named after a point half way up the Pearl River.

In June 1840 a sizeable British force sailed out of the bay at Hong Kong, already used illegally as an anchorage. The complement included three battleships, fourteen smaller ships and four armed steamers. Aboard the

troopships were the 26th (Cameronians) and 49th Regiments, a battalion
of Bengal sepoys, and supporting arms. Captain Elliot and his cousin, Rear-
Admiral George Elliot, were appointed joint Plenipotentiaries.[7] Palmerston
had recalled that Napier, in trying to negotiate locally at Canton, had got a
bloody nose. Taking much of William Jardine's advice, he now proposed a
selective blockade of several Chinese ports and rivers. The Elliots should
seize Chusan as a minimum, present his demands at the mouth of the
Peiho for transmission to Peking, and insist that the Chinese should send
emissaries to discuss terms on board the British flagship.

In more detail, Elliot was to demand payment for the surrendered
opium, reparation for the indignities suffered by Her Britannic
Majesty's representative, and access to four named ports. The cession of
an island could be raised, but need not be pressed if other demands
were met. The Elliot armada sailed to the Chusan peninsula, and the
town of Tinghai was captured before the expedition weighed anchor
again on 1 August. Reaching the Peiho, Captain Elliot tried to deliver
Palmerston's letter. After the normal delays and prevarications, Peking
authorized a parley, which took place on 30 August. The leading
Chinese spokesman, Kishen, the Manchu Governor of Chihli, was
amazed at the request for compensation, but as the talks went on, he
indicated that he was going to replace Lin Tse-hsu at Canton. Would it
not be more realistic for talks to continue there? Elliot, sensing that
Kishen might be more amenable than Lin, agreed. By the end of
November the British, leaving a small garrison at Chusan, were ready to
renew discussions at Canton. Rear-Admiral Elliot went home a sick man,
and his cousin took sole charge.

The negotiations took place against a noisy background of skirmishes
with the Chinese war junks and the exchange of fire with shore batteries –
the second battle of Chuenpi was fought on 7 January 1841 – but on
20 January Elliot announced tentative heads of agreement. Under what
became known as the Chuenpi Convention, though it was never signed, the
Chinese were to pay compensation of $6m over six years: relations with the
Emperor would be on an equal basis; the British would retire from Chusan;
trade at Canton would be restarted, and, in the first official mention, Hong
Kong would be ceded. On 26 January Elliot, without any authority from

London, sent a survey party to Hong Kong, where the Union Jack was raised and the Queen's health drunk. Next day Commodore Bremer led his squadron into the harbour.

But it was not to be so simple. The British merchants thought the Chuenpi terms were utterly inadequate, and Kishen, stalling and soon to fall from Imperial favour, would not put his seal to the Convention. On 26 February Elliot resumed the attack (the third battle of Chuenpi) and the British were soon masters of the river. Then, with Canton at his mercy, Elliot accepted a settlement, instead of pressing home his advantage. The compensation, unchanged at $6m, would now be paid in six days, not years, but there was no explicit reference to Hong Kong. Two days later, however, Elliot announced that there would be a public auction of plots of land on the north shore of the island, and he coolly sent Captain William Caine of the Cameronians to be local magistrate, while Alexander Johnston moved across from Macao to set up the first secretariat in a tent on the beach. But he had pushed his luck too soon and too far.

In London, Palmerston was furious that Elliot had disregarded his orders. Though he had been given a large force of ships and men, he had settled for terms far short of what he should have secured.

> Throughout the whole course of your proceedings you seem to have considered that my instructions were waste paper, which you might treat with entire disregard, and that you were at full liberty to deal with the interests of your country according to your own fancy.[8]

The $6m would not pay for the confiscated opium, far less the cost of the expedition, and Chusan had been given up as an additional trading port. To Palmerston's mind, there was no point in setting foot on Hong Kong. It was a barren island, with no port, no town and no houses. In any event, it was held illegally 'on sufferance in the territory of the crown of China', and the Emperor would not consent to alienate it. Queen Victoria, having listened to her Foreign Secretary, wrote peevishly to the King of the Belgians.

> All we wanted we might have got, if it had not been for the unaccountably strange conduct of Charles Elliot (*not Admiral Elliot*, for *he* was obliged to come away from ill health) who completely disobeyed his instructions and *tried* to get the *lowest* terms he could.[9]

Elliot had been the prisoner of events that were too much for him, circumstances that led inexorably to the Opium War. (Since there had been no official declaration of war, the term 'hostilities' was used.) The British at Canton, chafing under Chinese restrictions, wanted to end the Co-Hong monopoly and open other ports to trade, but William Jardine and his colleagues were convinced that none of this would happen without resort to arms. At Government level there was great indignation that the Imperial Court disdained to negotiate on equal terms. The Chinese, however, felt that they themselves had no need of goods from any other country, and if Europeans did not like the conditions, they should not sail to Eastern waters. Finally, the British condoned the opium trade, though it was pronounced illegal by the Emperor, and if any Mandarin at Peking tried to construct a balance of payments he would have found a large deficit caused by opium imports. Given such a heap of combustible timber, the wonder is not that the war started in 1840, but that a spark had not set it alight in 1834 when Napier was affronted.

Elliot had stretched his discretion to adopt a conciliatory posture whenever he could, even agreeing to address 'petitions', a method Palmerston especially deplored, to the Co-Hong. Strategically, he failed to see that a local understanding at Canton could not be translated into a wider concordat. Tactically, since his own belief was that the opium business was a sin and a disgrace he never secured the confidence of the British community. He received the formal notification of his recall on 29 July 1841.[10] Five days earlier, thanks to the superior efficiency of the mercantile network, the news had been circulated in the local press. His successor was to be a man of very different calibre.

CHAPTER TEN

Ningpo for a Cold Winter

Sir Henry Pottinger came home from India in poor health, early in 1840, but soon recovered his strength. Although still enjoying his well-earned *otium cum dignitate*, he began to think about a new assignment which he expected to be in Hindustan, but Palmerston's surprising invitation to go to China as sole Plenipotentiary and Chief Superintendent was at once attractive (as was the salary of £6,000 a year, twice that paid to the hapless Elliot). It was also made clear to him that a strong hand was needed in China – a compliment in itself.

This was not a routine, peacetime appointment. There had been mis-judgment and ineptitude, and now the war had to be won. Pottinger accepted the position only on the understanding that he would be in full charge, that his orders should be clear and precise, and that he could return to England as soon as his mission was accomplished.

He was to go out with a new naval commander, Sir William Parker, while Sir Hugh Gough would remain in charge of the land forces. Parker, a cousin of the Earl of St Vincent, was regarded as an experienced officer with few eccentricities, apart from a hatred of tobacco which led him to prohibit all smoking on his ship. It was thought that he would form an amicable partnership with Pottinger – an important factor, since the latter's relations with admirals and generals sometimes veered from the delicate to the downright fractious. In Canton, the press greeted the news of Pottinger's appointment with the comment that he was 'up to all the tricks and chicanery of the native courts, and rely on it will not allow himself to be humbugged'.[1]

Pottinger and Parker sailed in the new steam frigate *Sesostris* in June 1841. The intention had been to call at Calcutta for a final briefing from the Governor-General, but plans were changed when they reached Bombay. Auckland, realizing that the season was far advanced, and anxious that the expedition should not lose good sailing weather, sent a signal that they were to proceed straight to the China coast. Making good time, the *Sesostris* completed the voyage from London to Macao in a record sixty-seven days, including ten spent in Bombay, and arrived on the evening of 9 August.

Pottinger knew Auckland from his Sind days, and at Bombay he received a letter from him that was to have some future significance. Auckland did not share Palmerston's view that access to named Chinese ports was to be preferred to taking possession of an island, and he strongly recommended setting up a permanent base at Hong Kong, not only for the trading advantages,

> but because in the prospect of a protracted war, it has seemed to me absolutely necessary, that we should have in advance of Singapore, a secure position for Magazines, Hospitals, and reserves, and a Harbour in which naval repairs to some extent may be effected.[2]

Auckland had been First Lord of the Admiralty in 1834, and this hints that his strategic sense there had been stronger than he showed as Governor-General in launching the disastrous war in Afghanistan. (He returned to the Admiralty in 1846.)

Pottinger lost no time in letting the British merchants at Macao, the small contingent precariously occupying Hong Kong, and the Chinese authorities at Canton know that he meant business. On 10 August Elliot came aboard at Macao to pay his respects to his successor, and the Portuguese garrison fired a salute when the party landed. That evening James Matheson gave a formal dinner and he later wrote to Jardine in England that Pottinger had made a favourable impression on the local community. A young officer who was present at the ceremonies recalled, with some irony in view of later disputes, that 'He is a most popular character with the army and navy; his penchant for energetic measures, even of an indiscriminate nature, finding much greater favour than the vacillations of his predecessor'.[3]

'Energetic measures' were to be the hallmark of Pottinger's regime. Trading with Canton had been uneasily resumed, but winning the war was to have priority. In a Proclamation on 12 August he emphasized that he would devote his undivided energies and thoughts to secure a speedy and satisfactory end to the hostilities. He could not allow any interests, mercantile or otherwise, to interfere with the strong measures which he may find it necessary to authorise and adopt towards the government and subjects of China, with a view to compelling an honourable and lasting peace.

There was a sting in the tail. He had to

warn British subjects, and all other foreigners, against putting themselves or their property in the power of the Chinese authorities, during the present anomalous and unsettled state of our relations with the emperor; and to declare that, if they do so, it must be clearly understood to be at their own risk and peril.[4]

Next he despatched Major Malcolm to Canton with a formal letter intimating his appointment. On 18 August the Chinese responded by sending an emissary to Macao, but Pottinger declined to receive him pronouncing that he was not interested in a local discussion with an official. It was for the Imperial Government to reach a settlement that would safeguard the rights of British traders in China.

Admittedly this was what might have been expected of Pottinger. In Sind he had long been accustomed to take an obdurate line with the Amirs. But there, even as Resident, he was subject to direct, and frequent, orders from Calcutta. Here he was no longer a subordinate officer, and though the Governor-General's overall responsibility extended to China, distance made the link weaker and more intermittent. He therefore had to fashion and execute policy on the ground. Fortunately events were to show him equal to both tasks.

Before quitting Macao, he issued a notification that his predecessor's arrangements regarding Hong Kong should remain in force 'until the pleasure of Her Majesty regarding that Island and those arrangements should be received'.[5] He also appointed A.R. Johnston as his deputy to act for him while he was absent on the northern expedition. These actions gave the impression that the days of wavering in the face of Chinese intransigence were over. Local merchants were fortified in their belief that the permanent occupation of Hong Kong was very much in mind. A few days later Pottinger arrived at the island on board the steam-frigate *Queen* to undertake a rapid inspection of such building work as had been started. He approved the disposition of the naval force, including the

steamer *Hoogly* under Captain Nias, and the troops under Major-General
Burrell, a wing of the 49th Regiment, the 37th Madras Native Infantry
and the Bengal Volunteers, who were to defend the island. He returned
to the *Queen* overnight, and was then ready to sail. It had all been pretty
brisk.

In London, Palmerston was impatient to bring the Chinese to book. It was
fortunate, he wrote, tongue in cheek, to Pottinger,

> that the Emperor has given us such a good cause of Quarrel and thus
> enabled us to begin hostilities at the Commencement of the favourable
> season.[6]

He had been advised that after the south-west monsoon the Yangtse would
be navigable even by ships-of-the-line.

Parker and Gough had several hazards to overcome before they could
inform Pottinger that they were ready to put to sea. Two typhoons of
exceptional severity had swept Hong Kong on 21 and 26 July, causing
widespread damage to ships at anchor. Reinforcements, together with a
fresh regiment, the 55th, had been despatched from Calcutta during the
summer, but the whole complement was weakened by a fever that spread
through the ranks. At one time scarcely a tenth of the 37th Madras Native
Infantry was fit for duty. Ships' ratings were as severely affected: the *Conway*
had become a hospital ship, and when Parker eventually sailed his sick roll
was over 340. A Royal Irish officer describes the clutter on the ship decks –
'guns, howitzers, provisions, water casks, rocket tubes, brought on board
and thrown down in a heap'.[7]

On 21 August the armada, with Pottinger on board, got under way. For
the China station it was a formidable force – two 74-gun battleships, the
Wellesley and *Blenheim*, seven lesser men-of-war carrying ten to forty-four
guns, twenty-one hired transports and store-ships, a troopship, a survey
vessel, and the four Company steamers, two of which, the *Phlegethon* and
the *Nemesis*, were built of iron and had been invaluable in Elliot's
expedition. Gough's troops comprised the 18th (Royal Irish), the 55th,
parts of the 26th and the 49th Regiments, with artillery, sappers and
miners, and marines.

Taking full advantage of fair winds, the fleet reached Amoy, the first objective, on 25 August. Parker's captains were not greatly encouraged by what they saw in the approaches, for it was obvious that the Chinese engineers had been at work. The islets which protected the main channel were studded with gun emplacements, and Kulangsu, the island that guarded the eastern entrance was in itself a formidable fortress. The muzzles of a battery of seventy-six guns projected through the ramparts of rock, masonry, and earthworks. A two-hour bombardment by the warships' heavy guns made little impression on the granite-based defences. (Luckily for the British, the guns on Kulangsu were clumsily mounted and poorly serviced.) Even if the attack penetrated the necklace of islands, the high walls of Amoy town, seen through telescopes, would be hard to scale, and the beach in front was heavily entrenched.

On the day it was surprisingly simple, and Amoy was taken in a model amphibious operation. Two frigates and the light draught vessels took on the Kulangsu battery, while the steamers ferried troops to the subsidiary beaches. Meanwhile the full might of the *Wellesley* and the *Blenheim* was brought to bear on the main shore to cover the landings. The Royal Irish led the way in rolling up the defences from the flank. General Gough came ashore and the troops bivouacked, ready for the assault on Amoy in the morning, but the city offered no resistance; most of the Chinese had abandoned their dwellings, and native plunderers had already been on the scene. Gough's soldiers were disappointed that there was so little loot, but a large quantity of military material had been left behind, which the sappers gleefully destroyed. Pottinger, keenly observing the whole exercise from start to finish, wrote enthusiastically, 'Had the opposition been a hundred times greater than it was, the spirit and bearing of all employed showed that the result must have been the same.'

Bad weather kept the flotilla at Amoy for the next week, but on 6 September it was afloat again, bound for Chusan. Gough left behind a garrison of three hundred, who were to suffer more from fever, malaria, and cholera than from hostile natives. Parker detached the *Druid* (forty-four guns), the *Pylades* (twenty), and the *Algerine* (a 10-gun brig) to provide a show of strength.

This was the time when the monsoon changed: a vigorous gale scattered Parker's ships, and it was not till the twenty-ninth that they all reassembled to lie off the island of Chusan. Chinhai was the next objective, but the coast was so exposed to the north-east monsoon that it was decided to attack Tinghai on Chusan first. Only the steamers could make headway against the tidewater and reconnaissance showed that a battery even longer than the one at Amoy had been constructed to cover the full width of the valley, but again the Chinese had not protected their flanks. On 1 October Gough deployed the 18th and the 55th west of the battery and they charged up the hill. Gough was hit, but fortunately the musket ball was spent. Soon the hill was his: the 55th descended into Tinghai, while the 18th cleaned up the battery. Gough garrisoned Tinghai with a detachment 400-strong, though this continued dilution was to cause severe manpower problems. Pottinger issued a proclamation to the effect that Chusan would be occupied until the British demands 'were not only acceded to, but carried into full effect',[8] a statement intended for Peking rather than local hearing.

Gough and Parker now turned their minds to the agreeable prospect of seizing Ningpo, a distinct possibility for winter quarters. But first they had to take Chinhai, which lay on a narrow peninsula between the mouth of the Yung river and the sea. A high castellated wall surrounded the town, but from the invaders' point of view the most sinister feature was the enormous rock, 200 feet high with a citadel on top, which commanded the approaches. The citadel had batteries to each side and lines of stakes had been sunk in the river, which was too shallow to permit the passage of the '74s' or the frigates.

Despite these obstacles, the attack on Chinhai, starting on the morning of 10 October, had succeeded before nightfall, Colonel Mountain, on Gough's staff, describing the operation as 'the prettiest and smartest we have yet had'.[9] Thanks to skilful manoeuvring by Parker's ships, Gough put a battalion ashore east of the river mouth and threatened the enemy from the front; at the same time another column outflanked them from the rear. The *Wellesley* and *Blenheim* were daringly towed at high tide as near as possible to the citadel and kept up a steady bombardment. Marines and sailors scaled the rock, and the Chinese fled. Mountain later explained that this striking success had occurred because the enemy's arms were 'bad, and they fire ill'. But, he continued,

The Chinese are robust muscular fellows, and no cowards – the Tartars desperate; but neither are well commanded nor acquainted with European warfare. Having had, however, experience of three of them, I am inclined to suppose that a Tartar bullet is not a whit softer than a French one.[10]

British casualties at Tinghai and Chinhai numbered only seventeen dead and thirty-six wounded; the Chinese losses were heavy. Gough found Chinhai to be 'one great arsenal, with a cannon foundry and gun-carriage manufactory, together with war-like stores of various descriptions'. Over 150 brass and iron cannon were captured.

Two days later the steamers, with a frigate and two other vessels in tow, put what remained of Gough's force ashore before the east gate of Ningpo. The gate was soon opened, and the Chinese, stunned at the fall of their seemingly impregnable fortress of Chinhai, were not prepared to fight. Not a shot was fired as the band of the Royal Irish marched in to *St Patrick's Day*, before treating the astounded onlookers to *God Save the Queen*.

What was to be the next move? A decision could not be delayed, since the campaigning season was almost over. The expeditionary force was now isolated deep in hostile country, and its line of communication was extremely frail. It would have been tempting for Pottinger to take the bold course and push on the 100 miles or so to Hangchow, the capital of the province and, of greater strategic significance, the southern terminal of the Grand Canal. If Hangchow could be occupied and the Canal sealed off, the Emperor might find it expedient to negotiate before the winter set in. But that was wishful thinking. The sick roll was still alarmingly high, and with that and the casualties incurred, Gough reported that he had only about 700 men fit for action from which he had to find guards, picquets and patrols, and since security on land was his charge he strongly recommended a withdrawal to Chusan, which would be easier to defend. Pottinger, however, thought that to retire now from Ningpo would be seen as a British defeat, and would be so represented at Peking. Parker supported this view, and the force holed up where they were. Once the rains ceased, the colder climate, with frost and occasional snow, was not unhealthy. The commissariat at Calcutta had failed to provide blankets, or even greatcoats, but the troops

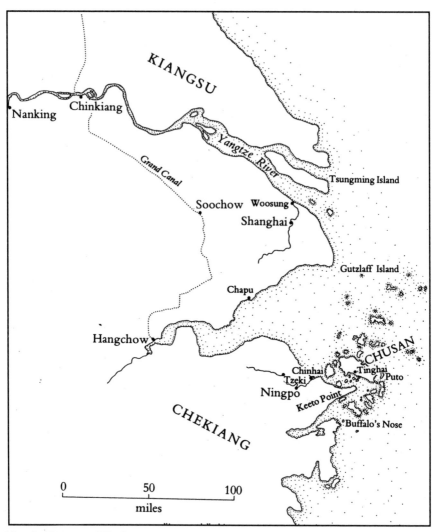

Map 5. *Ningpo and Nanking*

improvised with whatever they could lay hands on, and billeted themselves in abandoned houses. For the officers, there were sorties to shoot partridge, and morale began to rise.

Pottinger had expected a brisk battle for Ningpo, and in a minute to Gough and Parker he

looked forward with considerable satisfaction to the plundering of the city, not only as an act of retribution for the insults inflicted by its authorities on our people who were confined here, but as an example and warning to other places.[11]

To his mind there was a strong case for sacking Ningpo as punishment for the indignities suffered by the survivors from the *Kite*, which had grounded off Chusan in September the year before. Her master, Captain Noble, was drowned, but his widow, the mate and two boys, who had taken to a small boat, reached the Chusan shore. There they were beaten and tortured. Elliot Bingham describes how they were 'paraded to the hootings and howlings of the assembled savages'.[12] They were chained to the wall of a joss-house; irons were manacled on their legs before they were forced into bamboo cages and carried on display to Ningpo. It was the outrage to Mrs Noble that so affronted Pottinger. In his long experience, no white woman of the Raj had been so abused. He was now faced with an enemy even more barbarous than the Sind Amirs: the terrible story, embellished in retelling, was current among the troops and the appetite for retribution was keen.

Unfortunately for Pottinger, under the rules of engagement that were observed at the time, since Ningpo had offered no resistance he could not, much to his disappointment, sanction general plunder; at most he could insist that no public property should be spared, and he was emphatic that

> we should remove, carry away, or utterly destroy all public property (in which I include whatever belonged to the Emperor or his officers) together with the public buildings of every description or denomination, and the official residences of the authorities, the granaries, timber yards, war junks and boats. I would carry this work of destruction of whatever buildings may be public to the extremest point by even throwing down their walls, and burning any furniture or other articles found in them that may not be worth, or be too heavy, or cumbersome, for removal.[13]

Ningpo was going to experience a hard winter.

Gough objected; as he explained in a letter to his son-in-law, Pottinger's line was that harsh treatment for the provinces would eventually impel Peking to negotiate. This might, he argued, apply in France, where *vox populi* influenced the behaviour of government, but not in China, where

> the Government care not for the people, and I verily believe the most

annoying thing you could do is to prove to the people by our moderation
and our justice that our characters are foully belied.[14]

The discussion seems to have been carried on with good humour, for
Gough adds that Pottinger, Parker, and he 'are, however, great friends;
they all dine with me today – if I could carry my point, I would feed them
for a month'. Gough's proposition had some force, but it did not convince
the Plenipotentiary. Pottinger was determined that the Chinese should see
that he intended the sternest treatment, and, just as important, that they
should be made to pay the costs of the expedition. (Whether he served in
India, China, or the Cape of Good Hope, the public purse had no more
careful custodian.) On 6 December Gough agreed that there should be a
10 per cent levy on all merchandise in store. The most prized Ningpo
possession, the great bell from the Pagoda, was sent off to Calcutta. Rice
from the government granaries was sold to the local inhabitants at a knock-
down price to ensure purchasers. Stores of lead and copper were
impounded, and a sum of $160,000 was realized from this source.
Auckland, in one of his last minutes to Pottinger before he was relieved as
Governor-General, apparently sympathized with Gough. For his part, he
wrote, he would not have favoured a ransom on private property,[15] but this,
arrived much too late to be effective.

As a codicil to Ningpo, despite Pottinger's rigorous discipline, the
behaviour of the British was far from exemplary. They treated the Chinese
with invariable contempt. Tying their pigtails together, or cutting them off
completely was a favourite sport, and the natives carrying unwieldy sacks of
grain from the requisitioned buildings were mocked. The young
Lieutenant Alexander Murray noted with approval that it was the practice
to take leading citizens as hostage until a fresh supply of bullocks was
brought in.

> This is by far the best way of getting supplies in China, instead of sending out
> foraging parties; for, as soon as the people see a red coat coming, they drive
> away the cattle and hide them among the trees on the hills. They are also
> very dexterous in concealing their fowls, stowing them in all sorts of curious
> places, in baskets covered over with rubbish, or hung up to the ceiling.[16]

Late in November the British detachment learned that two months
earlier the Melbourne Government had fallen, to be replaced by the

second Peel administration. Palmerston gave way to Lord Aberdeen as Foreign Secretary, and the Earl of Haddington followed Minto at the Admiralty. Of equal importance to the three commanders at Ningpo was the transfer of responsibility for the war in China from the Foreign Secretary to the Secretary for War and the Colonies, Lord Stanley. Since Stanley was not well versed in Far Eastern affairs, the appointment of a new Governor-General of India, still retaining oversight of British interests in China, became more significant. Ellenborough was to be translated from the Board of Control to India; Peel admitted some reservations about his 'tendency to precipitation & over-activity',[17] but though he was appointed in October 1841, he did not reach Calcutta until 28 February 1842.

CHAPTER ELEVEN

The Chinese Puzzle

From distant Calcutta, Auckland's responsibility for Chinese affairs included making sure that the northern expedition was adequately provided with troops, ships, arms and equipment. The commissariat arrangements had scarcely come up to scratch, but, to fulfil a promise to Parker, he had ordered the delivery of more steamers in time for the renewal of hostilities. In December, however, he wrote to Ellenborough, his successor-designate, with doubts about the occupation of Ningpo. Unwittingly he endorsed Gough's view that, with overstretched lines of communication, it put too great a strain on the capacity of the force. To his mind it might have been better to return to Canton waters and await reinforcements before resuming the campaign in 1842.[1] The course of that campaign, he reminded Parker, must await the outcome of deliberations in England.[2]

The trouble was that the Secretary for the Colonies, though aware that decisions had to be taken before the end of the year, in time for next summer's deployment, still lacked enough up-to-date information to recommend a plan. Neither Ellenborough, en route for India, and quite likely to take his own line, nor Pottinger with the invading force, had any clear picture of what the Peel Government required of them. To compound confusion, both Auckland before he left, and Ellenborough when he arrived, were more than fully occupied with the signal catastrophe which had overwhelmed the Raj in Afghanistan. Ever since Surgeon Brydon rode into Jalalabad on 13 January with the news that the British had abandoned Kabul and that the entire force of 16,000 troops and camp-followers had perished, Afghanistan had had to be the Governor-General's first concern. So it continued throughout 1842: an Army of Retribution under General Pollock had to fight its way through the Khyber Pass and the rebels had to be put to the sword, before the British turned their backs on Afghanistan, leaving the country as it had been before Auckland launched his invasion. Compared with the necessity of restoring British prestige beyond the Indus, the Chinese war seemed pretty small beer, and as late as November 1842, the *Times* remarked, 'It is impossible to view that contest with the same exciting interest that attaches to the terrible realities of our Afghan war'.[3]

Many families were mourning the loss of relations in the retreat from Kabul – one of Henry Pottinger's nephews was killed and another was in captivity as a wounded hostage. Set against the Afghan débacle, casualties in the Opium War had been slight, but interest was maintained by letters sent home from the Far East. Peel's son and nephews of Earl Grey and Wellington were afloat with the expedition. Viscount Jocelyn and other returning officers began to publish their own accounts. The novelty of a Chinese Exhibition in a pavilion beside Hyde Park Corner drew large crowds to see all kinds of *chinoiserie* with eighty sinister mannequins in oriental costume as a centre piece. Then there was the vexed question of the ransom for the opium. Part of the silver was known to have reached the Mint, and the China lobby, led by William Jardine, now an MP, was demanding some payment on account for the confiscated chests. But the Treasury had no intention of relinquishing its grasp before the war ended.

For emotional, commercial, and strategic reasons, the Chinese business had to be settled, and Peel and his colleagues had to apply their minds to it. Charts were studied, advice was taken from anyone who had sailed the Far Eastern seas, from old hands who had traded at Canton, and from the Duke of Wellington, now increasingly infirm but a Minister without Portfolio in the Cabinet, and still deferred to as the fount of military wisdom.

In January 1842, while the Cabinet and the Board of Control at Leadenhall Street racked their brains to find a solution to the Chinese puzzle, Pottinger decided to come back to Hong Kong from Ningpo. Sailing in the *Blenheim*, he made a brief stop at Kulangsu to inspect the garrison that was wintering uncomfortably there, and arrived at the island early in February. He was not only the Plenipotentiary but also Chief Superintendent of Trade and he saw it as a duty to see how the mercantile community was faring. At the back of his mind, however, was the suspicion that the dubious British tenure of Hong Kong might be no more than temporary, to be

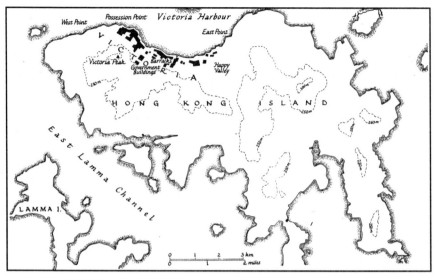

Map 6. *Hong Kong, c. 1842*

given up when claims against the Imperial Court had been met. From his Indian days he remembered that British disclaimers about having no wish to extend their frontiers had often served as a prelude to annexation, but there was always the possibility that the next mail would order him to stop all works and expenditure on the island. This he would regret. He did not need to look very far to be confirmed in his view that Auckland had been right; it would be folly to lose Hong Kong.

Whether or not the British presence was to be short-lived, there had been much activity on the island since Pottinger got his first sight of it the previous summer. One unreliable estimate suggested that there were now more than 8,000 inhabitants. The bulk of the Chinese sheltered in mat sheds, though the Tanka people lived in boats moored along the shore. A rudimentary thoroughfare known as the Queen's Road and already about four miles long, was being constructed along the northern shore from West Point, past Possession Point to East Point, where Jardine Matheson was establishing its undertaking. Most of the building was constructed in a mixture of clay and crushed stone, but a few public offices were made of brick. Ships' chandlers had set out their stores, missionaries were active, and there were said to be more than twenty whore-houses. In the words used by Auden about Macao,

Churches beside the brothels testify
That faith can pardon natural behaviour.

Following his unauthorized declaration of British sovereignty on 26 January 1841, Elliot had tried to be methodical. As Chief Superintendent of Trade, he took it upon himself to issue a proclamation on 29 January promising that the Chinese would be subject to the laws of China, 'every description of torture excepted', while British subjects and foreigners would be given security under British law. Further proclamations in February exempted Chinese traffic from British customs charges, and indicated that all traders could use the port of Hong Kong without duties levied at the port. Elliot saw the island becoming unmistakeably a major entrepôt. In a fair manifestation of oriental energy, ramshackle buildings began to appear along the coastline. Aware that squabbling over the allocation of land had already started, Elliot announced in May that building plots would be auctioned, leases subject to Crown rights going to those who offered the highest rents. Bidding at the first auction on 14 June was keen, but it had all been too hurried. There had been no proper survey, and later, both boundaries and the terms of the leases gave rise to confusion. All the trappings of permanent occupation were, however, being put in place.

Elliot's regime began to take shape with his first appointments. Captain William Caine, as magistrate, was to report serious crimes to Elliot, but he could try natives according to Chinese laws and custom, with powers to impose heavy fines, three months' imprisonment, or floggings up to a hundred lashes. A.R. Johnston, the Deputy-Superintendent, took overall charge in Elliot's absence on the northern campaign, and Lieutenant W. Pedder, who had served on the *Nemesis*, became harbour-master. (Their names are still to be found in street nomenclature.) Two days after his arrival, Pottinger temporarily endorsed Elliot's arrangements and confirmed the appointments he had made.

Palmerston, in his original instructions to Pottinger, had emphasized that his main objective was to obtain access, with the admission of British consuls, to four or five of the principal commercial towns. Alternatively, an island might be ceded, with the proviso that free commercial intercourse was permitted between it and the towns on the mainland. Palmerston was far from convinced that Hong Kong would be the best island station, but in a later letter, written on 5 June 1841, he appears to be moving reluctantly in that direction. Lord Aberdeen, the new Foreign Secretary, still wanted the claims against China to be resolutely pursued, but, significantly, the reference to the cession of an island was now omitted. Any island acquired during the hostilities would be useful for bargaining purposes, but it was not to be retained.[4]

Before Aberdeen's instructions arrived Pottinger had been persuaded of the advantages of keeping Hong Kong, and in March 1842, as much as a gesture as for efficiency reasons, he transferred the offices of the Chief Superintendent of Trade from Macao to the island, although British sovereignty had not been established. When he heard from Aberdeen, he wrote back, perhaps disingenuously, that 'this settlement has already advanced too far to admit of its being restored to the authority of the Emperor' without affecting British honour.[5] In short, Pottinger, like Aiken Drum in the old Scottish song, 'rode upon a razor' between these opposing points of view. Meanwhile, to pay lip service at least to the letter of his instructions, before he left to join Parker and Gough in June he suspended official building work and land auctions.

To Ellenborough, a sympathetic correspondent on this issue, he revealed his inner thoughts:

> I have done as much as I could to retard, without injuring, this Settlement, but the disposition to colonize under our protection is so strong that I behold a large and wealthy city springing up under my temporizing measures, and the chief difficulty I now have is the provision of locations for respectable and opulent Chinese Traders who are flocking to this Island.[6]

Ellenborough had never doubted that Hong Kong should be retained. For security reasons alone, the British must have a permanent base. He also thought that trade could best be conducted from 'Insular Possessions held by us on the Coast of China, to which the Chinese might and would come to trade' – a typical view that the Chinese should come to them, not vice versa.[7] By a strange quirk, Ellenborough, who supported Pottinger's subversive attitude towards Westminster, was himself hoodwinked by two of his Generals in Afghanistan. When Pollock had relieved the besieged garrison at Jalalabad, Ellenborough ordered all British troops to return to India. Pollock, ably supported by Nott, who had held Kandahar, was adamant that the hostages must first be rescued and the Afghan army defeated in the field. For months he deliberately misunderstood Ellenborough's orders till the Governor-General at last reluctantly consented to an advance on Kabul.

In Pottinger's absence on the Ningpo expedition, Johnston had continued, despite the embargo, to classify sites and to organize land sales, for which he earned a formal reproof from the Superintendent. The truth, however, was that the settlement was gaining its own momentum. The Government at home might instruct Pottinger to cancel the appointments of a Land Officer, or a Surveyor, but the work went on. Each tide brought in a new wave of jetsam – dubious traders and speculators.

Meanwhile the Plenipotentiary was undertaking a campaign of attrition in his correspondence with London. On 8 March he had assured Aberdeen that 'highly respectable Chinese merchants are flocking from Canton and Macao to settle here, or at least to form branches of their trading firms'.[8] Two months later he wrote enthusiastically about the warehouses that were going up, and added that 'Within six months of Hong Kong becoming a permanent colony, it will be a vast Emporium of Commerce and wealth'.[9] Was he misleading, devious, or simply ingenuous in the assessment he sent back to London? Whatever his motives, his views could not be disregarded. Vocal support for keeping the island came from the Jardine Matheson lobby; Pottinger was topping it up with personal knowledge and Aberdeen and Stanley were not receiving any contrary opinion based on local experience. Events might conspire to make retention more likely, but Pottinger was the fulcrum.

Riots at Canton in December 1841 had encouraged merchants to move their offices to Hong Kong and Captain Nias's squadron had been deployed to blockade the Pearl River. Pottinger, on his return from the North, cancelled the blockade; with an eye to the future he insisted on compensation for the Chinese whose junks and cargoes had been sold at auction. On 6 February, ignoring Elliot's earlier announcements, he issued a proclamation to the effect that the harbour at Hong Kong should be considered a free port, without duties, levies, or charges, a statement that was later to bedevil him. On 22 March he faced up to another vexatious question that was to run for a long time by appointing a Land Committee, with Major Malcolm and Woosnam among its members. The Committee was to settle the length and breadth of Queen's Road; a carriage and pair, imported from Manila, had already incongruously appeared on it. The main task, however, was to examine claims to land, boundaries, rents, etc. At the same time Pottinger emphasized that purchases would not be recognized unless they had been officially sanctioned,

> it being the basis of the footing on which the Island of Hong Kong has been taken possession of and is to be held pending the Queen's royal and gracious commands, that the proprietary of the soil is vested in and appertains solely to the Crown.[10]

Before rejoining the expedition, Pottinger issued proclamations to regulate currency. The dollar was taken as standard and the rate at which Indian coins and Chinese copper were to be accepted as legal tender was fixed. He also organized a postal service. Later in his career he was said to be an indifferent administrator, but in the early stages at Hong Kong, given the inchoate situation, his grasp was firm.

Trade, however, was not increasing as rapidly as had been expected. Tea was being sent to Europe, but it still came straight from Canton, and there was no reason to tranship in the new port. Sales of cotton and woollens were proving difficult, and only the market in opium was flourishing. Ships carrying the drug no longer anchored at Lintin: they came straight to Hong Kong, and Lt. Pedder in his harbourmaster's office recorded that one vessel in four had an opium cargo. In February 1841 the famous clipper *Red Rover*, which had brought much-wanted specie from sales at Amoy in the previous November, was back in Hong Kong with a new supply from Calcutta. Jardine Matheson made no apology for the size of the opium fleet maintaining that 'It is the command of money which we derive from our large Opium dealings, and which can hardly be acquired from any other source, that gives us such important advantages'.[11]

Opium posed severe moral problems for the missionaries who were arriving in numbers to fight the devil, and each other. Their plight is defined by Peter Ward Fay as a syllogism – 'Only Christ can save China from opium. But only war can open China to Christ. And the war actually in progress has been occasioned by traffic in the drug.'[12] Pottinger was mildly sympathetic to the societies, giving them grants of land and financial assistance. For the time being, Hong Kong could not rival the urbane atmosphere of Macao, still as lively and rackety as ever. Silveira Pinto, the Portuguese Governor, invited Pottinger to a ball to celebrate the Queen of Portugal's Birthday. There he enjoyed some brief relaxation, but his transfer of the Superintendent's office to Hong Kong was a clear pointer to how he saw the future.

While Pottinger had been discreetly supervising activities at Hong Kong, back in London Ministers had been vacillating about the orders to be sent to him for the summer campaign. They were still hamstrung by the lack of up-to-date news, and at the end of 1841 Stanley remarked petulantly that he had received no reports from China since 21 August. At the same time, however, he told Lord Fitzgerald, who had taken over from Ellenborough at the Board of Control, that the overall objectives were to obtain compensation for insults and injuries received at the hands of the Chinese, and to establish secure relations on a proper basis.[13] Pottinger would have smiled grimly at the repeated denial that Her Majesty's Government had any territorial ambitions.) To achieve its purpose, the expeditionary force must strike a decisive blow that would bring pressure on the Imperial Court at Peking, and the immediate plan was to sail up the Yangtse in order to seize the island of Kinshan and so blockade the Grand Canal.

Substantial reinforcements were to be sent. Luckily, Ellenborough's Army of Retribution made no demands on the Navy, so Parker was given another ship of the line besides the *Cornwallis*. The Admiralty would also provide half a dozen frigates, twenty sloops and brigs, and at least eight steamers, most useful in the changeable channels of the Yangtse. Gough too was given a stronger hand. His European regiments were to be brought up to strength, and another, the 98th, sent out from England. He would also get additional Bengal volunteers and five regiments of native infantry, together with artillery, and sappers and miners from Madras. On paper this increased Gough's command from 3,000 to 10,000 men, but most of the new troops were not to arrive until early June; in the event hostilities were resumed before then.

Stanley's proposal was based on the idea that Peking depended so heavily on produce carried on the Grand Canal, running from Hangchow through some of the most prosperous parts of China, that a blockade would rapidly bring the Emperor's advisers to the conference table. Bearing in mind that little was really known about the climate or topography of the area, it was a simple and ingenuous plan, but there was no unanimity about it in the Cabinet. Palmerston, while in office, doubted whether a blockade would be enough, and he wanted an advance up the Peiho to threaten Peking. Stanley thought the Peiho scheme was too risky, and Wellington dismissed it as the concept of a civilian.[14] Then the Duke, on being assured that there was a safe anchorage at the mouth of the Peiho, changed his mind; the Peking expedition was to be preferred,[15] and the Cabinet, pathetically keen to agree with him, concurred. After Kinsan had been taken and garrisoned, the force should return downstream, cross the Gulf of Pecheli, and sail up the Peiho to Tientsin. Fortunately there was a proviso that Parker and Gough should agree that this could be done.

This was not a good example of the decision-making process. The next step was to inform Ellenborough who, as Stanley admitted in his letter to him, was left at this distance 'absolutely to control our proceedings'.[16] Ellenborough promptly vetoed the Peiho plan and wrote to Gough emphatically that, 'I do not hesitate at once to direct your Excellency not to undertake that operation'.[17] Ellenborough was at heart a soldier *manqué* – he tried to revive for himself the old title of Captain-General of the forces in India – and he was shrewd enough to see that in an advance up the Peiho the links between the military and naval forces would be too vulnerable. He was also uncomfortably aware that, after the Kabul fiasco, the British in Asia simply could not risk another defeat. Mutterings of discontent were already apparent at Madras, and a reverse in China would have incalculable effects on the disposition of the entire Indian army.

The Westminster satraps' more ambitious plans had been negated by their middleman, Governor-General Ellenborough. Instructions transmitted by him to the expedition were on the way. Pottinger had been playing a 'Brer Rabbit' game at Hong Kong and was now about to rejoin Parker and Gough for the renewal of the campaign. The Chinese, however, had tried to seize the initiative at Ningpo.

CHAPTER TWELVE

Protocol at Nanking

As winter gave way to the spring of 1842, conditions for the British at Ningpo got steadily worse. The Chinese, having had time to assess the invaders' strength and weakness, became daily more insolent. Murder and kidnapping were frequent and British troops, finding the bodies of comrades who had been picked off and mutilated, became more violent in their response. Gough kept his men on the alert, and patrols who searched the surrounding country reported that the enemy were massing for a counter-attack. It came on the night of 9 March. Unusually, the Emperor had sent his cousin Iching to collect troops from neighbouring provinces to direct the assault. Several thousand Chinese, many in civilian disguise, attacked the south and west gates. The enemy carried the south gate and, driving the defenders back along the top of the wall, reached the market place in the centre. The detachment at the west gate held firm in the heaviest of the fighting. Soon the British, making good use of artillery and disciplined musket volleys, had the upper hand. Those attackers who could escaped, but many caught in the narrow streets were met by a hail of grape and canister. Five hundred Chinese bodies were counted, but amazingly, no British were reported killed. An attack with fire-boats on Chinhai, timed to coincide with the attempted assault on Ningpo, was also repulsed.

A week later, three steamers, *Nemesis*, *Queen* and *Phlegethon*, carried Gough and a punitive column sixteen miles upstream to reach Tzeki. The Chinese had taken up position on the hills north of the town, but they were engaged with great spirit and their camp was destroyed. Gough's resources, however, were being stretched to the limit, and every day it became more obvious that the British force, alone in the middle of hostile territory, was too vulnerable. On humane grounds alone, Pottinger never liked the policy of leaving isolated garrisons. Inevitably, they oppressed the inhabitants, and, as at Ningpo, created '"a wilderness", and a focus for strife and anarchy, which no measures we can adopt can possibly ward off'.[1]

Reluctantly it was decided to reverse an earlier decision and to quit Ningpo. Instead, the British would concentrate at Chinhai, where reinforcements were beginning to arrive. Gough made the best of it, and on 7 May embarked in good order with bands playing. Reports to the Emperor naturally spoke of the barbarians retreating after being defeated in a great Chinese victory.

The first objective of the summer campaign was to be Chapu, fifty miles across the Hangchow estuary and river, whose capture was to have more effect on the attitude at Peking than was realized at the time. A strong ebb tide made it unsafe to proceed up river towards the rich prize of Hangchow itself, which would have made strategic sense, but Chapu was there, and it was going to be attacked. On 16 May the *Nemesis* and *Phlegethon* steamed into the bay to make a preliminary probe, and the attack went in a day later. Gough and his staff were now expert at assaulting walled Chinese towns. Once the troops had been landed from steamers, they went for the enemy posted on the surrounding hills, from the rear and the flank. Skilful and experienced though Gough's troops were, this time they were confronted by the *élite* Tartars and the fighting was severe. The initial attack on the joss-house, the pivot of the defences, came under heavy fire. Lieutenant Colonel Tomlinson, leading by example, was rewarded for an impetuous charge with two balls in the neck. His men, enraged at the loss of their commanding officer, pushed on recklessly and the casualties were heavier than they need have been. In time artillery fire had its effect; gunpowder was exploded to blow a hole in the wall, and the joss-house was taken. The interior was piled with corpses.

Reflections on two incidents at Chapu remained to chill the minds of Pottinger and his commanders. First was the discovery of the body of a private in the 18th regiment. He had been mutilated with his own razor which the Chinese had taken from his pack to cut off his ears and nose and gouge out his eyes. Lieutenant Murray was amazed that they did this in the course of a losing battle. In his view, 'It is a great proof of their ferocity that they should commit such cruelties amidst the horrors of their own situation, expecting almost immediate death'.[2]

Second came the Tartars' universal suicide, in preference to capture, after defeat. Not only did the soldiers follow their commander in cutting their throats but men, women and children were found hanging from the beams of their houses, drowned in shallow wells, or poisoned. John Ouchterlony said the floors of the Tartar quarters were covered with bodies 'bloody from the wounds by which their lives had been cut short, or swollen and blackened by the effects of poison'.[3]

There had been reports that the Tartars would rather die than be dishonoured, but the horrific evidence on such a scale sickened even the hardiest veterans. As Pottinger stored up these happenings in his mind, he realized that he was dealing with a callous culture of a kind not previously experienced. If he needed any hardening in advance of negotiating with the Chinese, the experience of Chapu did it.

The batteries, magazines and foundries at Chapu were destroyed before the expedition left the port on 23 May. By 13 June the fleet lay off Woosung, before crossing the bar, which had been surveyed and buoyed, into the Yangtse to the point where it is joined by the River Woosung. Pottinger writing from the *Queen* a week later, described the action.

> The Chinese had erected immense lines of works, to defend the entrances of both rivers; and seem to have been so confident of their ability to repel us, that they permitted a very close reconnaissance to be made, in two small steamers, by their excellencies the naval and military commanders-in-chief, on the 14th instant; and even cheered and encouraged the boats which were sent, in the same night, to lay down buoys to guide the ships of war to their allotted positions of attack.

At daylight on 16 June the ships of war were towed into position by steamers.. They were met by a two-hour bombardment, but once they were outwith the traversing arc of the enemy guns they were safe. Sailors and marines landed under covering fire and cleared the batteries before the main body of troops had disembarked.

> Two hundred and fifty-three guns, {Pottinger goes on} (forty-two of them brass) were taken in the batteries – most of them of heavy calibre, and upwards of eleven feet long. The whole were mounted on pivot carriages, of new and efficient construction; and it was likewise observed that they were fitted with bamboo sights. The casualties in the naval arm of the expedition amounted to two killed, and twenty-five wounded. It appears almost miraculous that the casualties should not have been much greater, considering how well the Chinese served their guns. The *Blonde* frigate had

fourteen shots in her hull; the *Sesostris* steamer eleven; and all the ships
engaged, more or less.[4]

Ever since Pottinger took over as Plenipotentiary the war had been
prosecuted with vigour, but it is a fair question as to how Parker's flotilla
and Gough's troops achieved their monotonous series of successes. The
naval actions scarcely justified the term, in view of the poor state of the
Chinese ships and their inefficient manning. Parker had nothing more
formidable to face than a collection of junks, hastily assembled, and
incapable of making any effective reply to British fire-power. On shore, the
popular supposition had been that the Chinese could put innumerable
hordes into the field; in practice Gough was outnumbered, but not
seriously. His own estimate of the defenders at Chapu was about 8,000. The
Chinese seldom reinforced their garrisons from other provinces and when
they did, as in the counter-attack at Ningpo, the troops had never trained
together. The Chinese army was recruited from two sources; the best
fighters were the Tartars or Manchu bannermen, the name being derived
from the flags, like regimental colours, borne by each contingent. Fine
warriors, their efficiency was impaired by being allowed to vegetate in
separate quarters in lonely outposts. The Tartars were supplemented by
native levies who made up the Army of the Green Standard, troops who
were posted in even smaller detachments and who acted as a form of police
force under the control of local mandarins. Altogether, the military lacked
an efficient organization.[5]

Without any proper artillery apart from the fixed coastal defences, the
Chinese relied on the gingal. Mounted on a tripod and served by a team of
two or three, it fired a ball of about half a pound in weight. Their musket
was a small calibre matchlock, badly made to an obsolete design.
Gunpowder was slow, often failing to ignite altogether. Equipped with a
variety of antique weapons – bows and arrows, spears, halberds and
strangely designed battle-axes – they went into battle wearing brass helmets
and sometimes chain-mail. The Chinese infantry made a tremendous din as
they shouted imprecations from behind their rattan shields, covered with
grotesque designs. The total effect was, if nothing else, dramatic. Could
they give the British a fair fight? On the day, probably not: they were no
match for controlled artillery fire, disciplined musketry, and, finally, the

bayonet, but the expeditionary force was at risk in remaining indefinitely so far from a secure base.

As Pottinger took counsel aboard the *Queen*, he had few worries that Gough could do what was asked of him, provided that Parker's ships could steer a course through the treacherous waters of the Yangtse. So far, the Admiral had coped well. Looking ahead, his problem was still to convince the Emperor that British power was such that he should come to terms.

Shanghai, as Gough recalled, was taken without breaking sweat. Expecting only slight opposition, he sent a regiment of the Madras Native Infantry, with artillery and sappers, to advance overland from Woosung. At the same time four warships were towed up the Hwangpu river. The footsoldiers, often moving in single file over the tops of dykes as there were no proper roads, aroused the curiosity of the natives, but there was no resistance. Captain Granville Loch recalled that when the ramparts had been scaled, 'the gates were opened, the bugles struck up, and the troops marched through'.[6] The flotilla met some perfunctory fire as it approached the town, but the battery was soon silenced, and the men of the 55th were landed from the *Nemesis*.

Shanghai fell on 19 June. Parker then led a small survey party of three steamers up a branch of the Hwangpu seeking for Soochow, whose exact location was not charted, but he turned back before catching sight of the town. Pottinger did not want to lose time before making for Nanking, and he fretted impatiently while the force remained at Woosung for a full fortnight. Reinforcements were arriving, and all had to be in order before starting on the 170-mile journey. Gough's troops had suffered more from the vagaries of the climate, and conditions aboard ship, than from the enemy. With the latest arrivals, including the 98th under Lieutenant Colonel Colin Campbell, later Lord Clyde, he felt he could face anything that might be thrown at him.[7] For Parker it was a different matter. The Yangtse presented every kind of hazard to navigation; heavy tides, changing currents, violent eddies, rapids, and the great coils as the river turned course in sharp bends, all lay ahead. Pilot boats would have to lead the way, and there would have to be sounding, marking, and buoying before the men-of-war could proceed up river. On 4 July the *Phlegethon* returned from its reconnaissance to report that a navigable channel had been marked, and two days later Parker was on the move. The fleet of seventy-two vessels, including two ships of the line, ten steamers, two survey schooners, and forty-eight transports, was more formidable than had been seen on the Yangtse. Though it started impressively in five divisions, it could not hope to keep formation as it ascended the Yangtse, and between Woosung and Nanking almost every ship had run aground on mud banks at least once, with attendant delays until it could be refloated. Despite this Parker pressed on inexorably.

For the most part, there was no resistance. The landscape, though studded with villages, appeared deserted, and only one small battery had to be destroyed before the fleet lay off the island of Kinshan, at the entrance to the Grand Canal, on 15 July. At this point the Canal runs through the suburbs of Chinkiang, and there a shock awaited Gough's braves. (Woosung had been a naval occasion; this was military.) On 16 July Parker and Gough steamed up river past the walled town, and could see through their telescopes no sign of organized defences. On the 19th the *Cornwallis* took station almost under the city walls, to be followed next day by most of the remaining ships. Still there was no welcoming fusillade. A further reconnaissance detected troops encamped on hills to the south-west of the city. Gough, thinking he could dispense with the usual bombardment, sent in a task force that quickly routed the enemy in their camp. The two regiments assaulting the city got an unpleasant surprise. When they had blown in a gate and made an entry passage, they were at once set upon by the Chinese who had been hiding in strength behind the walls. This was a new stratagem. About half the enemy – later estimates gave their number as 2,600 – were Manchu bannermen, who fought with their traditional suicidal courage. This was a fierce hand-to-hand battle, the most bitter of the whole campaign. Gough lost forty-four men killed, with over 100 wounded.[8] As the British gained the upper hand, the bannermen fought their way back to their quarters, where, disgraced by defeat, they killed themselves and their families. At the height of this self-immolation the Tartar commander threw himself onto a funeral pyre. Of a total Manchu population of 4,000, barely 500 were left alive. Captain Loch noted the contrast between the sickly stench of death and the fragrance of the flowers surrounding the houses.

A small garrison under Major-General Schoedde was left stationed on the hills above Chinkiang, to command the city, and more importantly, the Canal.[9] Meanwhile the city of Kwachow, opposite Chinkiang, offered $500,000 to save it from assault.[10] On 2 August the fleet was ready for the most difficult part of the voyage. Earlier navigational hazards were repeated, the current alone causing severe problems, and skilful towing was needed before the *Cornwallis*, the *Blonde*, and some of the steamers came to anchor before Nanking's outer fortifications. Pottinger in the *Queen* lay alongside Parker's flagship, and a council of war decided that the assault, preceded by a heavy bombardment, should begin on 15 August. Gough had devised a clever plan to attack the east and north-east sides of the city, but it was never put into operation; at the last moment a Chinese representative came to the *Queen* to say that if the attack was suspended, serious negotiations could begin. There had been earlier unsatisfactory comings and goings between the two sides, but this offer seemed more purposeful so Pottinger complied.

The Chinese relied on three negotiators to deal with the barbarians. The most influential was Kiying, very much a Peking man who had spent little time in the provinces, and had never come into contact with the British. He was an Imperial Clansman and held the honour of being junior guardian to the heir-apparent. He had recently been appointed Tartar-General at Canton and was diverted to the Nanking negotiations. The venerable Ilipu, courteous, deceptively mild and reasonable, had arranged the truce with Elliot in 1840. He had since been ordered to retake Chusan, and when he tried to explain that this was not practicable, had been degraded. With the apparently unstoppable advance of the invading force in April 1842, he was rehabilitated and ordered to the Yangtse basin. Chang Hsi, one of Ilipu's assistants, also took part in the negotiations, often acting as intermediary.

While Parker's pilots were leading the way up river, Pottinger had tried to imagine what the enemy's attitude would be. At first the Chinese, seeing that the invaders had abandoned Chapu and turned back from Soochow, had entertained a glimmer of hope that this might be no more than a temporary raid. But the Yangtse was now completely dominated by the

British, and trade had come to a stop. A frigate had been left at Woosung to prevent access to Shanghai, and as the flotilla advanced, Parker destroyed or captured every junk that was met. (It might be said that he pre-empted Admiral Cunningham's signal off Cape Bon in 1943 – 'Sink, burn, destroy. Let nothing pass.') On shore, villages were plundered for provisions. Keppel in the *Dido* saw it as a form of sport. The plan, he said, was to seize the village chief and give him 'until 4.00 p.m. to supply twenty-five bullocks or have his tail cut off, which had the desired effect'.[11] Gough protested, as he had done at Ningpo, but Pottinger had no qualms.

> Our period of operations is limited, and we cannot therefore afford to follow half measures. The Government and people of England look to decisive results from the operations of the ample forces placed under the orders and guidance of your Excellencies.

Since, on past form, the enemy would certainly procrastinate, it was essential to let the Emperor

> see that we have the means, and are prepared to exert them, of increasing pressure on the country to an unbearable degree.[12]

The Imperial Court might shrug off the capture of individual ports as temporary depredations, but had the barbarians not seized the island of Hong Kong? Might they not have the impertinence to appear before the gates of Peking itself? With this alarming possibility in mind, Tientsin was rapidly reinforced, and when Kiying and Ilipu left Peking on 15 April they knew what they had to do. They could play for time, delay, quibble as much as they thought expedient, but they had to get a concordat that would ensure that the barbarians turned in their tracks.

The first tentative overture from the Chinese came on 20 May, when Ilipu sent an official to see Karl Gutzlaff, accompanying the expedition as an interpreter, but his approach was so vague that it was ignored.[13] In June, after the Chinese had begun to appreciate the full significance of the fall of Chapu, when for the first time a Tartar detachment had been annihilated, Ilipu sent another emissary, proposing in effect that the advance should come to a halt while discussions began. Pottinger's response was crucial. Recalling how Elliot had been bamboozled in inconclusive talks, his reply admitted no ambiguity. He would talk only to representatives who had full plenipotentiary powers, and who could negotiate without referring back to Peking. Ilipu and Kiying were left to think again.

The British did not falter. A final blow to the Tartars' reputation came with the fall of Chinkiang and on 5 August Parker's fleet was anchored before Nanking. Meanwhile Peking had given Ilipu and Kiying authority to proceed. After they had consulted Niu Chien, the Nanking Governor, they sent Chang Hsi to the *Queen* with a plea not to bombard the city. Pottinger, who did not intend to give up one scrap of his demands, received Chang Hsi with two interpreters, John Morrison and Robert Thom.[14] Chang tried to bluster, but the British Plenipotentiary was unmoved. In an intercepted and often quoted letter to Peking occurs the realistic sentence; 'to all his representations, the barbarian, Pottinger, only knit his brows, and said "No"'.[15] However, suspecting that Ilipu now knew he had to make progress, he agreed to a brief intermission.

The tempo changed. On 9 June Ilipu forwarded a commission which was said to prove that he had full powers, but after scrutinizing it, Morrison reported to Pottinger that this was not good enough. It was time to remove the tampions from the seventy-two guns of the battleships as the *Cornwallis* took up a menacing station within range of the walls. Ilipu sent Chang back to the *Queen* with the offer of an immediate ransom of $3m, but Pottinger was implacable. (Meanwhile, Gough was using the time profitably to smuggle his artillery, which included a troop of horse gunners, ashore.) In the ebb and flow of the non-negotiations, Major Malcolm, Pottinger's secretary, handed the Chinese a draft treaty, but when their emissaries met him (Ilipu and Kiying were still in the background), they were not ready to discuss it. Malcolm saw another web of delay being woven: he knew Pottinger's mind. He called the Chinese bluff and said that the bombardment would start in the morning.

It worked. Early on Sunday 14 August a suppliant Chang came aboard the *Queen* to say that if the guns remained silent, Kiying's authoritative commission would be produced as evidence of good faith, and his seniors would negotiate on the British terms. Pottinger, taking the air on deck, knew that he had won, though it was not till 17 August that he formally asked his colleagues to regard hostilities as suspended.

On the same day, Morrison and Thom examined Kiying's commission and found it satisfactory. Pottinger was now content to let intermediaries get to work on the draft treaty, and by 19 August the Chinese had accepted a version which they despatched to Peking for approval. Peace was very much in the air, and on the 20th Pottinger met Ilipu, Kiying and Niu for the first time when the Admiral's barge brought them to the *Cornwallis*. The occasion was formal but friendly; cherry brandy and tea were served, and the Chinese, being informed that a portrait in the wardroom was of Queen Victoria, rose and made their obeisance.

The fourteen-year-old Harry Parkes who had been learning Chinese under Morrison was interested spectator.[16] Pottinger, intrigued by the boy's studious habits, had brought him aboard the *Cornwallis*. Kiying, who apparently suffered from frustrated paternal feelings and later tried to adopt Pottinger's son, took 'a bit of a fancy' to the youthful Parkes, who recounts, 'I tried to talk as much as possible, but could only stammer out a few words, while I could not understand Kiying in the least, who speaks northern Mandarin very broadly'. He liked Kiying's appearance, 'for he has a fine manly honest countenance, with pleasantness in his looks', but he thought Ilipu and Niu seemed dull and heavy, with coarse features, which suggested that they were opium addicts.

The subsequent Treaty of Nanking was silent on the subject of opium, which, after all, had been the real *casus belli*, but the omission was not accidental. In the short interval before Peking's consent to the settlement was given, there were further exchanges of courtesy visits, and in a more serious session Pottinger raised the question of traffic in the drug. The Chinese reply was even more cagey than usual, and Loch noted that they would not talk 'until Sir Henry assured them he did not wish to speak of it but as a topic of private conversation'. Even then it was no more than fencing, adopting the conventional postures. Why did the British, the Chinese led, not stop production in India? Pottinger parried with the argument that if it did not come from there, it would come from somewhere else. The solution was up to the Chinese. 'If your people are virtuous,' he argued, 'they will desist from the evil practice, and if your officers are incorruptible, and obey their orders, no opium can enter your country.'[17] This was a recipe for perfection, so surely it would be preferable to make the trade legitimate, and tax it? This would have met British legal, and to some extent moral, difficulties, but the Chinese politely reiterated that they had no mandate to discuss the matter further.

On 27 August Kiying told Pottinger he had received news of Peking's assent to the treaty, and two days later everyone assembled on board the *Cornwallis* for the final ceremonies. The principals, Pottinger, Parker and Gough, along with their Chinese counterparts, Kiying, Ilipu, and Niu Chien – and as many officers and mandarins as could crowd into the cabin – were all present for the historic moment. Full oriental protocol was observed. Four copies of the treaty, in English and Chinese, were spread out, bound in silk. Seals were attached before Pottinger and the Chinese Commissioners signed. A 'grand tiffin' with much toasting followed. During the celebrations Kiying insisted on Pottinger opening his mouth, into which with great dexterity he shot several large sugar plums, claiming that this was an old Manchu custom denoting mutual confidence. The Union Jack and the flag of China were raised at the mizzen and the main, and a 21-gun salute was fired.

When the Emperor's formal notification arrived from Peking on 5 September, some of Parker's fleet, with crews greatly weakened by fever, had already started to withdraw down river. Pottinger despatched Major Malcolm on his urgent journey home in the steam-frigate *Auckland,* carrying the treaty document. Eventually making use of the overland route, he reached London on 10 December in record time. Four ships, the *Blonde, Herald, Modeste* and *Columbine* had also sailed with $6m in silver, the first instalment of the ransom to be paid by the Chinese under the agreement. By the end of October the entire fleet had left the Yangtse, to regroup at Tinghai and Chusan.

Pottinger and Parker were to have an increasingly awkward relationship in Hong Kong, but Gough soon departed for a post as Commander-in-Chief in India. He was succeeded by Major-General D'Aguilar, who had already gained some diplomatic experience on a military mission to Constantinople.[18] Of the Chinese, Ilipu became High Commissioner at Canton, where he died in March 1843; Kiying, who had been titular Nanking Viceroy, took his place. Niu Chien was less fortunate. He was degraded in October 1842, and the following June was tried at Peking, apparently for the loss of the Woosung batteries, for which he was condemned to death.

CHAPTER THIRTEEN

The Bones of Government

The First Opium War, which had begun without any formal declaration on either side, was ended by the Treaty of Nanking. Pottinger had been resolute – unreasonably obstinate to Chinese eyes – and with one exception, the settlement followed the lines set out in the letter which Palmerston had hoped would be presented to the Emperor in 1840. The Treaty contained seven articles:

1. Hong Kong was to be ceded to Britain.
2. Five ports – Canton, Foochow, Ningpo, Shanghai, and Nanking – were to be opened to foreign trade. (Canton was opened on 27 July 1843; Amoy and Shanghai in November; Ningpo in January 1844 and Foochow, for which the Chinese had earnestly pleaded exclusion, in June. After the signing of the Treaty, but before its ratification, Kiying tried to restrict British residence at the ports to the period of the trading season. Pottinger rejected this as intolerable, demanding that a quarter be set aside where his countrymen could stay as long as they wished.)
3. Resident consuls were to be appointed to each of the five ports.
4. An indemnity of $21m would be paid for British losses and expenses. (Chusan and Kulangsu would remain in British hands till payment was made in full, and the first $6m was to be paid before the British left Nanking. The total of $21m was a very severe impost – on paper roughly equal to half the annual Chinese revenue.)
5. The Chinese merchant monopoly of the Co-Hong would cease to operate.
6. There was to be a uniform and moderate tariff on imports and exports.
7. Equality between officials of corresponding rank in the two countries was to be recognized.

For the Chinese, this was the first treaty they had signed with a foreign power since the Treaty of Nertchinsk with Russia in 1689. But, bearing in mind that to the Asiatic no single decision is binding indefinitely, their attitude to the outside world had not changed. Once the barbarians had destroyed the famed Manchu warriors at Chapu and Chinkiang and taken control of the Yangtse, they had seen the need to come to terms, but the effect on the rest of the Emperor's domain was minimal. No substantial concessions had been made. The arrangements at the treaty ports would be no less restrictive than had existed at Canton and the admission of consuls was consistent with the view that foreigners should be supervised by their own people. Of more importance was what the treaty document did not include – there was no reference to an ambassador being received at Peking as the ultimate symbol of parity of esteem. However, Pottinger had inflicted a deep blow to Chinese pride and the resentment lingered. He had achieved the immediate objective of lifting specific trade barriers, but the Imperial Court remained determined to resist any encroachment by foreigners.

Later, John Stuart Mill, always contentious, took the more cynical view that 'Probably a Chinese statesman thinks that when concessions galling to national pride, or adverse to national policy, have been extorted by force of arms, and as it were under duress, he is doing no more than his duty in regarding the treaty as a nullity'.[1] Mill concluded that the more extensive the concessions the more certain it was that they would be violated, and that in a vicious circle, once one expedition had exacted a treaty, another more powerful one would be required to enforce it. The force of Mill's argument, written in 1860, eventually became apparent, but for the time being Pottinger succeeded in persuading the Chinese to pay lip service at least to the Treaty, and to allow the new colony to take root.

Immediately, however, the news from Nanking was taken at face value and welcomed with euphoria. When it reached Hong Kong on 9 September, merchants took the news as endorsing their belief that the British were going to remain on the island. They had not yet realized the effect that the opening of the five ports to British trade would have on the commerce of the colony. In the local *Friend of China* (22 September 1842) the editor was bewildered at the magnificence of the prosperous career that seems now before us. Our Island will be the single British possession in China. What more in praise of its prospects can we say than this? Already we hear of teeming projects fraught with good for our Island.[2]

For the time being, Pottinger was acclaimed as Jupiter.

In London, Stanley suggested that a *feu de joie* would be appropriate, and since a report had just indicated that the tide had also turned in Afghanistan, Prime Minister Peel enthusiastically agreed.[3] Salutes were fired from batteries in Hyde Park and in the Tower. Stanley did his humble duty at the Palace, informing Queen Victoria that there had been a triumphant outcome to two gigantic operations, one in central Asia, 'the other in the heart of the hitherto unapproachable Chinese Empire'.[4] (The *Times*, which had always disliked the Opium War, commented wryly that the soldiers of the Queen could now cease 'sweeping away with cannon or bayonet whole crowds of poor pigtailed animals'.[5]

Pottinger had gone beyond his remit in obtaining Hong Kong, as well as admission to the treaty ports. To his mind the logic of acquiring an island base was clear. First, it had not taken him long to see that arrangements at Canton, the original trading port, had become too tortuous, and were never going to be entirely satisfactory. Occupation of an island would remove some of the main grounds for merchants' complaints. Second, the strategic case for having a permanent naval base was compelling, since further warfare was likely. Third, on the Bombay and Singapore precedents, an off-coast island would serve as a great entrepôt for trade. There was also a strong argument based on domestic stability. Law and order could only be enforced by a court operating on its own – British – territory.

If the island option, as opposed to secure arrangements at the treaty ports, had to be chosen, Palmerston's preference would have been for Chusan, a view shared by the East India Company's agents. Chusan would have been more convenient for trading in the Yangtse basin, and eventually with the northern provinces; but the approach to the small harbour at Tinghai was notoriously hazardous, while Hong Kong had a deep, sheltered anchorage with entrances from both east and west for sailing ships. Unenthusiastic and sceptical as he was, it is no surprise that when giving

Sir Henry Pottinger with the Treaty of Nanking *by Sir Francis Grant*

Marquis Wellesley

Major Eldred Pottinger *by George Duncan Beechey*

Mountstuart Elphinstone

Viscount Palmerston

Dost Mahomed Khan

The death of Sir Alexander Burnes

The Bala Hissar, Kabul

Canton factories, c. 1830

HMS Nemesis *in action*

Chinese artillerymen and gun

General Sir Hugh (later Viscount) Gough

Ningpo

Firing from the Josshouse, Chapu

Hong Kong, early view

Nanking, early view

Chinese diplomacy at Nanking

Signing of the Treaty of Nanking

Jardine Matheson's first factory at Hong Kong

Howqua, Head of the Co-Hong, Canton *by George Chinnery*

Hong Kong street, 1846

The SS Pottinger

Marquis of Dalhousie

Sir Frederick Pottinger

SACRED TO THE MEMORY OF

LIEUT. GENERAL THE RIGHT HONOURABLE

Sir HENRY POTTINGER, Baronet,

KNIGHT GRAND CROSS OF THE MOST HONOURABLE ORDER OF THE BATH,
AND ONE OF HER MAJESTY'S MOST HONOURABLE PRIVY COUNCIL;
LATE MINISTER PLENIPOTENTIARY AND AMBASSADOR EXTRAORDINARY
TO THE EMPEROR OF CHINA;
GOVERNOR AND COMMANDER-IN-CHIEF OF THE COLONY OF THE CAPE OF GOOD HOPE;
AND GOVERNOR AND COMMANDER-IN-CHIEF
OF THE PRESIDENCY OF MADRAS, IN THE EAST INDIES, &c., &c., &c.

BORN AT MOUNT POTTINGER, COUNTY OF DOWN, IRELAND, ON CHRISTMAS-DAY, 1789,
AND DIED AT MALTA, ON THE 18TH OF MARCH, 1856, AGED 67 YEARS.

DURING HIS ACTIVE PUBLIC CAREER OF 53 YEARS, FROM MIDSHIPMAN TO GENERAL,
HE FILLED MANY OF THE MOST PROMINENT OFFICES UNDER THE CROWN,
WITH DISTINGUISHED ADVANTAGE TO HIS COUNTRY AND GREAT CREDIT TO HIMSELF,
AND HIS UNBENDING INTEGRITY, HIGH SENSE OF HONOUR,
AND GENEROSITY OF CHARACTER AND DISPOSITION,
SECURED HIM THE UNBOUNDED RESPECT AND ESTEEM OF ALL WITH WHOM
HE BECAME ASSOCIATED IN THE PUBLIC AND PRIVATE RELATIONS OF LIFE.

ON CONCLUDING HIS SUCCESSFUL TREATY WITH CHINA IN THE YEAR 1842,
HE WAS DESTINED FOR THE PEERAGE,
BY HER GRACIOUS MAJESTY QUEEN VICTORIA THE FIRST,
BUT LOST THIS HIGH DISTINCTION THROUGH THE SAME HOSTILE INFLUENCE
WHICH WAS EXERTED IN VAIN TO PREVENT PARLIAMENT REWARDING
HIS EMINENT SERVICES TO THE STATE.

THIS MEMORIAL IS PLACED HERE
BY HIS ONLY SURVIVING BROTHER WILLIAM,
A.D. 1861.

Sir Henry Pottinger's memorial, St George's Church, Belfast

Pottinger his instructions on 31 May 1841 Palmerston was lukewarm about acquiring any island, especially Hong Kong. He admitted grudgingly that it was 'supposed to be in many respects well qualified' to become important commercially, and he enjoined Pottinger to examine its capacity, for use as a bargaining counter. (This letter casts some light on the character of both men. Palmerston recalled that in the Elliot negotiations Kishen had not altogether dropped that 'tone of affected superiority' which the Chinese used to cloak 'the real weakness of the Empire'. But since Pottinger knew the Asiatics so well, and was so accustomed to dealing with them, he need not be instructed 'to stop at the outset any attempts of this kind'.[6] Palmerston was not to be let down.)

On taking over at the Foreign Office, Lord Aberdeen was equally unconvinced by the need to retain an island base. Writing in November 1841, before he heard that the expedition had holed up in Ningpo for the winter, he correctly assumed that both Hong Kong and Chusan had been occupied. These 'island positions' would be useful for negotiating purposes, but – and here the heavy hand of the Treasury is revealed – to keep them under the Crown 'would be attended with great and certain expense'. It would lead to undesirable political involvement with the Chinese, and 'a secure and well regulated trade' was the only objective of Her Majesty's Government.[7] There was nothing here to encourage Pottinger in the pursuit of his plan for Hong Kong. Nor did Stanley at the Colonial Office give him any help. At the end of January 1842 he wrote that the island was to be regarded as 'a place militarily occupied, and liable to be restored to the Chinese Govt. on the attainment of the objects which H.M.'s Govt. seek from China'.[8] For good measure, he wanted all building on the island to be halted.

It was the Spring before Stanley's embargo on construction work reached Hong Kong. Pottinger was, of course, aware that Aberdeen was opposed to any acquisition, but he also observed that Stanley's later letter had been silent about actually giving up the island, and from this he concluded that he could still find room for manoeuvre. He could not see that the forthcoming campaign, whatever its result, would make a permanent base less desirable; he was the man on the spot, he knew more about the tactical and strategic imperatives than Westminster, and he was not going to yield.

To Aberdeen he wrote a deliberately ingenuous letter. The point, quite simply, was that developments put in hand by Elliot before his own arrival had gone too far to be abandoned.[9]

Pottinger was not a visionary, though on the Hong Kong issue he saw further ahead than most. He was a resolute but unpolished diplomat in his negotiations with the Chinese Commissioners, though he was very shrewd in dealing with a distant Government in London. Knowing that the outcome at Nanking would be welcomed at home, and would create a favourable climate, he seized the opportunity to justify his disobedience. Forwarding the Treaty to Aberdeen, he confessed that:

> the retention of Hong Kong is the only point in which I have intentionally exceeded my modified instructions, but every single hour I have passed in this superb country has convinced me of the necessity and desirability of our possessing such a settlement as an emporium for our trade and a place from which Her Majesty's subjects in China may be alike protected and controlled.[10]

Pottinger got his way. The acquisition of Hong Kong was not disowned. With hindsight, a nexus of events and trends can be constructed to make the permanent British presence there seem inevitable, but the crucial factor – the fulcrum – was the dogged determination of Sir Henry Pottinger. There is no need to indulge in the hypothesis of what might have happened if he had not been sent out as Plenipotentiary in 1841. He has left his mark on history.

It was clear from Aberdeen's letter of 4 January 1843 that the Cabinet had accepted the *fait accompli* at Hong Kong. The Foreign Secretary, acknowledging the Treaty with which Malcolm had hurried home, was happy to add that Pottinger's despatches had been laid before the Queen, and that 'Her Majesty highly appreciates the ability and zeal which you have displayed in the difficult circumstances in which you have been placed, and entirely approves all your proceedings'.[11]

As though to confirm that there were no hard feelings, no resentment that he had been outwitted, Aberdeen continued, 'So long as you remain in China, the entire control of affairs shall rest exclusively in you.' As soon as possible after the Ratifications of the Treaty had been exchanged he was to assume the Government of the island, which would then become a possession of the British Crown, and he was to issue suitable proclamations to that effect. No doubt the civil servants at the Foreign Office had been beavering away, because Aberdeen ends with an odd assortment of administrative instructions, ranging from the siting of barracks to the leasing of land and the appointment of consuls, who would report direct to Pottinger as Chief Superintendent of Trade. At a distance of a century and a half, there is a touch of irony in the advice to leave ample space for streets, so as to ensure good ventilation, and to guard against 'the evil consequences which might ensue from too crowded an occupation'.

Events on the island moved rapidly, even before the actual ratifications, now regarded as a formality, had been received, and before the proclamation of the new Colony on 26 June 1843. Stanley meanwhile summed up Hong Kong's unique status. The island was occupied not with a view to colonization, but for diplomatic, commercial, and military purposes. The three principal tasks of the governing officer were to negotiate with the Emperor of China or his officers, to superintend the 'trade of the Queen's subjects in the Seas, Rivers and Coasts of the Empire', and to regulate the settlement's internal economy. 'Hence it follows,' Stanley admitted, 'that methods of proceeding unknown in other British Colonies must be followed in Hong Kong, and that the Rules and Regulations . . . must, in many regards, bend to exigencies beyond the contemplation of the framers of them.'[12] Stripped of its jargon, this conceded that geography and government policy combined to give Pottinger an exceptionally free hand.

After ratification, he held three offices under two masters. As Governor, he reported to Stanley, the Secretary for War and the Colonies, while as Chief Superintendent of Trade, and Plenipotentiary and Minister Extraordinary he came under Aberdeen at the Foreign Office. Much would depend on how he discharged his triple responsibility.

Nine instruments of various kinds had been sent out from London to provide the bones of an administration which would last till they were fleshed out as a proper constitution. (Their terms bore the stamp of the indefatigable Sir James Stephen, Permanent Under-secretary at the Colonial Office, known as 'Mr Over-secretary Stephen' for the influence he exercised.) They extended to setting up a court to try British offenders, and the disposal of claims to land which had been illegally leased before the island had been ceded. The naval and military commanders were to be given guidance by the Governor-to-be on the deployment of their forces – later a source of much dispute.

From his hastily-constructed quarters on the island – until October 1843 he often resided at Macao – Pottinger reported, as requested, with 'the utmost unreserve' on the powers to be allocated to the Governor and the Legislative Council which would be required. This led to a constitution which was embodied in the 'Charter', publicly proclaimed on Ratification Day. The Governor, advised by the Legislative Council, was authorized to make domestic laws, provided they were not in conflict with the interests of the Crown. He was to keep the seal of office, issue grants of land, make appointments, and apply the prerogative to pardon criminals. The Governor was effectively in control of the Legislative Council, since no law could be passed, nor any motion debated, unless proposed by him, though a member could have his opinions recorded, for transmission half-yearly to the Secretary of State. The Governor had a casting as well as an original vote, and could override the Council. Stanley in his Instructions of 6 April 1843, had told Pottinger that

> in the very peculiar circumstances of Hong Kong, H.M. Government have thought it right to confer upon you the extraordinary power of passing laws independently of their assent, should the necessity for such a proceeding arise.[13]

The Government did not invent the Hong Kong structure *de novo*. There were general precedents in the arrangements that had been adopted in New Zealand and Ceylon, but the exceptional freedom allowed to Pottinger is a measure of Stanley's confidence in him.

To complete the impression that the members were 'hollow men going round the prickly pear', the Governor was to choose them himself, though they held their appointments from London. There was also to be an Executive Council of three with a quorum of two, exclusive of the Governor presiding.

In the view of the Home Government, Hong Kong was still a rocky outpost, sparsely populated and without any substantial local community calling for representation. The route to acquisition had been tortuous; it was not a normal settlement. Realistically, no popular element could be expected in the 1843 set-up, though some eventual devolution was apparently in mind, since Pottinger was told that in levying rates he should give householders 'the power and obligation to assess themselves and each other'. No such refinement was reached in his time. If the Charter and the accompanying Instructions appear to impute dictatorial powers to the Governor, in practice there were two restraints. First, the mercantile community, wanting to be left alone to trade and earn profits, expected the Governor to protect the broad Imperial interest and confine himself to a limited field, i.e. law and order, public works, etc. It was intended that the Chinese on the island should be subject to Chinese law, though this caused problems. Second, there was the safeguard, albeit distant, provided by the Secretary of State, subject to the vigilance of the Opposition and responsible to Parliament. The Hong Kong constitution, which Pottinger was the first to operate, was designed to safeguard trade and protect native customs.

Pottinger met unforeseen snags in setting up the Councils. On 24 August 1843 he nominated as members of the Legislative body A.R. Johnston, to be his deputy, J.R. Morrison who had succeeded his father as Chinese Secretary and Interpreter and had been prominent at Nanking, and William Caine, the Cameronian officer who also became Chief Magistrate. They were also to form the Executive Council and be styled 'Honourable'. But Morrison died of fever almost at once, and Johnston had to go home on sick leave. Pottinger could not find adequate replacements, and it was only in January 1844 that he could establish the councils, with a bare quorum of two members – Caine and Major-General D'Aguilar.

Soon after he succeeded as Governor, Sir John Davis wrote home that the Legislative and Executive Councils had been 'blended under Pottinger'.[14] Ignoring the requirement that they were each to have a minimum of three members, he had conducted them as a single body (as the Minutes confirm).[15] Pottinger belonged to the school that regarded the ideal size of a committee as two, with one member in hospital. He knew that committees were useful for defusing crises, or delaying awkward decisions, provided he did not himself have to attend prolonged debates.

Starting on 11 January 1844, the Legislative Council passed seventeen Ordinances within four months. Their first Instrument was designed to forbid the Chinese form of slavery (bond-servitude) in the colony, but it was ruled *ultra vires* because the relevant British legislation already applied. Other Ordinances dealt with such matters as the regulation of printing books and papers (thought to be premature), the settlement of civil suits by arbitration, the limitation of interest to 12 per cent, the unlicensed distillation of spirits, the licensing of public houses, and the establishment of a police force.

It is surprising that Pottinger managed to act with such speed, since, for the most part, he had to create the nucleus of a civilian establishment from personnel already in Hong Kong. Caine continued as Magistrate, Pedder as Harbour-Master, and the much-travelled Malcolm became Colonial Secretary. The Governor was in urgent need of legal assistance, and fortunately, but possibly not accidentally, a fellow-Irishman, Richard Burgess, was recruited, a barrister previously in Bombay and 'happening to have come to China'.[16] Pottinger persuaded an army surgeon, R.W. Woosnam to be his Private Secretary. Though he was often distant with subordinates, he developed a warm relationship with Woosnam, who later accompanied him to the Cape of Good Hope. The Rev. Vincent Stanton was nominated Colonial Chaplain – the Church of England was given some financial assistance, as befitted its official status in the colony. Stanton, previously Chaplain at Macao, had already suffered much tribulation as a soldier for Christ. Taken prisoner by the Chinese in 1840, he had been kept in chains at Canton.

Policing the new colony – more trade meant more robbery and burglary – was always going to be difficult, and Pottinger was criticized, rather unfairly, for the failure to recruit a competent force. As he carried on a testy exchange of missives on this subject with the Colonial Office, robbery was on the increase. In the last week of April 1843 Government House, and three mercantile houses (those of Dent, Jardine and Gillespie) were all burgled. On 10 May a curfew was imposed, preventing ships in the harbour leaving their moorings after 9 p.m. Chinese were to carry lanterns after dark, and not leave their houses after 10 p.m. The leading merchants mounted their own guards, and Jardine, Matheson & Co. employed twelve armed men at £60 a month to protect their warehouses. Each private house had a night-watchman who had to strike a hollow bamboo at intervals to prove he was awake. Europeans might carry their own weapons, and a pistol under the pillow at night, but robbers seemed to be getting the upper hand. In February 1844 an impertinent gang occupied James White's bungalow till they were driven out by rifle fire from the military. Chinese vagrants were not discouraged by the floggings ordered by Caine, and the prison was often more comfortable than their own dwellings.

Pottinger applied for a cadre of fifty inspectors and policemen from England but the Colonial Office deemed this too expensive, confirming that officers would be sent out, but that the rank and file should be enlisted locally. Pottinger, whose blood pressure was not improved by the pettifogging response from London, finally squeezed authority for as superintendent and two inspectors out of the Colonial Office only a fortnight before he left the island altogether. Meanwhile, he had assigned a detachment of Indian Soldiers, under an officer of the Madras Native Infantry, to police duties, though they were severely, sometimes comically, handicapped by their linguistic deficiencies.

Someone in the Treasury then raised the fascinating question whether the cost of running the Colony before the Treaty was ratified was properly a war, or a colonial, expense. The Legislative Council had not yet passed a taxation Ordinance, and though Pottinger was normally a meticulous accounting officer, no revenue had been collected from Hong Kong residents when he left the island in May 1844.

The British had a habit of setting up their own administration in foreign territory as though it was a divinely protected oasis. There was no need, it seemed, to take notice of the customs, wishes, or ambitions of the native inhabitants. But the outcome was not always as serene as had been envisaged. Pottinger was only too well aware of recent events in Afghanistan, where the British, on arrival at Kabul, had built cantonments, sent for their wives to join them, organized gymkhanas, and erected all the totems of permanent occupation. While this went on, the tribesmen were sharpening their knives, and Sir William Macnaghten, who had failed to comprehend the Afghan temper, was assassinated as a prelude to the rebellion that forced the ignominious retreat. Pottinger was not going to make the same mistake. His policy at Hong Kong was to honour the Treaty of Nanking in the spirit as well as in the letter, to avoid irritating the Chinese, and to do his utmost to gain their confidence and trust for the future. In order to achieve these ends, he was prepared to face criticism, even downright hostility, from his fellow countrymen on the island.

CHAPTER FOURTEEN

Bloody but Unbowed

Omnipotent on the island, at least in theory, Pottinger was a lonely man. He was surrounded by Service chiefs who fought their corners, merchants eager to assert trading privileges, adventurers who lurked everywhere, cadging what they could, and the Chinese, always likely to infer that the British were intruders, allowed a temporary presence by the Emperor's generosity. He knew that orders he implemented or arrangements he improvised might be cancelled by the arrival of despatches written in London six months previously and, in the light of events, already out-of-date. He could confide only in his private secretary, Woosnam.

In India, the Governor-General at Fort William, or even the Governors of the Presidencies, could point to a panoply of precedents and a whole tradition of service. Compared to them, Pottinger was a mere frontiersman, stubbornly nursing his concern for the public interest. He may have known that his 'Redeemer liveth', but he was not an overtly religious man, though he helped the missionary societies who zealously took the Cross to the heathen. His temper, which had got him into trouble in his Indian days, had not improved in the insalubrious climate, and his Irish brogue, never fully suppressed, became more apparent in moments of stress.

He knew from the start that his problems would not all come from the Chinese, though their resentment at the Treaty still smouldered, writing, 'I am convinced that it will be a far more difficult undertaking to control than to protect British subjects.'[1] He had just returned from Nanking when he was met with clamours for compensation for damage done during riots at the Canton factories. Under the Treaty, the Chinese High Commissioner was required to protect British subjects, and the factories, in all the treaty ports, but this was far from effective at Canton, where attacks on foreigners were always likely to happen. On this occasion a skirmish with Lascar sailors from the opium ships had developed into a patriotic demonstration. There had been threats to lives and property, but it was not clear whether the

Cantonese were initially at fault, and Pottinger dismissed the merchants' claims. Instead, he enquired whether they could

> assert that you have studied the complexion of the times, that you have in any single iota or circumstance striven to aid me in my arrangements, by endeavouring to dissipate and soothe the very excitement and irritation of which you so loudly complain.[2]

The Home Government supported the Governor's view that there should be no compensation for those who 'render themselves obnoxious to the Chinese Government or People'.[3]

Though he often deplored the behaviour of his fellow-Britons, Pottinger had not gone native, as proconsuls were known to do. At Nanking he had urged Ilipu and Kiying to stop their contemptuous references to Europeans. He tried to persuade them that, in the apparently improved atmosphere of the Treaty, there should be an Imperial edict against the 'low and scurrilous language hitherto at times published officially against foreigners'. It was worth trying, but with the Manchu regarding merchants as a grossly inferior class, it was not likely to change the attitude of centuries.

Since the Treaty had been drawn up and signed in a hurry – the Chinese wanted nothing so much as to see the sterns of Parker's ships sailing down the Yangtse – many details had still to be settled. Pottinger invited the views of a committee of British merchants on tariffs and trade regulations, but their replies verged on the insolent, some going as far as to regret the prospect of a peaceful régime. The fact was, Pottinger wrote to Aberdeen, that every individual was out for himself, 'open to corruption and ready to evade payment of the just dues of the Chinese Government by the most barefaced and wholesale smuggling'.[4] If this sounds pious, Pottinger justified himself by declaring his intention to propose terms that would be approved by Peking and would persuade the Chinese 'that their confidence in my fair dealing is not misplaced'.[5] The negotiations were delayed by the death of Ilipu, the result of 'apoplexy brought on by repletion'[6] – here Pottinger's understatement matches oriental politeness – but the new rates were agreed soon after Kishin took his place at Canton. Naturally, not everyone was pleased; the rooting out of corruption, even if only partial, is seldom popular.

Exchanges with the Foreign and Colonial Offices revealed confused arguments, more theoretical than practical, about the jurisdiction over the Chinese in Hong Kong. Were they, as the original instructions provided, to be subject to Chinese law, with the patronizing rider that it should not be 'repugnant to those immutable principles of morality' which Christians regarded as binding? Was there to be any distinction between transient Chinese and those who became domiciled in the colony? The Colonial Office eventually decided that the Chinese should have their own law and custom, administered by their own judge on the island, though Pottinger thought this a derogation of Crown authority.[7] Kiying argued forcibly that Chinese freedom from English laws was the same as the English refusing to abide by the laws of China. The final agreement left it to the Legislative Council to arrange for the Chinese to be subject to Chinese law.

After much discussion of a courteous nature with Kiying, Pottinger negotiated a Supplementary Treaty, called the Treaty of the Bogue, after the Bocca Tigris or Bogue, the main entrance to the Canton river, which was signed on 8 October 1843. The Americans and the French both obtained similar treaties a year later. Their most lasting effect was twofold. A 'most favoured nation' clause extended the same concessions from China to each treaty power. The provision on 'extraterritoriality' ensured that foreigners would be subject only to the jurisdiction of their own country's representative in China.

On the regulation of trade, Pottinger was embroiled with an indignant mercantile community. When, on 22 July 1843, he announced agreement with the Chinese on rules for the conduct of trade at the open ports, accompanied by a tariff of duties, he seized the chance to issue a sharp exhortation, calling upon all subjects of the Crown, not only to conform strictly to the new provisions,

> but to spurn, decry, and make known to the world, any base, unprincipled, and traitorous overtures which they, or their agents or employees, may receive from, or which may be in any shape made to them, by any subject of China – whether officially connected with the Government or not – towards entering into any collusion or scheme for the purpose of evading, or acting in contravention of, the said provisions of the Commercial Treaty.[8]

He promised 'the most stringent and decided measures' against offenders, and if his existing powers were inadequate, he was confident that the Home Government would indemnify him. This was good minatory stuff, with a pungent turn of phrase, but the merchants were furious at the implication that they were nothing but opium dealers and smugglers intent on disregarding the law.

There was an even louder outcry when the terms of the Supplementary Treaty became known. Going back to Palmerston's plan, the original objective had been for goods to be freely admitted to any port in China once Chinese custom duties had been paid at Hong Kong. The Chinese, however, cited the Nanking Treaty and insisted that foreign trade should go only to the five open ports. This in itself was annoying, but could have been foreseen. After complex arguments, however, the Treaty of the Bogue in effect gave the Chinese control of all native ships entering Hong Kong. This was anathema to British merchants, who complained that it negated the status of the colony as a free port.

To make it worse, the first version of the Treaty to be published did not contain the objectionable clauses, and it was alleged that Kiying had baffled the Governor by inserting them. (As rumours multiplied, it was even claimed that the interpreter had been bribed.) Pottinger, embarrassed for once, explained that the first copy was not meant to be complete. With confusion worse confounded, even G.B. Endacott, the distinguished Hong Kong historian, concludes that 'the whole incident is a little obscure'.[9] As Pottinger made clear on returning to England, he felt that he had been misrepresented. At a reception in his honour at the Merchant Tailors' Hall on 11 December 1844, he was at pains to correct the 'very erroneous impression' that there had been some mistake in the Bogue Treaty.

It arose from the necessity of my making public an abstract of the Treaty, while the Chinese published the whole, and a translation was made with many important omissions. Having been asked seriously whether there was any ground for the allegation that mistakes had been committed, I am happy to say that there was no cause for alarm.[10]

This sounds like an Irish obfuscation, but the point at issue was that the

British merchants wanted freedom for Hong Kong junks to enter all Chinese ports, thus undermining the Nanking Treaty. Pottinger had meticulously observed the Treaty requirements, and on this account met with sustained obloquy. The main criticism was that he took credit for acquiring an island trading station, but had not protected its trading conditions. Resentment at the Bogue Treaty provisions on this matter was so strong that they were largely ignored – a typical oriental reaction. Overall, Pottinger's prestige and popularity had taken a knock.

With the Chinese officials, however, he remained on good terms. During the final days at Nanking he had reported that Ilipu, Kiying, and their colleagues were no longer affecting 'that tone of exclusiveness and arrogance' which had so exasperated Palmerston,[11] and cordiality was carried a stage further when he got back to Hong Kong. At the beginning of 1843 he made a ritual journey upstream to Whampoa, where he was received by the High Commissioner and the Governor of Kwantung Province. Two assistant Chinese Commissioners came, more informally, to Hong Kong, where they behaved 'with easy politeness and total absence of constrained feeling'. There followed one of the highlights of Pottinger's term of office, and of his policy of encouraging social intercourse, when Kiying paid a return visit with some ceremony. Two steamers had been sent to escort the High Commissioner and his attendants from Whampoa and, after the obligatory pavane had been completed, he was entertained to dinner.

Pottinger's account brings the scene to life and illustrates, more clearly than many of his despatches, his own zest and competence.[12] In the drawing-room, before dinner, Kiying, observing two miniatures of the Governor's family, regretted that he did not have an heir. He requested permission to adopt Sir Henry's eldest son, and 'allow him to visit' China. The tactful reply was that 'the lad's education must first be attended to, but stranger things had happened than his seeing Kiying hereafter'. The Chinese Commissioner persevered; the boy was now adopted and would be known as 'Frederick Kiying Pottinger'. Meanwhile, he would keep the miniature. Next he wanted the picture of Lady Pottinger, which he placed on his head, 'the highest token of respect and friendship', and drank a glass of wine while holding it before him. What, he enquired, could he give the Governor's wife? Sir Henry, politely demurring, asked for time to consider, which provoked Kiying to exclaim 'What! Am I Governor-General and cannot get my orders obeyed?' Some embroidery, it was amicably agreed, would be appropriate.

After dinner came the more formal exchange of gifts. Kiying took a gold bracelet from his arm; it was one of two his father had given to him, and which he had worn for upward of forty years. Engraved with his name in mystic characters, if it was produced anywhere in China the wearer would be received as his brother. In return, Pottinger gave him a sword and belt which he had commissioned Malcolm to bring from England. The evening ended with much jollity, toasting – Kiying's taste for wine and cherry brandy had been a feature at Nanking – a spirited rendering of Tartar songs matched by contributions from British officers, and many professions of friendship. Before leaving, Kiying put his prized silk shawl over Pottinger's shoulders. The whole occasion had been skilfully stage-managed, and the contrast with the humiliation Elliot had suffered at Chinese hands was inescapable.

As a postscript, next morning Kiying and his two colleagues were given a trip round the island in a steamer. The young officer detailed to escort them remembered that 'all three were stretched at full length on the deck nearly the whole time, vomiting freely'.[13]

Pottinger was entitled to feel that his policy was progressing when Kiying asked to be called his 'familiar friend'. This was important since the High Commissioner was both in control of the nearest treaty port, Canton, and the channel of communication with the Imperial Court. But there were undercurrents. The Cantonese, for example, hated losing their monopoly, whose value was obvious when Howqua, the long-time Head of the Co-Hong, died in September 1843, worth $20m dollars. They were aggrieved at the new controls. Pottinger had to admit that he was still dealing with 'an Empire and people who have no notion, however small, of international law and rights'.[14] He had not exorcised isolationist China's suspicion of industrial Britain.

Scottish clan chiefs in the Highlands, it was said, could carry out a discussion in Gaelic for a whole day without the subject that was on all their minds ever being raised. The 'Great Thing' hung like a cloud above them, but it was never mentioned. In Hong Kong so it was with opium. Though it was widely believed in England that the war was fought to ensure that the Chinese would continue to import opium from India, and buy it with silver, there is no reference to the drug in the Treaties of either Nanking or the Bogue.

The British position was clear. The Chinese officially banned imports, but conveniently ignored smuggling. Pottinger had suggested that if China made the trade legal, it would earn revenue and put the smugglers out of business. But the Chinese did no more than say they would only prosecute their own nationals for involvement in the trade. Aberdeen pompously told Pottinger that even if sales were legalized, 'it will be right that Her Majesty's servants in China should hold themselves aloof from all connection with so discreditable a traffic'.[15] When Hong Kong became a colony it was thought that something more positive might be needed, but the idea that traffic might be made legal at one port, Canton, with a ban elsewhere, came to nothing. So long as the Chinese embargo on imports remained absolute, in Aberdeen's view, 'Her Majesty's Government can do no more for China in that respect than prevent the Island of Hong Kong from being a resort and market for British smugglers'.[16]

It was, ironically, for reasons connected with opium that Prime Minister Peel had made the island a dependency of the Crown instead of investing control in the East India Company, which was the alternative. The Honourable Company, he told Stanley, had too strong a pecuniary interest in the opium trade to be unbiased in dealing with China. He believed that a regulated trade would be the wisest policy for the Chinese, and

> the Home Government is more likely to speak with authority upon this point
> – I mean the authority of reason and not of force – than a party immediately
> interested on the double ground of commercial profits and of reason.[17]

Now the ambivalence appears. From Calcutta, Ellenborough was emphatic that Her Majesty's Government should not do anything 'to place in peril our opium Revenue. As for preventing the manufacture of opium and the sale of it in China, that is far beyond your Power.'[18] Ellenborough had good cause for alarm. In India opium was a government monopoly, and its value to the Indian government varied from £6m to £8m; about a sixth of total revenue. (Twenty-five years after Pottinger left Hong Kong there had been no change in the attitude at Fort William.) Sir Richard Temple is typical. 'If the Chinese will have opium, they may as well get it first rate from us, as second rate at home, and they may as well consume it taxed as untaxed.'[19] Sir George Campbell, the Lieutenant-Governor of Bengal had no qualms. Whatever the moral aspect, 'economically there is no fault to be found'.[20]

In this pull devil-pull baker situation, Pottinger was given wide discretion to act in advance of instructions from home. He indicated that steps already taken to discourage traffic in Hong Kong might simply result in opium ships carrying foreign flags. Other countries might be asked to cooperate, but he concluded wearily,

> For whatever the terms in which the trade in opium is spoken of in this and other (official) communications, I have the strongest causes for doubting whether even one in a hundred of the officers of the Chinese government is at all disposed to check the trade.[21]

This opinion was fully confirmed by the sapient Consul, George Tradescant Lay. For many months, he wrote, the sale and use of opium had been marked by a 'universal toleration' throughout the Chinese Empire. The High Authorities saw that any measures against it would be futile; if imports were stopped, opium would be cultivated in Yunnan Province, to the detriment of the essential grain harvest. Lay gave an insight into oriental thinking when he identified one objection to legalizing the trade. This was that to do so would violate Imperial decorum since the Emperor had so strongly condemned it. One ingenious solution considered was to refer, not to opium, but to the 'juice of the poppy', a preparation which found a place in the native pharmacopoeias.[22] But this interesting piece of chicanery made no progress, and Lay, like the other consuls who reported to Pottinger, was operating a policy of laisser-faire with the Chinese officials.

Against this background, the Foreign and Colonial offices not surprisingly took the view that Pottinger should stop excluding opium ships from the harbour, if he thought it expedient. (The ban had anyway largely been evaded by moving to outer anchorages.) By the time he went home in 1844 he had made no progress in regulating, far less stopping, traffic in the drug. He had not expected that he would. Personally, he was opposed to traffic in the drug, if not with Elliot's theological fervour, but he was conscious that there were things that no Plenipotentiary could hope to achieve.

The allocation of land for building, and the disposal of competing claims by merchants, speculators, and officials who wanted plots for public purposes, was bound to be contentious, and chaos marked the earliest stages. Elliot had sold allotments with a dubious title, Johnston had auctioned more land despite the embargo, and there were many squatters with no title at all. Pottinger sent home a detailed assessment and asked for instructions. Aberdeen's reply was summed up in a feeble circumlocution: grants were not to be made to persons who intended 'to dispose of them again with advantage to themselves'.[23] Freeholds were not to be sold, and leases were to be for terms up to seventy-five years. No grants made before the island became a colony would be recognized as valid. It was, however, soon recognized that this was too drastic, especially where building had already taken place.

Meanwhile, before hearing from London – the time-lag in transmission again comes into play – Pottinger had tried to deal with the whole land question on his own, calling for details of claims, and setting up a Land Committee to settle titles and fix rents. The Committee's work was held up by the need to take some rudimentary decisions on the location of the main town buildings, and by a severe fever that put all the officials concerned out of action. Everyone, from the principal officers down, was speculating in land to the limit of his resources, and Pottinger, with his aggressive integrity, was outraged. In January 1844, the Committee recommended in favour of keeping the 75-year leases, but suggested a revaluation. Vigorous complaints about these proposals continued for the rest of Pottinger's tenure.

The army wanted far more land for quarters and stores than Pottinger thought reasonable, and he did not care for the plan drawn up by Major Aldrich, who had been sent out to suggest a scheme to meet the garrison's requirements. He denounced Aldrich's blueprint, which he said would make the island into a fortress, instead of 'a vast emporium of commerce and wealth', and he was determined to reduce the barrack area in the centre and preserve the Queen's Road frontage. This dispute, too, outlasted Pottinger, but the army did not get all they wanted. The navy also aroused his wrath by occupying a prime site and refusing to relinquish it. These disagreements were only facets of the worsening relationship between the Governor and his military and naval commanders.

Pottinger had got on well with Gough during the Nanking operation, but he did not like his estimate of the future military strength at Hong Kong. Gough, before departing for his new post in India, had suggested a garrison of 4,500. Pottinger, consistent with his belief that the island should be primarily a trading station, not a military one, argued that a smaller strength, of perhaps 1,000 men, would be adequate. He also deplored the inattention to the health of the troops, and on good grounds, during the fever epidemic. Relations with the army did not greatly improve with the arrival of a new military commander in Major-General D'Aguilar, though Pottinger knew he had earned a good reputation in India and was, like himself, a veteran of the Maratha campaigns.[24]

Relations with the Senior Naval Officer were worse. The trouble was that Parker resented Pottinger's overall authority as Governor, while Pottinger did not refrain from intervening in matters that were properly Parker's concern. The barometer was set for storms.

These disagreements are the more surprising, since, with one possible exception, there is little evidence of a lack of rapport when Pottinger, Gough, and Parker were all cabin'd and confined on the way to Nanking. At the outset, the allocation of responsibility could scarcely have been more precise. Auckland, as Governor-General, had been given the overall direction of the campaign, India being nearer than England to China. (At the time, he pointed out that the return of messages between Calcutta and Hong Kong took from four to eight months.)[25] Writing to Parker, Auckland was explicit; 'Sir Henry Pottinger will decide, in communication with me, upon the manner and object of your measures.'[26]

All seems to have gone well between the Plenipotentiary and the Naval

Commander, at least during the 1841 campaign. Parker reported to Auckland from the *Modeste* that Pottinger had accompanied him on a reconnaissance on board the *Phlegethon* before the attack on Amoy, and that he had been present on the *Wellesley* during the actual assault. Similar dispositions were reported at Ningpo.[27] Gough, as already recorded, dissented from Pottinger's severe policy towards the Chinese at Ningpo, but they did not, apparently, quarrel.

Then came a pregnant minute from Stanley to the Admiralty, on 4 June 1842. After reiterating that it was for the Foreign Secretary to designate the duties that devolved on Pottinger entirely, he continued that in naval and military matters Parker and Gough could each pursue 'without control, so far as he is officially concerned, the most expedient course'. Straightforward so far, but where civil, naval, and military issues were all involved, the three leaders 'should meet and confer together with the utmost possible frankness and unreserve'. They were not to decide on a course of action by voting, and, if they could not agree, the officer who would have to execute the decision should take it on his own.[28] The clear inference from the need to issue an instruction at this stage is that there had been a row.

Once the Treaty had been signed at Nanking, however, nothing but sweetness and light could be seen through the Admiral's spyglass. Reporting on events to the Admiralty on 29 August, he referred to the 'cordial and friendly understanding and intercourse which had invariably existed' among the three leaders. 'The judicious, firm, and courteous bearing of the Plenipotentiary, and the energetic, chivalrous spirit of the intrepid General and his gallant army', had led to their success. There had been no disagreement, but 'a degree of harmony and kindly feeling' that had never been surpassed.[29] (Pottinger's eulogistic address when Gough, authorized by the First Lord, invested Parker with the Grand Cross of the Order of the Bath on board the *Cornwallis* can be discounted as a routine element in the ceremony.)[30]

Did Parker go over the top in a moment of exultation, or were his remarks merely cynical, intended to cover up past discord and safeguard his own reputation as a cooperative colleague? Whatever his motive, any semblance of harmony was soon dissipated when they were both back in Hong Kong.

Friction between proconsuls and naval commanders was endemic in the colonies during the nineteenth century. The Governor, supreme in his territory, had no doubt that the job of the naval commander-in-chief was to deploy his ships to assist the execution of policy. The navy, always a self-contained, self-regarding service, was uncomfortably aware that it owed allegiance to the Lords of Admiralty, but in practice was subject to orders that emanated from, or were approved by, the Foreign Office. In Hong Kong, Pottinger had, from the background to the acquisition of the colony and for simple reasons of geography, been given exceptionally wide powers, which were paradoxically inflated by the availability of the squadron in the harbour. This made for further exacerbation. Pottinger and Parker had, for their own survival, to get on together on the Yangtse, but this imperative no longer applied. As the summer of 1843 wore on, the thermometer climbed to 97°F, there were few remedies for the 'winged plagues' of mosquitoes, and tempers rose. Parker became more and more crusty, and Pottinger increasingly tetchy. Examples of their conflict, sometimes comic, occasionally serious, are not hard to find.

In April 1843, Captain Hope, the senior naval officer at Chusan, had tried to arrest a Jardine Matheson schooner, the *Vixen*, which he suspected was carrying opium to Shanghai, a port not yet officially open to trade under the Treaty. The *Vixen* evaded pursuit, but four other British ships found at the mouth of the Yangtse were ordered out. The Hong Kong merchants were vociferous in their anger at this interference with their trade, known to be condoned by the Chinese. Pottinger was embarrassed because he could not openly endorse trading in the drug. Fortunately, an enquiry did not actually establish that the *Vixen* was carrying opium, and so he reprimanded Hope for being too quick on the draw. The indignant officer was posted away from Hong Kong, complaining bitterly about his treatment.

Pottinger assured Aberdeen that the *Vixen* business was no more than a hiccup, but Admiralty papers say otherwise. Pottinger, Parker wrote, was trying to place Naval officers under his control.[31] The Governor, however, claimed that his authority covered everything that could be construed as political. To Parker he wrote that it was odd that, as Governor, he did not know where the ships of the squadron were – apart from his flagship, clearly visible in harbour. Ships had sailed from the island without the Governor's knowledge and this would not do.

> The impression I have is, that the Naval Commander and Squadron is precisely placed on the same footing as far as I am concerned, as the Military Commander of the Land Forces. It is clear that your Excellency does not subscribe to that impression, and it is surely clear that one of us must be in error. To have that error cleared up is, as I have said, equally necessary and proper.[32]

A logical, though heavy-handed conclusion, but the Admiralty naturally took Parker's side. Pottinger, who had disavowed 'the smallest wish to cavil at trifles', was meanwhile claiming that he could delegate his authority over ships on detachment down to consuls and his Military Secretary. He went too far when a consul ordered the flogging of 'refractory merchant seamen' not liable to martial law, on board the *Dido*. Parker told Captain Keppel that this was contrary to 'that dignity and high bearing which should distinguish a British ship-of-war' and was not to be repeated.[33] Aberdeen also disapproved.[34] However, Parker had the last laugh when Pottinger wanted to hoist the same flag as the Lord High Admiral, and to receive a similar salute, when he went aboard ship; Parker referred gleefully to an Order in Council which forbade this kind of personal recognition.[35]

The Foreign Secretary and Haddington as First Lord of the Admiralty were now alert to the testy missives flying between Pottinger and Parker, and sent out a stream of emollient letters which the clerks engaged on despatch must have found hilarious. Parker was still complaining that it was not the Governor's orders he objected to, but 'the manner in which he assumes the right of promulgating them'.[36] There were, however, more serious aspects. Under the Treaty of the Bogue a cruiser had to be stationed at each of the Treaty ports. Parker said that to do this would impair his ability to carry out other essential duties such as anti-piracy patrols, convoys, and ferrying home the silver coinage of the Chinese indemnity. Moreover, ships rot if permanently tied up at a quayside. After lengthy discussion the Law Officers of the Crown also weighed in, and the Admiralty and the Foreign Office were persuaded that regular visits would comply with the Bogue Treaty.[37]

Pottinger was displeased at this rebuff (which came after Parker had gone). The significant point is that, with more experience of the oriental mentality than the pundits at home, he was firmly of the belief that he had to take Chinese sensitivity into account. (He always emphasized how essential it was 'to study the peculiarities and feelings of the Chinese people'.)[38] The Treaty terms must be meticulously observed, and only in this way would the Chinese learn the meaning of European conventions. He grieved, he told Aberdeen, that there had been carelessness in infringing the settlement.

> I mean, that things are often done, or attempted to be done, which though not expressly prohibited by the Treaty, I do not consider would be considered admissible with regard to independent states in Europe.[39]

He was consistent in doing everything he could to avoid irritating the Chinese, even if this meant assuming the impossible task of overseeing every detail himself. He would not allow Parker to undertake a ceremonial cruise in his flagship the *Agincourt*, lest it should seem to have some sinister implication, and he persuaded the Admiral to prohibit British ships from travelling north of 32° of latitude, i.e. the mouth of the Yangtse. He had the better of the argument when it was proposed that Captain Sir Edward Belcher should survey the five treaty ports. Belcher was highly experienced in survey work, but notorious for his bellicose attitude. Pottinger said that he was not to go and upset the Chinese. Parker climbed down, and eventually Lieutenant Bate was deputed to do the survey.[40] The atmosphere was just as tense after Rear-Admiral Sir Thomas Cochrane replaced Parker in December 1843. Pottinger would not let Cochrane move the *Agincourt* into the Canton River, where barnacles could be released in fresh water, and in March 1844 he reprimanded the Captain of the *Plover* for attacking pirates near the shore at Amoy.[41] On a strict reading of the Treaty, this was not allowed. Cochrane was provoked to disagree with Pottinger's conception of duty, calling him vain, vengeful, and impudent.[42]

The Governor, so called for convenience, though much of his work was done in his capacity as Superintendent of Trade, or as Plenipotentiary, was satisfied enough not to be over-concerned at the irritation of the Senior Naval Officer. But he was tired. He had stood alone, he wrote to Stanley, and had to act on his 'unassisted judgment', and yet he was accused of being 'the originator and approver of all public mistakes and oversights'. He had long made it known that he wished to return to England when the Opium War was ended, and had offered his resignation in July 1843, but did not finally leave until his successor, Sir John Davis, arrived in May 1844.

Pottinger had expected, and always had an abrasive relationship with the Hong Kong merchants. Like settlers elsewhere, they clamoured for Government protection and security for their own activities. Having got it, they did not like the regime set up in the interests of law and order, equity, and responsibility towards the indigenous population. In short, they were basically anti-colonial, wanting to be left alone to operate in an area free from customs and excise exactions. Parodying Adam Smith, they saw no situation so bad that government interference would not make it worse. If they took a selective view of past, pre-Treaty, events, they could persuade themselves that, with a little lubrication, they had always overcome difficulties with Canton.

His critics said that Pottinger, unremitting in his approach to work, had gone too fast for what was still an incipient colony. There is some force in this, but it is a matter of degree. While he was hurrying his Ordinances through the Legislative Council, the colony could muster at least a dozen large English firms, some with huge floating warehouses in the harbour, as many smaller concerns, and a growing number of Indian companies. Three newspapers had offices, and the first ship to be built in Hong Kong, the *Celestial*, weighing 80 tons, was launched on 7 February 1843. The merchants, however, croaked that the Governor would not recognize leases granted by Elliot and Johnston, and complained that they had been misled. (It might not be too fanciful to suggest that the hysterical speculation in land started Hong Kong's notorious gambling fever.) They niggled about the delay in organizing a proper police force, though this was not Pottinger's fault. He had, however, little success in improving public health. In the summer of 1843, 24 per cent of the troops and 10 per cent of the European civilians died during a fever epidemic. In the same year records show 1,526 troops needing 7,893 admissions to hospital.[43] If these grim figures are correct, it appears that on average each man was admitted more than five times in the year. In August 1843 Pottinger appointed a Committee of Public

Health and Cleanliness, with authority to enforce sanitary rules, and passed an Ordinance on 20 March 1844, but he could not point to any great progress.

Senior merchants were offended that he seldom socialized with them. He was not, like Major-General Lord Saltoun, disposed to be President of the local madrigal society. But if he lived too much in seclusion with his staff, this was in the character of the man who was determined to impose his own template, and who had learned in India that the Governor should not mingle too closely with the governed, if he was to retain respect and an unsullied reputation.

In his last months on the island Pottinger had been greatly distressed by the death of his nephew Eldred, who had come to visit him before going home on leave. Eldred was last heard of defending Herat against the Persian army (Chapter Seven). For his services he was appointed Political Agent in Herat, and a graceful acknowledgement in the Gazette recorded the Governor-General's pleasure in 'bestowing the high applause which is due to the signal merits of that officer'.[44] His next appointment was as Agent at Charekar in the Kohistan. There he was soon besieged by rebellious tribesmen and after another, equally heroic, defence he and a fellow-officer made a hazardous escape to Kabul. The city was already under attack but Eldred managed to get through the Afghan lines by addressing the enemy's guard in Persian. Lady Sale noted laconically in her diary for 15 November 1841, 'Major Pottinger and Mr Haughton have made their escape from the Kohistan; the former has a ball in his leg; the latter has lost his hand and is severely wounded in the back and neck'.[45]

After the murder of the British Envoy in December, Eldred reluctantly negotiated terms with the Afghans for withdrawal. Made a hostage during the retreat, in which the British force was wiped out, he survived months of captivity in appalling conditions. When his captors had been bluffed into changing sides, he impertinently set up his own administration before being rescued. A Court of Enquiry into the Kabul disaster concluded that his conduct was marked by energy and manly firmness that stamped his character as worthy of high admiration.[46]

Eldred was cast very much in Sir Henry's mould, and they shared a strong bond of affection. Writing to his brother John on 23 August, he said that Uncle Henry was 'too much engaged with public correspondence' to have time for private letters.

> He is generally at work before sunrise; and, except while dressing, he continues till it is too dark to see in his office. He sleeps very little and I quite wonder how he keeps his health. He has asked me to stay as Consul at Canton till he can procure an officer fitted for that purpose. I was rather reluctant, but I have consented. My leg is still annoying me a great deal, and I am afraid it will give me much more trouble than I calculated on.

His next paragraph was more sinister.

> This place is very sickly at present. A sort of typhus fever is laying hold of people and doing much to thin our numbers. My uncle thinks he will go Home at the end of the year, in which case I think I will accompany him.[47]

It was not to be. Already ill when he landed at Hong Kong, he fell a victim to the fever that was ravaging the colony. There is no record of the actual circumstances of his death on 15 November 1843 beyond the official notification that reached Calcutta in December.

CHAPTER FIFTEEN

A Sort of Hero

Sir Henry Pottinger was not an introspective man, or, if he was, he suppressed any evidence of such a tendency in his letters. But on his way home after the most surprising assignment of his career, there was time to take stock. When he returned to England from Sind in 1841, he was a sick man, but his spirits rose after a period of recuperation. He became restless and began to think of continuing his climb up the hierarchy in Hindustan. In time he might hope for one of the plum jobs, as Lieutenant-Governor of a Province, or even as Governor of one of the three Presidencies. Given his record, this was not vaulting ambition; it was a reasonable prospect. He had not expected the China appointment. It had come as a shock, but it was over. Now, en route from Hong Kong – he was peeved not to be given the sole use of a ship for the first stage to Bombay – he could reflect on what had happened since he got his first sight of the Pearl River. Boring friends with reminiscences would come later, but he could draw up a rough balance sheet.

In one sense his castle was built on sand because, although he was the chosen instrument to carry out the wishes of Her Majesty's Government, there was very little that could be described as a coherent foreign policy. There was, admittedly, an objective – to develop trade with the China coast, which in turn meant obtaining equality of diplomatic status. But neither the rhetoric of Palmerston, primarily interested in Europe, nor the more moderate attitude of Aberdeen, could disguise one basic feature. Looking to the Far East, the British Government was seemingly content with reacting to events as they occurred, and the more adverse the event (bearing in mind the indignities suffered by Charles Elliot), the more positive the response. But if the Government was distracted by developments in Europe and India, traders on the China coast, volubly supported by mercantile opinion at home, saw a great future for expansion. To this end they wanted free trade, subject to no regulations, but protected by British gunboats. It was in this maelstrom that Pottinger had to supervise the founding of the new colony.

Was Hong Kong becoming a great emporium of trade and commerce, attracting 'highly respectable and affluent Chinese merchants' in large numbers, as he had visualized? Not entirely, for two years after his departure, the Rev. George Smith concluded regretfully:

> There are but faint prospects of any other than a migratory or a predatory race being attracted to Hong Kong, who, when their hopes of gain or pilfering vanish, without hesitation or difficulty remove elsewhere.[1]

Pottinger had certainly obtained the cession of the island by treaty: the constitution was taking shape and the first decisions on how to run the colony had been taken. But he had been so deep in negotiations, both with the Home Government and with the Chinese, that he had little time to put many of the practical measures required into effect. Roots, first shoots, could be seen, but so far few flowers to garland the fragrant harbour.

Estimates of population growth are largely speculative, but the first Registrar-General, Samuel Fearon reported, using the earliest official data, on 24 June 1845 that in the last two years thousands of Chinese had swarmed ashore, bringing the total up to 23,000. Building, another yardstick to measure activity, had gone in fits and starts, and Fearon recorded over 700 houses, together with public offices, barracks, a hospital (with subscriptions from Jardine Matheson and other firms) and, as the inevitable postscript, a gaol with eleven cells for prisoners awaiting execution.

Though it was much the youngest colony, a vigorous social life quickly took root among Europeans even in Pottinger's time. In the House of Lords, in March 1843, the Marquess of Lansdowne said his fellow peers might be amused at some aspects of Hong Kong's rapid advance, including the announcement of a theatre with 'actresses whose virtues surpassed even their accomplishments'.[2] In 1844 that habitual manifestation of British colonial life, the amateur dramatic society, appeared, though only briefly. (The final bastion, the Hong Kong Club, had to wait until 1846.) There was already a market for delicacies, as the *Hong Kong Gazette* showed;

> Notice – The gentry of Hong Kong, and the public generally, can be furnished with fine English mutton [at one half dollar a pound] by sending orders to *The Briton's Boast* on Saturday mornings.[3]

Despite misgivings that troubled missionaries, the Governor, and sometimes the Home Government, opium was still the staple item of trade. The year after Pottinger left, the Hong Kong Auditor-General reported that eighty clippers (nineteen belonging to Jardine Matheson), and several small schooners, which made use of the harbour, were carrying the drug. There was also an extensive trade in smuggling salt to the mainland, in order to get round the Chinese monopoly.

Otherwise, trade grew more slowly than Pottinger had expected. In 1845 the ubiquitous Gutzlaff, now Chinese Secretary to the Superintendent of Trade, tried to explain why Hong Kong had not become an emporium as quickly as had been hoped.[4] This was not due to the restrictions imposed by the Treaty of the Bogue as much as to the competition of the treaty ports. (No one at that time foresaw the spectacular growth of Shanghai.) Piracy hindered trade; Pottinger, anxious not to impair his good relations with the Chinese, had been reluctant to sanction counter-measures against pirates. There was no reciprocal market for Chinese products in Hong Kong. The Chinese used British ships for imports, and while this benefited the shipping lines, it did nothing for the island's economy. Chinese merchants were still finding it more profitable to trade directly from Canton. The basic problem, however, was that the assumption that Canton's monopoly of foreign trade would be replaced by Hong Kong had been undermined by the opening of the five treaty ports. It was more economic to use the facilities there, avoiding transhipment at Hong Kong.

Pottinger left no easy legacy, as successive Governors were to find. The longer he stayed on the island, the more he was criticized – a common fate of innovators, especially those with supreme power. At times he seemed to be increasingly at odds with everyone. He had long-running disputes with the armed forces; the mercantile community blamed him for enforcing regulations and for the Treaty of the Bogue. For his part, he inveighed against those, including his own officials, who speculated in land. He buried himself in details as he tried to ensure that no item of government business escaped his vigilant eye. He grew more short-tempered, and his subordinates were not all sorry when he left. (His successor, Sir John Davis, fared no better, eventually becoming the most unpopular Governor the colony was ever to have.)

On the credit side, apart from persevering in his determination to secure the island for the Crown, he had made a very fair shot at coping with the problems which arose in the colony's initial stage. No one questioned his honesty, or his intense, often solitary, belief in upholding the public interest. He was most successful in his relations with the Chinese High Commissioner and his staff. It was not just a matter of personalities, though he and Kiying got on amazingly well; he enjoyed the respect of the Chinese officials for always sticking to his word. Obstinately he upheld the two Treaties, holus bolus, and in so doing he overlooked the extent to which the Chinese nourished their resentment against the terms he had imposed at Nanking. He also underestimated the barely concealed hostility of the Cantonese who wanted to go back to their immensely profitable, wholly unregulated, trade pattern. But his policy of conciliation was endorsed by Peel's Cabinet, and it was a confident ex-Governor who returned to receive the plaudits of his fellow-countrymen.

Soon after he reached London in October 1844, he paid his official call on the Foreign Office where, according to Aberdeen, he made a number of points very much in character. He said that as long as his friend Kiying, who had become more influential, remained in authority, relations should not cause difficulty. The Chinese, he thought, would eventually make the opium traffic legal. There was no limit to the expansion of trade originating in the colony. 'But,' said Aberdeen, 'he spoke with strong censure of our merchants and their practices in China, each of whom, he said with a genuine Irish accent, was a bigger rogue than the other.'[5]

Aberdeen accompanied him to Windsor, where he was received in audience by The Queen. The Foreign Secretary noted from the conversation that the Sovereign 'seems to take a peculiar interest about China'.[6] Aberdeen was, he told Peel, impressed by the ex-Plenipotentiary's friendly manner and his outstanding integrity. 'He is evidently a remarkable man, and is perhaps the more striking from his comparative ignorance of Europe and European affairs.'[7]

Even before he came home, Pottinger had some idea of his standing with the Government from the peculiar exchanges which had already taken place in Parliament. On 7 February 1843, Peel, in answer to a question about the regulation of courts in Hong Kong, remarked that, 'It was impossible for any man to act with greater moderation, discretion, good sense, energy and firmness than Sir Henry had done.'[8] A week later, after Stanley moved an address conveying thanks to the armed forces for the successful outcome of the Opium War, two Members, Sir George Staunton[9] and Mr Hume,[10] asked why Pottinger was not included in the resolution that named Gough, Parker, and other senior officers. Peel, in reply, referred to what he had said the week before, expressing the wish that 'it had been consistent with usage' to have included Pottinger's name. He was, however, adhering to precedent and there was no instance of Parliament thanking a diplomatic agent for the conclusion of a treaty. His Government had endorsed Pottinger's appointment by its predecessor, and he had been entreated to stay at his post. He added that, 'If he will recall his decision and remain permanently in China, he will possess the entire confidence of Her Majesty's Government'.[11]

This was heady stuff, but the House of Lords was even more complimentary. Lansdowne regretted that it had been necessary to make the omission on technical grounds. Pottinger had not only been the Plenipotentiary, but 'he was throughout the whole of the late operations aiding and assisting in person the exertions of the forces upon every occasion', and he had contributed largely to the conciliatory nature of the settlement. Wellington, very much on the defensive, said that if all the papers could be laid before the House, 'at that moment would be furnished sufficient to attract the admiration of every man in England to Sir Henry Pottinger'.

This was surely enough, but Aberdeen had to have his say. After offering his tribute to Pottinger's discretion, judgment etc, he concluded that he had earned the respect and good feeling of the Chinese – hardly to be expected in the circumstances. 'The Government was very satisfied to have, at such an immense distance, someone in whom they had full confidence.'[12]

Was this any more than Parliamentary flannel? Clearly there was some real regret that Pottinger's name was not to be recorded along with his sometime Yangtse comrades. But the unworthy thought remains that, just because Ministers were persuaded by some senior bureaucrat that precedent prevented this, on that very score they were more fulsome than they would otherwise have been. Faute de mieux, he got the best of all.

In an extraordinary postscript, on 3 May 1843 Lord John Russell asked Peel if he would now object to a vote of thanks to Pottinger. Peel said he would 'decidedly object', as Pottinger had not been abused in the House, and the Treaty had not yet been ratified. Russell said he would postpone his motion, and that he hoped, for Pottinger's sake, that someone could be found to abuse him before ratification reached this country. Peel commented that, 'The abuse will not come from this side of the House'.[13] The great expert on Parliamentary practice, Erskine May, even at his most arcane, would find it hard to justify this contorted exchange.

Almost a year later, on 2 April 1844, the question came up again. Peel, laying the Supplementary Treaty before the House, again paid tribute to Pottinger, but added that 'I believe that sometimes panegyric is weakened and diluted by words'. This was intended to put a stopper on further questions, but Palmerston obstinately had his point to add. He had appointed Pottinger on his own merit, not for his political opinions, unknown at the time, and for the ability he had displayed in India. Another year passed and Parliament was not allowed to forget Sir Henry. On 17 March 1845 Mr Hume popped up again to ask if there was to be a vote of thanks.[14] Peel wearily replied that he meant no disrespect, but once again it 'had not been the normal course to vote the thanks of the House for civil or diplomatic services'. He recalled that Sir Henry had been made a Baronet for his time in Sind, and had been awarded the Grand Cross of the Bath when the Treaty was ratified. The clear implication was that these honours, and his membership of the Privy Council (to which he was admitted on 24 May 1844), were enough.

Meanwhile, Pottinger had to endure a round of municipal frolics that tested his stamina as severely as the Yangtse expedition. Merchants (who could hear the tills ringing with Chinese trade), and local corporations, vied in doing him honour. He was given grand banquets by London,

Edinburgh, and Glasgow, and made a freeman of these cities. Liverpool (where Stanley spoke in his praise), Manchester, and Belfast were not to be outshone, and commemorative pieces of plate overloaded his sideboard. The general reaction was summed up by the Lord Provost of Glasgow: 'Tell him in the plain language of British merchants that he has done us good, and we are grateful for it.'[15]

The P&O shipping line resolved to give him an 'entertainment' at the Albion Hotel, Aldersgate Street on 28 June 1845, and eventually named their new ship for the China run after him.[16] The Bombay Chamber of Commerce, the Merchant Tailors Company of London (where Aberdeen added his own felicitations), and the East India and China Association came forward with their tributes. A striking testimony was provided by the 14,000 workers in Manchester who signed an address within hours of the list being opened. When he spoke to a crowded meeting of cotton merchants, he assured them that all the mills in Lancashire could not make enough stocking-stuff for a single province of China. Delivered in his richest Irish brogue, this was an extravagant claim. China simply did not have the purchasing power. Its revenue, derived from tea, silk and silver, was limited, and the more spent on opium, the less was available for other goods – as a Select Committee of the House of Commons found in 1847. For the time being, however, Sir Henry was the hero of the hour.

Sir Francis Grant, the fashionable artist (and later President of the Royal Academy) painted a portrait of Pottinger holding the famous Treaty, and when crowds thronged to see it at Graves' Gallery in Pall Mall, the Duke of Wellington pronounced himself 'highly satisfied' with the likeness.[17] But what was the Government doing for its faithful servant? The answer was nothing tangible, and it seemed as though the ex-Governor, heavy with honours, would have to eke out a penurious existence.

On 3 June 1845 the tenacious Mr Hume was on his feet once more. (There is no suggestion that Pottinger put him up to it, and Hume said explicitly that he had never met him.) In the Commons he moved for an address to The Queen to provide Pottinger with a pension. He was seconded by Viscount Sandon and eloquently supported by John Hobhouse,[18] speaking with the authority of his experience as President of the Board of Control. Meeting no opposition, they referred to Pottinger's distinguished service, the acclaim he had received in the country, the pensions given to other diplomats, and the expectations of high office he had lost from not being allowed to continue his career in India. In reply, Peel did nothing but waffle. There were rules regarding the minimum service required, there was the danger of creating precedents, and so on. But exceptions could be made, and taking note of the feeling in the House he was prepared to move the necessary address. It was all done with some reluctance.[19] Lord John Russell and Palmerston added to Peel's embarrassment by enthusiastically endorsing his fairly graceless concession.

On 16 June Peel announced that Pottinger's pension was to be £1,500 for life – not over generous when compared with Gough, who eventually got £2,000. Peel, however, had the nerve to invite Members to save the country 'from the discredit of allowing him to remain in poverty'.[20]

CHAPTER SIXTEEN

The War of the Axe

Having surveyed the problems affecting his Ministry, Earl Grey, the new Secretary of State for the Colonies, did not like the news from the Cape of Good Hope. He had already made up his mind that his guiding principle must be 'to protect the Colonists from the depredations and constantly recurring wars with their savage neighbours, by civilizing and reclaiming the Kaffir tribes'.[1] But first the tribesmen had to be subdued. The present campaign in the prolonged contest for land between white settlers and black inhabitants on the Cape's eastern frontier, at best inconclusive, was not achieving this objective. The Kaffir Wars, mainly skirmishes, cattle-raids and the burning of crops, did not give rise to spectacular battles that might fire the public imagination, but they were a drain on manpower and on the Exchequer. The latest phase – known as the 'War of the Axe' after Sandile, the head of the western Xhosa (the Ngqika), refused to give up one of his men accused of stealing an axe from a store at Fort Beaufort – had started in April when the Cape Governor decided to take the offensive.

The Governor, Sir Peregrine Maitland, a Waterloo veteran, was actively involved in the hunt for the leading Kaffirs, but back in London, Grey was not satisfied with progress.[2] The next step was to decide on a scapegoat, and in January 1846, Maitland was told that he was to be replaced. He replied tartly, but too optimistically that an end to military operations was imminent.

Pottinger had been home for more than a year and was taking his ease in Cheltenham when he received an unexpected letter from Grey. It came straight to the point. Because of the unhappy condition of the Cape colony a younger Governor was needed, and Pottinger was invited to accept 'this very important and arduous duty'.[3] (Grey later wrote that 'the state of the colony required the services of a Governor of the greatest ability and energy that could be found'.)[4] The offer was not received with any great exuberance. On one reckoning, it was flattering to the ego to be selected for another challenging assignment, or, as he suspected, to clear up another mess. But, as he told Grey, he would have much preferred another appointment in India, and moreover, the remuneration attached to the Cape job was, he thought, inadequate.

Public servants can only protest so far. Lord John Russell, now Prime Minister, was emphatic that Grey should persuade Pottinger to go to the Cape. As a sweetener, he was told that if he were to go, it would be on the understanding that he would be relieved as soon as peace was restored, and that 'your claim upon public grounds to employment in India will become very strong upon any ministry which may be in power when an opportunity of offering you such employment may occur'.[5] It was a pretty guarded undertaking, but it was the best he could expect, and he notified his agreement. He had, however, made his point about pay, which was met by giving him the new, additional, office of High Commissioner 'for settling the affairs of the eastern border of the colony'.

Grey's Journal for 6 December 1846 carries an unmistakeable note of relief. Pottinger had left for the Cape 'with all the instruments it seems possible to give him at this distance. The state of things at the Cape is by all accounts most wretched, and I believe mainly owing to mismanagement.'[6] His instructions admitted, realistically, that, in another hemisphere, the new Governor would at times have to take his own decisions on matters of policy. There was the usual disclaimer, with which Pottinger was only too familiar, that the Crown had no wish to extend its dominions or responsibilities. Nevertheless, 'sound policy and enlightened regard for the welfare of the colonists require that the Kaffir tribes no longer be left in possession of their territory'.[7] They were not to be governed as part of the colony, but armed forces were to be stationed on their land. It was a pudding of an arrangement.

Pottinger, pondering over his new remit, and still served by Richard Woosnam, his private secretary from Hong Kong days, sailed for the Cape. Travelling by way of St Helena, he reached Table Bay on 27 January 1847. It was a pity he could not have made the journey on board the good ship *Pottinger*. A three-masted paddle steamer, belonging to the P&O line, she made her maiden voyage from Southampton, arriving at Table Bay on 9 April 1847, in the record time of thirty-four days and three hours. (When she was launched in March 1846 – at which event a toast was drunk to Sir Henry's health – she was said to be the largest iron steam-ship built, apart from Brunel's *Great Britain*.)

A sly journalist, reporting on the new Governor's disembarkation from the *Haddington*, noted that he was 'somewhat stout', his countenance was 'thoughtful' and time had thinned his flowing hair.[8] Pottinger did not stay long in Cape Town. A rapid but searching appreciation soon convinced him that John Montagu, the Secretary to the Government, and Sir Henry Young, the Lieutenant-Governor of the eastern districts, could be left to deal with day-to-day domestic questions. Keen to get near to the action, he left on 11 February for the eastern frontier, and there he remained during his time as Governor, either at Grahamstown, where he rented Government House for £300 a year, or at Fort Peddie. He did not doubt that this was what the tactical situation required, but it meant that his contact with the colonists at large was severely restricted.

The Cape was also to have a new Commander of the armed forces in Sir George Berkeley, recently promoted to Lieutenant-General, who had come out with Pottinger.[9] Although he had a good military record (including service in the Peninsula and at Waterloo), he received a muted welcome at the Cape where it was thought that Colonel Henry Somerset, very popular in local circles, should have been preferred.[10] Personal relations between Berkeley and the Governor were clouded by Pottinger's strong views on the division of powers between the civil and military authorities, but for the most part they respected each other.

At Grahamstown, Pottinger found that intelligence reports on the movements of the Kaffir chiefs were often contradictory, the troops' morale was low, and that general confusion reigned. After a lengthy conference, he and Berkeley concocted a plan to attack the chief Pato, and either secure his submission or drive him further east over the Kei River. On 3 March 1847, Pottinger issued a proclamation calling on white settlers to assist the regular forces in a final campaign to end opposition by the Xhosa tribesmen. Burghers who came as frontier volunteers were promised that they would not be absent from their families for more than a mouth.[11] Writing to Berkeley from Fort Peddie on 26 March, he confirmed that the first objective was to establish a line on the Buffalo River. Later, thinking ahead, he proposed that 'Beyond the Buffalo as far as the Kei, I intend to place the whole country under the protection of the Queen of England under the name of British Kaffraria'.[12] Kaffir chiefs could reside there, and British political agents would take post amongst them to administer justice. It was to become apparent that he had in mind to apply a template very similar to that which the Raj had imposed in India.

Berkeley's advance eastward was constantly impeded by Kaffirs 'swarming in every thick bush', marauding, ambushing, but never fighting a pitched battle. By mid-April, when it was clear that he would not be able to move beyond the Buffalo, Pottinger began to consider indenting for reinforcements from Mauritius, and he was 'strongly impressed' with the idea of getting native troops from India, preferably from Madras, as they were 'less tied down by scruples of caste'.[13]

Berkeley was back at Fort Peddie in early May, but he and Pottinger were still exchanging pompous notes about the extent of their respective jurisdictions. Previous governors had held a joint post, but Grey advised Pottinger that since he was technically under the jurisdiction of the East India Company, and not a Queen's man, he could not, under Army rules, be invested with the direct command of Her Majesty's troops. Grey tried to clear the air with a despatch written on 14 July, but not received till the end of October.[14] He indicated that while the Governor had no authority over the Queen's forces, he could call up any supplementary levies he thought were needed. The conclusion is splendidly oracular:

> To yourself, I need hardly observe, it exclusively belongs, to state and explain to the lieutenant-general the policy of Her Majesty's Government and the military measures by which that policy is to be attained. With him it must rest to direct the execution of those measures . . .[15]

Regrettably, both were too obdurate to admit that this was the basis of a common-sense solution.

Berkeley's advance, now reduced to pursuing cattle thieves and protecting convoys of supplies, was still halted on the Buffalo River, and Pottinger, for once, had to confess that he was not well. He wrote that 'This sickness of mine is most tedious and inopportune, but I find it necessary to work, else the wheel would stop. I have not been out since this day week. In fact I am often in such pain that I cannot walk.'[16]

Pottinger showed at best a sharp concern for the public purse, and at worst an ill-informed prejudice, in his treatment of the Kat River Settlement, a mountainous area of about 200 square miles on the northern frontier, with a population of 5,000. The settlement contributed a very high proportion of its able-bodied men for military service, and as a result farms were not worked and families left behind were nearly destitute. Despite a sympathetic report from Colonel Somerset, Pottinger was impervious to appeals for rations and clothing for women and children, and when in mid-April over 270 settlers decided to lay down their arms and go home, he was furious, claiming that 'Never was a greater deception practised on any government than speaking of it as a flourishing settlement. It is a concourse of rebellious, idle paupers.'[17] Gout, the climate, and frustration at the lack of progress in the field, had made him less than generous. To get this into perspective, within a week of arrival at Grahamstown, he was urging Grey to allow compensation for those who had suffered losses in the war, but he received a response typical of the Treasury. Were they to compensate colonists 'in every quarter of the globe'? Pottinger confessed to Berkeley that he thought this was most unfair.

Throughout the War of the Axe the regular British force had to be supplemented by irregulars. The colonial Burghers were not keen to turn out, and when they did were very likely to return home. The Kat River settlers, not surprisingly, were increasingly reluctant to do so, and there was no alternative to raising local levies from both whites and friendly tribesmen. But this was done in a chaotic way that soon attracted Pottinger's special ire. He had agreed with Berkeley that the levies were to come under his own supervision until they were deployed, when they would be subject to military command – a certain recipe for confusion.

Pottinger was trying to transform a gaggle of part-time, unenthusiastic, civilians, into an efficient force, and, of course, it did not work. As reports of the levies' activities reached him at Fort Peddie, it seemed to him that each day revealed more negligence, incompetence, or fraud, and his tendency to bury himself in minutiae, already apparent when he was in

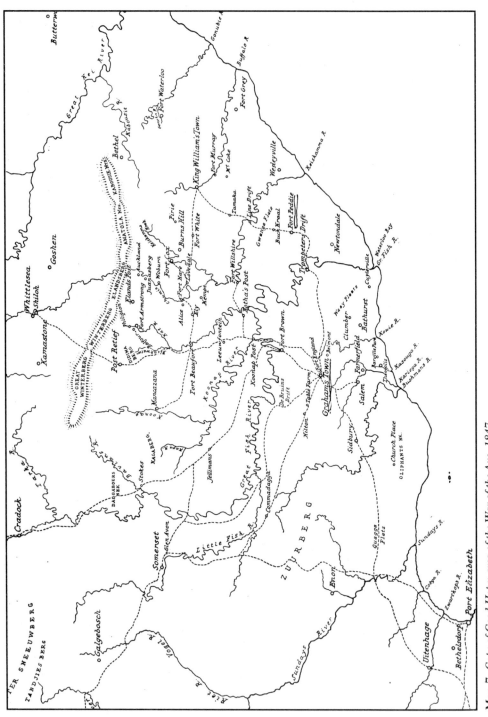

Map 7. *Cape of Good Hope; area of the War of the Axe, 1847*

Hong Kong, became an obsession. He issued a General Order calling for details of personnel, pay, equipment, etc, but the outcome was tardy and incomplete. Convinced that he was fighting a lone battle against inefficiency, he disbanded the levies on 6 May and dismissed most of the officers. He attempted to start afresh, but managed to effect only marginal improvements. He thought he had discovered a typical case at Fort Beaufort, where a requisition was forwarded for 400 suits of clothing. But when he pounced, the strength of the levy was only 223 – so where were the remaining 177 suits? A court of enquiry was convened to deal with this matter of great pith and moment, and he was annoyed with the finding that the 223 levies were, properly, wearing suits, while the remainder were lodged in store.

Immersed in trivia, Pottinger began to think that the supplementary force was being recruited for fun. He told Grey that at Grahamstown,

> Merchants, tailors, shopkeepers, editors of newspapers, hotel-keepers, etc. were all dignified with the military titles of captains, lieutenants and ensigns, besides paymasters, quartermasters and all the paraphernalia of a regular army. Most of these men were following their usual occupations, and only did *duty* by drawing pay! Others were occasionally employed in hunting straggling thieves, and used to report on these events as though they had fought the battle of Waterloo![18]

On 3 December he informed Berkeley that he was having the 'accompaniments' to his despatch No. 154 of 20 October printed – this would show the 'total absence of system' which he found in every branch of public expenditure.[19] The result, a blue book of 253 pages, was published after he left the Cape and produced the volley of abuse that he expected. A compendium of perceptive criticism, it does not contain a word of praise for anyone. Sir George Cory's view was that the violation of red tape regulations had horrified him more than the destruction caused by the Kaffirs. It was his opinion that: 'Apparently the principle which actuated him was to regard every man as utterly dishonest until proof of the reverse was forthcoming.'[20]

The *Cape Frontier Times* said he would have been sued for defamation if he was still in the Colony. How long, it asked, was 'this callous, unprincipled libeller to bask like a crocodile in the favour of Her Majesty's Government?' An embarrassed Grey referred the Despatch to the Treasury audit office, which said that at such a distance no conclusions were possible. Inefficiency there had certainly been, but in his zeal to root it out Pottinger infuriated many of the officers – which he always did cheerfully if he thought he had detected laggards.

The summer of 1847 was not Pottinger's happiest time. The press was derisive about his attempts to bring the Kaffirs to book. While they were carrying off thousands of cattle, it was said that 'our arms and our people have rivalled each other in blundering and stupidity' and the tribesmen were 'contemptuously laughing us to scorn'.[21] This polemic found a ready response from local readers and it was difficult to rebut.

A strong column that set out to take the Ngqika chief by surprise proved to be an embarrassing failure. The wily Sandile had vanished, and the returning party, made up of units from the 7th Dragoons, Cape Mounted Rifles and the 45th Regiment, was harassed by a force of about 2,000 Kaffirs all the way back to Fort Hare. On 20 June Pottinger had to agree with Berkeley that further operations would be futile until they could put more troops in the field. He was enquiring whether 'the Burghers and Boors' could be induced to turn out for a short period if they were allowed to retain plunder. He also proposed to detain any British regiments that might touch at the Cape on their way home from India.[22]

By the end of July Pottinger had spent a great deal of time in drafting memoranda on future action, though always disowning any ambition to interfere in military matters. On 16 August he authorized Henry Calderwood, the Commissioner with the Ngqika, to make Sandile a final offer of peaceful terms (a token surrender of arms, etc.),[23] and on 27 August, when this had made no progress, he issued a formal proclamation declaring Sandile to be a rebel. Colonists were urged to make up commandos to support the regular troops and levies, and were promised that they could keep all the cattle and other booty captured.[24] While the columns were being assembled for the advance into Sandile's territory, Berkeley put some pertinent questions to the Governor about the treatment to be afforded to the Kaffirs. Were they to be taken prisoner or merely disarmed? Were their cattle to be killed, or kept?

Were kraals to be burned?[25] In his reply, perfectly reasonable and polite in itself, Pottinger could not refrain from another canter on his hobby horse; in his view the division of political and military authority was a serious difficulty.[26]

Two problems still faced the Governor and the Lieutenant-General as they completed their plans. First, the Kaffirs were on home ground. Somerset, who knew them and the territory well, warned what would happen:

> As fast as fire and smoke can travel (their usual signal that an enemy is in sight) so fast would their parties assemble on the numerous commanding points of this most difficult country; and then, biding their time, they would by concerted signals and an overwhelming force, rush on and attack any small bodies or weak parties attempting to pass with cattle.
>
> Any attempt on our part to pass out with small parties must meet with failure and defeat, as the cattle would inevitably be recaptured (which with the Kaffirs is the test of victory) and the parties so detached will in all probability be destroyed.[27]

The second problem was that though Pottinger had recruited Hottentots and scrubbed around for reinforcements, he had got little support from the Burghers. He told Berkeley that 'the Cradock races are likely to interfere with the attendance of many, which is another proof of the patriotic zeal and high feelings of the colonists'.[28] But action there had to be, and on 11 September Berkeley marched out of Grahamstown.

On 22 September Berkeley reported from his headquarters in the field that his three columns were all making good progress and that 'the enemy has been everywhere driven from his possessions, and his property and habitations laid waste and destroyed'.[29] But this was all too rosy a picture of the attack on the Amatola Ridge. The experienced Somerset was nearer the mark, explaining that all his movements had been successfully executed, 'but the Kaffirs have not shewn'.[30] The Xhosa seldom stood his ground or returned fire, so that Berkeley's troops were engaged in shooting a flying enemy, rounding up his cattle, and burning his home. The business of climbing up the face of mountainous ridges or cutting a path through the dense bush was slow and exhausting, but casualties were slight.

Pottinger, exchanging signals with Berkeley, repeated his determination to expel Sandile, but soon exhausted his fund of sarcasm about the Burghers, very few of whom had enrolled for service. They would not do what he wanted them to do; the frustration was exceptionally galling. In character, he was also worried that a letter from Grey threatened that there would be 'the devil to pay' when the cost of the campaign was tallied.[31]

On 27 September he received a formal reply from London, written on 26 July, to his various requests for reinforcements. It was distinctly dusty. Pottinger would have to make do with what he had. (The total force in the Colony amounted to 5,470 and about 3,270 of them were at the frontier.) There was no possibility of regiments on the way home from India, or of troops from the garrisons of Mauritius and St Helena, being rerouted.[32] With the same steamer, however, came much more welcome news. He was to get the one post which he had long coveted; he was to be Governor of the Madras Presidency. Grey sent a friendly private letter, wishing him well 'in the more important government even than that of the Cape', and added that 'for myself it would have been more satisfactory that you should have remained to carry your measures into complete effect'.[33]

Pottinger was also told about two other appointments, though formal notification came later. Sir Harry Smith, who had served in the Peninsular War and at Waterloo and had been Quartermaster General in the Cape from 1829 to 1840, was to succeed him. This would dispose of the problem arising from the division of command. Pottinger had most recently written to Grey on 23 August arguing that the divided practice 'utterly destroys that oneness of purpose and decision' which were the only surety of success. In proposing that an officer competent to discharge the 'double authority' should be sent out, he emphasized that he was not prompted by personal considerations. Bearing in mind how strongly he felt about this issue, his letter is remarkably free from pique.[34] The second appointment would also take Berkeley to Madras, as Commander-in-Chief of the army of the Presidency. Pottinger wrote to him in warm terms about his new posting, but Sir John Hall, the Chief Medical Officer at the Cape, had doubts. He wondered how they would fare together in Madras, since 'no cordiality has existed between them here'.[35]

The scouring of the Amatola ridge continued. Soon after he saw the scale of the operation, Sandile had put out feelers for a settlement, but the curt reply was that no terms could be negotiated, only his personal safety would be guaranteed. In the first weeks of October there had still been no pitched battle, only skirmishes as Xhosa marauders scuttled back into the bush, but Berkeley's relentless, plodding advance had eroded Sandile's authority. His position was becoming hopeless; he had very nearly been captured; and other tribes would not join him in continuing resistance. On 19 October he surrendered.

The search for Sandile had ended at a good time for Pottinger, who admitted that for once he was 'overwhelmed with colonial references'.[36] Though making the war his first priority, he was in the habit of getting through civil business with despatch, not to say élan. At present, however, he was engaged with the Treasurer-General's account, petitions for a better steamship service, and a horde of other questions requiring decision. In the midst of these domestic preoccupations he was outraged at reports that Sandile had not surrendered unconditionally, but had merely come in to parley. This, he told Berkeley, he regarded as 'quite a Kaffir trick'. The colonial newspapers would seize on any suggestion of his bad faith, though, he added defiantly, 'You know how little I care for them or their opinions.'[37]

Tempers became frayed as the argument continued over whether the surrender of the Xhosa chief had really been due to a misunderstanding, or whether he had been 'cajoled' into giving himself up continued. In a sharp exchange, Berkeley denied that Sandile had been too generously treated after his capture. He and his followers had only been given rations, a blanket each, and half a bottle of spirits among eleven of them.[38] Pottinger, had he been going to stay in the Colony, would have deported Sandile at once, but he told Grey that he was going to keep him in confinement until the new Governor arrived, so that he might not be 'shackled by any steps I might adopt on the occasion'.[39]

A General Order had intimated that Sandile was now in custody, and Pottinger hoped that the other Xhosa chiefs, and Pato in particular, would now make their submission.[40] As this did not happen, Berkeley organized his forces to move against them on and beyond the Kei River. Successes were only intermittent, mainly because the Kei was often impassable at this season. Somerset, especially prominent in the action, had a hard time coping with floods, and a party of five officers was ambushed on

16 November.[41] In the second half of the month severe inroads were made on the Kaffirs, but while these operations continued, some of the initial impulse had been lost. Both Pottinger and Berkeley, looking towards Madras, were preparing to leave the frontier.

Pottinger was not sorry to be quitting the Cape. 'This is a sad colony to deal with', he told Grey, writing as one who had served in India and in the Far East. Though his reasoning is not easy to follow, he suspected that many colonists did not want the war to end, which explained why the press had thwarted his measures 'by misrepresentations and even falsehood – both of which are greedily followed'. He was severe on the missionaries, whom he had prevented from interfering in politics. To his mind they had made far too little progress 'in civilizing or teaching the natives of any class the common decencies of life'.[42]

At the end of November Pottinger and Berkeley received their official letters of appointment to the Madras Presidency. On 8 December the inhabitants of Grahamstown presented the retiring Governor with a farewell address. This was a time for healing old wounds, for offering a soothing reply, but that was not his way. He would, he said, always watch the progress of the colony. Though he had often differed in his views, and found reason to condemn and reform much of what he saw in operation, he conscientiously believed that he had acted for the public good.[43] This was no doubt true, but it was not opportune. Though he would have been horrified at the comparison, there are traces of Coriolanus in his obstinate disregard of criticism as he stuck to the path of duty.

Sir Harry Smith, who had arrived at Table Bay on 1 December, travelled to Sidbury, between Port Elisabeth and Grahamstown, a fortnight later. Pottinger met him there, and after handing over the seals of office, continued on his way to Cape Town. He sailed for India on 6 February.

Smith had Sandile and his councillors brought before him at Grahamstown. He asserted imperiously that 'the Kaffirs were his dogs', made Sandile kiss his foot, and ordered his release.[44] Smith then issued a proclamation which extended the boundary of the colony to the Keiskamma River, and declared that the lands which the Xhosa occupied between the Keiskamma and the Kei would become British Kaffraria. But the Xhosa were far from content; three years later Smith deposed Sandile and another frontier war, more violent than the War of the Axe, had started by the end of 1850.

A warm letter from Grey – somewhat ironic in the light of later events in the Cape – reached Pottinger in Madras. Grey was anxious to give him 'the credit you deserve of having completely finished the war before Smith took over'. Pottinger derived some wry satisfaction from the envoy writing that. 'I have no doubt that this would have been accomplished much sooner if the foolish etiquette of our service had not prevented your holding the military command with the civil government.'[45]

He had spent only a year at the Cape, mostly at Grahamstown or Fort Peddie, and his impact on the colony at large was limited. He was roundly denounced when his Despatch 154 on the levies was published after his departure. But when the *Cape Frontier Times* compared his tenure with Smith's bluster and hasty decisions, it admitted that for all his political blunders and contempt for everything colonial, he was 'going the right way to subdue the Kaffirs'. Given another year, he would have brought them to submission. 'He never made speeches to them. He never held interviews with them. The power which they felt was crushing them by degrees was unseen. The result was that they feared him – and in a savage fear is the child of respect.'[46] This is, palpably, a contemporary verdict, and today's ethics would lead to a different judgment. In the temper of the time, however, he did his job. He was faced with a different enemy and a different structure compared with what he had met in Sind, or China. No one could call him malleable, or flexible in his response, but his steadfastness was sufficient for the demands made on it, and he retained the confidence of the Secretary of State for the Colonies. Grey's considered view was that he 'performed the duties most ably', and dealt with abuses 'in a vigorous and determined manner'.[47]

His flaw was to spend far too much time on minor administrative matters, poring over details, and calling for returns of equipment, etc. to a comic extent. He was determined to win the war, and one of his last acts was to authorize the formation of a second division of Kaffir police, whose role he had energetically promoted. He had, however, little time to look further ahead or contemplate wider issues affecting the Kaffirs. This was most evident in his attitude to the Kat River settlement. In one error of judgment he declined to meet A.J.W. Pretorius, who had journeyed to Grahamstown to represent the plight of the Dutch emigrant farmers. This was a serious issue, but Pottinger said that he was overworked, and Natal must remain for his successor's attention. Otherwise he handed over an administration in better shape than he had found. The renewal of hostilities four years later was due to a Governor more headstrong, and less shrewd, than Pottinger.

Subscribing to the 'warts and all' requirement, it has to be recorded that an anonymous writer to the press described Pottinger as a man 'who enjoyed his glass and his lass, smoked his cigar and took things easy'.[48] The historian Theal went much further:

> He left without the esteem of a single colonist. No other governor of the colony ever lived in such open licentiousness as he. His amours would have been inexcusable in a young man; in one approaching his sixtieth year they were scandalous. In other respects a cold sneering unsympathetic demeanour prevented men of virtue from being attracted to him. He was much better adapted for office in India than in South Africa.[49]

Two comments may be made on this diatribe. The first is that Cory and others have noted that Theal cites no sources, and the Cape press, as already indicated, took a very different view of his conduct.[50] The second observation on the question of sexual impropriety, is that again there is no evidence, and his critics would certainly have grasped at it, had any been available. Whatever his proclivity, in the long months at the frontier post of Fort Peddie, he did not have time for dalliance.

CHAPTER SEVENTEEN

His Excellency

Sir Henry had hoped that appointment to the Governorship of Madras would be a fitting culmination to his career, though no one knows why he so much preferred this of the three Presidencies. It can scarcely have been purely because of its seniority, though Madras was the first territory in India to come under Company rule, earlier than either Bengal or Bombay. In 1639 a Hindu potentate allowed the British to occupy Fort St George in return for a yearly quitrent, but the tenure was seldom peaceful. From the decline of the great Mogul dynasty after the death of Aurangzeb in 1704, native rulers, fragmenting and feuding as they competed for their share of his empire, were involved in frequent struggles with troops from Madras.

Throughout the eighteenth century the Company had another reason to look to its arms due to the presence of the French, anxious to push out from their fortress at Pondicherry. On the French side, Dupleix of many wiles was a brilliant commander, and the British had their own heroes. The accomplished Stringer Lawrence, who had fought at Fontenoy and Culloden, arrived at Madras in 1748 and started recruiting native infantry for the Company's service. Robert Clive, originally a 'writer', or clerk, at Madras before he was commissioned as an ensign, learned his soldiering from Lawrence and became a great commander. His successful defence of Arcot, together with his later victories, marked the beginning of British ascendancy in India.

Recurring battles with French forces, in parallel with wars in Europe, or with native states, ending with the defeat of Tipu Sultan at Seringapatam in May 1799, are outwith the scope of this book, as are the changes in the structure of the East India Company under the Regulating Act of 1773 and the India Act of 1784, which effectively made it subject to Crown control. Meanwhile, however, the Madras Presidency was far from being a model of integrity or efficiency. A low point was reached when it ingloriously signed the Treaty of Madras in 1769 with Haidar Ali, the Muslim ruler of Mysore.

This proclaimed a nominal alliance with him and returned all captured territory on each side. But, instead of fighting Haidar Ali, Madras should have made friends with him as a bulwark against the warlike Marathas. Sadly, the Madras Council had none of Clive's expertise in dealing with native rulers.

In 1775, following a dispute over the restoration of the Raja of Tanjore, the Directors of the East India Company sacked the Governor, and Lord Pigot, who had earlier defended the Presidency against the French, was reappointed for a second term. Internal dissension, however, became more acute, and the Council itself imprisoned Pigot. He died eight months later, in 1777, while still confined. His successor, Sir Thomas Rumbold, who had been Clive's ADC at Plassey, notoriously applied himself to enlarging his own fortune during his two years in office. Next came the inordinately vain Lord Macartney, the first Governor to come from outside the Company. (Macartney's career was curiously similar to Pottinger's. After five years at Madras, Macartney was briefly Plenipotentiary to China, and later Governor of the Cape of Good Hope, all posts held by Pottinger but in different order.) The patrician Robert Hobart, son of the Earl of Buckinghamshire, went to Madras with high hopes of eventually becoming Governor-General, but, too conscious of his noble birth, he quarrelled with the socially inferior Sir John Shore, the incumbent at Calcutta, and the Court of Directors recalled him in 1798. In his place came Edward Clive, the son of the heroic victor of Plassey. Wellesley, by now Governor-General, described him as

> a worthy, zealous, obedient, and gentlemanlike man, of excellent temper; but neither of talents, knowledge, habits of business, or firmness of spirit equal to his present situation. How the Devil did he get there?[1]

Clive gave Wellesley no trouble.

By far the most distinguished and influential Governor of Madras was Sir Thomas Munro. During his seven years (1820–27) he developed the *ryot* system of land tenure and established a pattern of district administration with power devolved to the Collector. Like Elphinstone in Bombay, he had a keen sense of the imperial mission. He also predicted the course of the Mutiny, writing that the sepoys would rebel 'not for the sake of asserting the liberty of their country but for plunder and power'.[2] It was Munro that

Pottinger should seek to emulate when he reached Madras, rather than his immediate predecessor, the much wounded Peninsular veteran, the Marquis of Tweeddale.[3]

If a visitor to Madras earlier in the century is to be believed, Pottinger may have found that conditions at Madras were reminiscent of those in the newest colony of Hong Kong.

> A worse situation for a great capital could scarcely have been chosen, being placed in a large, arid plain, the vegetation scanty, and the soil, except in the gardens of the white inhabitants, producing little for general use; the action of the sun upon the sand renders the heat often excessive; it is likewise exposed to burning winds, loaded with suffocating fiery dust that occasions much distress, keeping the thermometer for days together at 100°.[4]

The official buildings were admittedly superior to those at Victoria Harbour, being described thus:

> Government House is a spacious though heavy pile of building. The banqueting-room is magnificent. . . . It was erected after his own design, I believe, by the celebrated Lord Clive.[5]

Madras society had one unusual feature.

> Spinsters, indeed, to the discredit of male gallantry, are by no means so uncommon here, as might be expected. I know not the cause: some attribute it to the men having become fastidious, some to the reluctance of a battered Indian constitution to encounter European vigour and beauty . . . some to increased illicit intercourse with the native women.[6]

In the years before Pottinger assumed office there had been many developments in the city's amenities – if not in the balance of the sexes – and he adopted a routine which he found agreeable. He lived at the Government Garden House at Guindy, riding in every Tuesday to hold a public breakfast. Thereafter he was available to anyone who sought an interview, before taking the Chair at the Executive Council's meeting.[7] One of his innovations was to hold durbars 'for the reception of native gentlemen', an experiment that raised eyebrows among the members of Council.

His voyage from the Cape had taken exactly two months and writing to Hobhouse on 22 April 1848, soon after his arrival, he started on a confident note.[8] From the outset, he resolved to make it a rule, in issuing invitations to Government House, to assume that all his guests were 'on the most cordial terms', as he did not consider that he should recognize 'any party dissensions and consequent misunderstandings and coolnesses'.Tweeddale had apparently intervened in private feuds, but fortunately for Pottinger 'the most volcanic of the belligerents' had left before he reached Madras. Six months later he was pleased to report that he was still treating everyone as though they were friends; he had succeeded in 'burying all past differences', so that the Europeans were 'all pleased with his rule'. Madras was 'in a state of perfect tranquillity'; he was glad to say that 'the people at large are happy and contented', and had set him down as 'a lucky Governor'.[9]

The following year he was still preening himself that 'we continue quiet here',[10] and he assured Melville, the Secretary of the East India Company, that the only complaint was that grain was too plentiful – and cheap.[11] The atmosphere was certainly calmer, more serene, than Madras had experienced a few years earlier. In 1842 there had been signs of disaffection in the army, especially in two regiments about to embark for China who were angry about changes in the *batta* (field allowances) and pension rules. Ellenborough, who happened to be in the port at the time, fortified the Madras Government not to give way, but to buy peace with the promise of an enquiry. Two years later the 6th Madras Cavalry at Jabalpur mutinied for more pay, and when the 47th Madras Infantry Regiment, posted to Bombay for service in Sind, learned that they were not to get the allowances promised by Tweeddale, they broke into open mutiny on parade. Some of the leaders were arrested; the rest were pacified with an advance of cash. But it was now clear that the Madras army could not be relied on for the defence of Sind, a task which would have to be undertaken by troops from the Bombay Presidency.

Reinforcements from Madras were needed however during the Second Sikh War, which started in September 1848 when General Whish was forced to abandon the siege of Multan because of the defection by Shere Singh.[12] In November Pottinger sent three regiments to replace Bengal troops who had been despatched to the North West.[13] In December, six companies of Her Majesty's 25th were put on notice to embark for Calcutta at a moment's call, and he had been warned that further demands might be made on Madras.[14]

The upshot was that Pottinger was not required to find further reinforcements, and he was greatly relieved when the British victory at Gujerat brought the war, and the threat of more extensive depletion of the Madras army, to an end. Before that he had been horrified by the mismanagement at Chillianwallah, where, as he put it, British troops were sent to be slaughtered without their Commander, Gough, having any idea of the enemy positions.[15] Pottinger remembered Gough as a skilful tactician in the Opium War, but his old comrade was now over seventy, and it was true that Chillianwallah was a muddle. Gough threw his force into battle without an adequate bombardment, and, according to Dalhousie, he later told a Brigadier, 'Indeed I had not intended to attack today, but the impudent rascals fired on me. They put my Irish blood up, and I attacked them.'[16] The British casualties amounted to 3,000, and nothing had been achieved.

In the Second Burmese War, Madras troops were required to make up the British expedition, totalling 6,000 men, which arrived off Rangoon in April 1852. When the province of Pegu was annexed at the end of the brief campaign, there was a problem in requisitioning regiments for garrison duty. The Bengal army was unwilling to cross the sea. The Madras Government was prepared to provide detachments, but not on a permanent basis, since, if a Burmese tour came round too frequently, it would discourage recruitment.

Throughout both these wars Pottinger remained impassive, though he was sometimes critical of the way the operations had been conducted. But the Plenipotentiary who had sailed up the Yangtse and brought the Opium War to an end showed no nostalgic sign of wanting to be actively involved. The former ensign in the Bombay Native Infantry, the veteran of the Sind campaigns, the wars in China and the Cape, had no wish to sniff gunpowder again. To use another metaphor, his olives had been gathered, and his grapes were in the tun.

The antics of the current Nawab of the Carnatic frequently exasperated

Pottinger, though the history of the Company's dealings with that state had always been tortuous, and was at times highly questionable. In 1801, Wellesley, on the most flimsy evidence, decided that Muhammad Ali and his son had been guilty of treachery, and that the Company should take over the government of the Carnatic, leaving the Nawab with a pension of one fifth of the state's revenue. Dishonestly, it is now agreed, the Company assumed control of a state which its own servants had ruthlessly exploited for the last forty years by insinuating themselves as creditors at the most usurious rates. Inevitably the Nawab, disgruntled, stripped of any real authority, remained a source of perpetual irritation to the Governor of Madras.

At the end of 1848 the Nawab impertinently claimed that a letter from The Queen, in reply to his tiresome representations, should be handed over to him formally by the Governor, Members of Council, Judges, and their ladies, and that protocol required no less. Pottinger refused and insisted that the letter should be transmitted by the Chief Secretary of Council. While this, in itself, was hardly a matter of crucial importance, Pottinger had no sympathy for the Nawab, whom he regarded as 'a most despicable character who is trying to go bankrupt and get away with paying 9% of his debts – and that with Treasury money!'[17]

He greatly regretted agreeing to give the Nawab an additional sum for his wedding expenses and not long afterwards, confided to Sir James Lushington that 'He has just married a common dancing girl who came with his wife from Hyderabad'. She now travelled about with an escort and a guard of honour – and had tried to stipulate that her own son should be acknowledged by the British as his successor. But even the Nawab had not dared to bring forward 'so disgraceful a proposal'.[18] In the event, when the Nawab died without a natural male heir, Governor-General Dalhousie abolished the titular sovereignty. This aroused no great concern, except for the family, and Pottinger was well pleased.

Relations between the Governor and the Court of Directors of the Company in London for a time went smoothly. The Court was most appreciative of Pottinger's detailed inspection of the Commissariat.

We anticipate that Sir H. Pottinger's continued, careful supervision of that department will, with the aid and support of the Commander-in-Chief and other Members of Council, stimulate the officers employed in it to a constant and minute personal and zealous management of the native establishments placed under their orders . . .[19]

No flagging here – Pottinger was still applying the jeweller's glass to the minutiae of administration.

In a peculiar despatch the Court approved of his 'animadversions on the improper application of the term "heathen" by Mr Bird [the Collector and magistrate] to designate the Hindoo inhabitants of the village in question'.[20] This referred to a complaint by villagers that Mr Hobbs, a missionary, had interfered with their religious services. Since his days at Ahmednagar Pottinger had acquired a more sensitive tolerance of native customs. It was at this time that his seniority was recognized by a Warrant signed by The Queen, appointing him 'to have the rank of Lieutenant General in Our Army in the East Indies' with effect from 11 November 1851.[21]

One class with whom he never struck up any rapport was the local clergy, particularly the official chaplains. He complained that Archdeacon Shortland overwhelmed him with long letters on trivial points, and he asked the Bishop of Calcutta to exercise his diocesan authority and curtail the correspondence. To Sir Archibald Galloway he confessed 'I have had a great deal of trouble with the Ecclesiastical Authorities who do not appear to understand their proper position as military chaplains',[22] and he intended to ensure that future orders were obeyed to the letter. He had been most incensed at the delay in burying a soldier who had died from falling off a verandah. The Chaplain had refused to officiate until he got the report of the court of enquiry, and the body was meanwhile decomposing.

For all his initial euphoria, there was some discontent with his regime, and signs can be detected in his adverse comments on those who habitually aired their grievances in the press because they felt they had been overlooked for promotion.[23] An observation by the Court of Directors on what seemed at first a minor matter is more serious. It arose from a proposal to erect a large tiled shed to shelter officers and men of the artillery 'while carrying out a system of repository exercise' at St Thomas's Mount. Pottinger had minuted that, so far as he could judge, 'neither in

this nor in any other case' had the Military Board shown the slightest wish
to economize in public money – their first duty – and that with these
remarks he had sanctioned the outlay 'to save himself from further
annoyance'. The Court seized on this as 'very unsatisfactory', both as
regards the vigilance of the Board and on the motive which had influenced
the President. They hoped he would use 'on public grounds only' the
powers entrusted to him, unaffected by the personal considerations to
which he had referred.[24] Pottinger's irritation is not hard to understand,
but that he should put it on record in this way, aware of the reproof he
would receive, shows that he was becoming tetchy – and bored.

The truth was that while, tongue-in-cheek, he could solemnly seek the
views of the Board of Control on the precedence to be afforded to the
wives of local dignitaries, his interest in maintaining a vigorous personal
direction of the Presidency had declined.[25] He was content to sit aside and
watch developments. For example, in 1850 Dr Hunter, a Surgeon in the
Black Town, opened a school of arts at his own expense, the first in India.
In 1851 a school of industry was started, but the Government showed little
interest until 1855, when it took over both schools. Pottinger was keen to
see the building of the *annicut* (dam) on the Godavery completed, and he
was alarmed when it overflowed, but, as usual, his primary concern was with
the mounting expense.[26] By the end of 1853 Madras was linked to Calcutta
by telegraph, which brought the Presidency more within the daily ambit of
the central government. There had been disappointment that Madras had
not been included in the first plans for railway construction, but 50 miles of
line were ready for opening at the end of 1855. Events were moving too fast
for the aging Governor.

In 1850, Hindus at Madras, as Pottinger reported, were outraged at
Governor-General Dalhousie's Act allowing converts from Hinduism to
retain their property. Some of Dalhousie's other reforms, such as the
inclusion of an officer from each Presidency in the Governor-General's
Legislative Council, and the appointment of a separate Lieutenant-
Governor for Bengal, which left the Governor-General, who had also been
directly responsible for this Presidency, freer to keep a vigilant eye on
Bombay and Madras, came too late to have much effect on Pottinger
before he retired. But times were changing.

Dalhousie had a somewhat distant view of the Governor of Madras:

As for Henry Pottinger, I know nothing about him. He does not encourage much communication, and we hear very little of that Presidency. You will know whether the silence is that of smooth prosperity or of lifelessness.[27]

Possibly because he and Pottinger never took each other's measure, Dalhousie strongly recommended that future Governors of Madras and of Bengal should be chosen from within the Company, and not politicians despatched from England. He made a point of contrasting the progressive administration in the Punjab and the North-Western Provinces under promoted Company officers with what he termed the 'stagnation' in Madras and Bombay. This was a bit hard on Pottinger, having regard to his years in Cutch and Sind, and to the very real climatic and other differences between Madras and the northern territories.

Dalhousie's proposal was not received with any enthusiasm in London, as it would have curtailed Crown patronage, but in a concession to him, a highly esteemed Company officer, James Thomason, then in charge of the North-Western Provinces, was selected to succeed Pottinger. The plan misfired; Thomason died on the day the news reached him; and the appointment went to Lord Harris, who had been Governor of Trinidad.[28]

When he disembarked at Madras, Pottinger had already painted on foreign lands and skies his 'odyssey of battle', and if, in the Presidency, he did not repeat his master-stroke at Hong Kong, or his modest achievement in the Cape, there were probably three reasons. To start with, there was not the same opportunity during his time at Madras for dramatic exploits that would catch the public eye. Secondly, his nature was such that he was better fitted to take a firm grip on a crisis than to busy himself with ordinary administrative duties. Lastly, he was tired. Apart from two short intervals, he had spent over forty years overseas in three very different theatres. He had done the State some service.

His health was very poor when he came home to England, and he sought a gentler climate in Malta, where he died on 18 March 1856. He is buried in the Maida Bastion Cemetery, now in bad repair as a result of neglect, vandalism, and bombing in the Second World War.

Epilogue

In 1861 Colonel William Pottinger, late of Her Majesty's 6th Foot Regiment, Henry's only surviving brother, had a marble tablet erected to his memory in St George's, Belfast. After recounting Henry's career, it reads:

> On concluding his successful Treaty with China in the year 1842 he was Destined for the Peerage by Her Gracious Majesty Queen Victoria the First, but Lost this High Distinction through the same Hostile Influence which was exerted in Vain to Prevent Parliament Rewarding his Eminent Services to the State.

This is odd. Fraternal resentment is understandable, and there was some feeling that Henry, tardily awarded a pension, should have been made a peer for his exploits in China. But was there a conspiracy, as William implies?[1] The conferring of Honours is, at best, a Byzantine business, and there was no exact precedent – which might have helped – for what Pottinger had done. His attitude was often abrasive, but only the Senior Naval officers at the China Station, Admirals Parker and Cochrane, might have nourished their hostility, and they would not have enough clout, even at the Admiralty, to keep Pottinger from the ermine – if it was being considered. Probably it was not. Under the 'totting up' system, he might, just, have been ennobled for the sum of his high offices, but in the last, at Madras, he had not been a great success. If he was to reach the peerage, it would have had to have been for the Opium War. His misfortune was that a Whig Government made him Plenipotentiary, but the Tory Peel was in power when he came back from China.

At the end of his time as Resident in Sind Pottinger had applied for a grant of arms, which was approved on 13 July 1840. As described by the present Clarencieux King of Arms, the achievement consisted of 'Vert an Eastern Crown Or between three Pelicans in their piety proper on a

Canton Argent a Cross Gules. Crest: a dexter Arm embowed in Armour grasping a Sword all proper surrounded by an Eastern Crown Gules. Motto: Virtus in Ardua.'[2] By 1845 Pottinger had acquired the Grand Cross of the Bath as well as his Baronetcy. In heraldry terms he was now entitled to supporters, and the grant by Garter King of Arms on 23 September provided for blazoning 'On the dexter side a Figure intending [sic] to represent a Chinese Mandarin habited and holding a Scroll in his exterior hand all proper, and on the sinister side a Sindian Foot Soldier habited, armed, and holding a Matchlock in his exterior hand also proper.'[3] These symbols are apposite, but there is a point to be added. Normally supporters in a coat-of-arms are granted only for life, but in Pottinger's case a special Royal Warrant declared that they were to be enjoyed by those to whom the Baronetcy descended. The origin of this minor concession is unknown, but it may have been meant as a small recompense for the non-appearance of a larger honour. In any event, Frederick Pottinger, when he succeeded to the title, needed more than heraldic supporters.

Henry's wife Susanna Maria remains a shadowy figure. She bore him three sons, the eldest of whom died in infancy, while the other two succeeded in turn to the Baronetcy, and a daughter. For long periods, however, she was separated from her husband because of the nature of his assignments, and no one could say that theirs was a close marriage. In India, she was the Collectrix at Ahmednagar before moving with Henry to Cutch, where they lived at Bhooj. Fred was born there in 1831, and his brother Harry three years later. As Bhooj was not a healthy place for children, Susanna took them home to England.[4] Leaving them with relations, she returned to India in 1839. On 9 March she sailed from Falmouth on board the *Inglis*, acting as chaperone to her nieces Eliza and Anne, the daughters of the improvident Thomas by his second wife Eliza Fulton.[5]

The two girls went out, like others collectively termed the 'fishing fleet', hoping for husbands. In G.O. Trevelyan's verse, they were described as

> Fair dames, whose easy-chairs in goodly row
> Fringe either bulwark of the P. and O.[6]

The Misses Pottinger were desperately unlucky. They reached Bombay on

14 June, but within three months Eliza, who had been staying with Uncle William, was buried at Poona. Anne then went to join Uncle Henry and Aunt Susanna at Bhooj. On 6 April 1840 she married Parr Willesford Hocking, a regimental surgeon, but things soon took an adverse turn. Henry and Susanna went home – they were delayed at Alexandria 'on account of the Plague, greatly to his annoyance'; the Residency was downgraded under Captain Melville, who was only designated Political Agent; Uncle William left for Aden to command a wing of the 6th Regiment; and, worst of all, Hocking had fallen into debt. In March 1841 Anne travelled back to Ahmednagar, and there she died on 20 September 1841.

At the time of Eliza's death the family thought that Aunt Susanna had behaved well and shown the 'most motherly affection' to her grieving sister.[7] Before long, however, Anne tells a different story. Writing to her mother, she complains of Lady Pottinger's 'utter indifference', and continues

> I have often thought before of writing to you and putting you on your guard that anything that you say before her is repeated to anyone who chooses to listen to it. Do not think I would say so ill-naturedly even though I have often experienced how little is to be trusted to her veracity.[8]

No doubt tempers frayed in the heat of Bhooj. Incidentally, years later Henry agreed with Hobhouse's view that ladies should be barred from countries where their presence might compromise the public interest, 'and so long as I was in Sinde I set my face against any coming there'.[9] Apparently he made some exceptions in Bhooj.

The hectic career of Henry's eldest surviving son, Frederick William, provides a perverse epilogue. Frederick thought himself a bit of a card and in temperament he was nearer to his Uncle Thomas than to his father. (His young brother Harry cut a more serious figure.) At Eton Fred was more interested in the stable gossip of Windsor and Ascot than in construing Virgil, although he enjoyed scribbling verses and left a collection of juvenilia.[10] He had got his first sight of Agar's Plough in 1845, but two years later, when Henry had left for Madras, his mother withdrew him from school and together they enjoyed fashionable jaunts to Paris and Bad Homburg. In 1851 he was commissioned in the Grenadier Guards.

With charm, money, and a secure social position, his future should have been set fair. But he had the devil in him – it could well be as a reaction against his famous father's reputation – and he was soon outdoing his fellow-officers in the extravagance of his behaviour. Gambling and the pursuit of actresses took up his time as he galloped down the primrose path.

News of his sons's exploits reached Henry at Madras, and he at once sent orders for Fred to be sent out as an ADC. But his doting mother would not have it. Lady Pottinger, asserting that she could no longer stand the rigours of the Orient, had remained in Eaton Place, and she was not going to lose her darling boy. He was far too useful dancing attendance on her when he could spare time from the green table, or from his minimal regimental duties. The scenario was now predictable: Fred lost £10,000 when 'Lord of the Isles' failed to win the Derby, his mother sold her diamonds, and the breach with his father was complete. There was, however, a near-deathbed reconciliation in Malta, when Harry and his sister Henrietta Maria, with misplaced generosity, persuaded the failing Baronet to allow Fred to remain his heir.

Fred did not take long to run through his patrimony, the £100,000 he had been left, his property and all its contents. With a fine disregard for sentiment, he sold the silver plate that Liverpool had presented to Sir Henry, the huge candelabra from the Bombay merchants, and the gold armlet from Kiying (ignoring the tale that Kiying had claimed him as an adopted son.) With overwhelming debts, he had to leave the Brigade and, as society of the time decreed, to emigrate. In 1859 he sailed for Melbourne aboard the *British Trident.*

The resemblance to the plot of a Ouida novel becomes more acute in what follows. (Rolf Boldrewood's slightly fictionalized account, where Fred appears as Sir Ferdinand Morringer, found a place in Australian folk-lore.)[11] A scapegrace Guards officer in the bush was bound to arouse comment, but Fred showed no interest in the daughters pushed forward by local matrons. In 1860, on his twenty-nineth birthday, he opened a diary, which he did not keep for long. He had enlisted in the New South Wales Mounted Police, and as a lonely trooper in the outback he admitted 'I have fallen as far below the position and expectations I was born to, as previous to my fall I was raised above them'. He ruefully recalled the old days at Eaton Place. At tea-time, 'Mother again opens her novel or goes on with her patchwork – Father falls asleep over the day's paper in the long low-backed chair. Henry gently touches (as the French aptly say) the piano.'[12] This is the nearest to a cosy domestic scene that can be found in the Pottinger archives.

Fred eventually overcame his self-pity and obtained a Police commission. He was most famous for hounding the notorious bushranger known as 'Starlight', and his gang of convicts. In time Starlight fell to the carbine of one of Fred's troopers. According to Boldrewood, as Fred held the dying man in his arms, Starlight murmured:

> 'Well, it's over now. I don't know that I'm sorry except for the others. I say, Morringer, do you remember the last pigeon shoot you and I shot in, at Hurlingham?'
>
> 'Why, good God!' says Sir Ferdinand, bending down and looking into his face, 'It can't be – yes, by Jove, it is –'
>
> Starlight muttered a scarcely audible name, then put a finger to his lips and whispered 'You won't tell, will you? Say you won't!'
>
> Fred nodded.
>
> Starlight had been a close friend of his in the Grenadiers.[13]

(Sadly, an anonymous contributor to *The Field* in 1937, who knew Starlight's identity, has not been traced.)[14]

Fred's death was as inconsequential as most of his career. He had been summoned to a board of enquiry to face a charge that he had not tried to arrest three known bushrangers at a race meeting. On the day he had been too busy acting as Chairman of the Wowingragong race committee, and riding his own horse in two events. Answering the summons, he boarded the western mail coach at Bathurst as the only inside passenger. Shortly before reaching Lapstone the driver heard a shot. He climbed down to find Fred bleeding from a wound in his chest, with his silver chased pistol lying on the seat. In Sydney, Fred refused to go to hospital and was taken to the Victoria Club. The wound mortified, and he died on 9 April 1865.[15]

The official conclusion was death by misadventure, but there were ugly rumours in the press that he had killed himself to avoid the enquiry. This is most unlikely. He could expect nothing worse than a censure, and it was well known that he loved playing with his pistol and explaining its mechanism. It was probably an accident, and the correct verdict on his demise – and on the rest of his life – might be that 'He should have known better'. A monument over his grave in St Jude's Cemetery, erected by 'his friends in the Colony', commends him as 'a zealous and active Officer of Police'. Harry, a barrister, succeeded to the title, which lapsed when he died without an heir.

A pompous Major once asked Sir Henry how, with his serious occupations, he could find time to share the folly of his children. 'I have my folly for everyday's use,' was the reply, 'and my wisdom for state occasions.'[16] Fred's end would have provoked only a grim smile. Sir Henry would, however, have been amused to read in the *Gazette* that his widow had been decorated twenty-three years after his death. The Imperial Order of the Crown of India, restricted to ladies, had been inaugurated in 1877. It was given to the wives and other female relatives of those who had held the highest offices in India. On 10 June 1879 Queen Victoria admitted Susanna Maria, Dowager Lady Pottinger to the Order. The Sovereign had been retrospectively generous.

Notes

INTRODUCTION

1. G.B. Endacott, *A History of Hong Kong*, 1958, p. 3.
2. Henry Ellis, *Journal of the Proceedings of the late Embassy to China*, 1817, p. 59.
3. Stanley to Pottinger, 3 June 1842. No. 8, CO 129/2.

CHAPTER ONE

1. Sir John W. Kaye, *Lives of Indian Officers*, 1889 edition, Vol II.
2. Colin Johnston Webb, *Irish News* and *Belfast Morning News*, 28 July 1949.
3. Major-General Sir Robert Rollo Gillespie (1776–1814), served in San Domingo (1796) where he killed six potential assassins; in Jamaica (1801); in India, where he rescued the 69th Regiment in the Vellore Mutiny (1806), and where he commanded the cavalry against Runjeet Singh (1809). He was killed in the fighting at Kalunga, Nepal, and buried at Meerut. His name was still remembered with respect in Madras, when Henry Pottinger became Governor of the Presidency in 1847.
4. The family was descended from James Hamilton (1559–1643), first Viscount Claneboye. An original fellow of Trinity College, Dublin 1592, he was knighted and given large grants of land in Ulster in 1605. He was MP for County Down in 1613, and was created an Irish Peer in 1622. He armed the Scots in Ulster in 1641.
5. Quoted *Belfast News-Letter*, 16 December 1929.
6. Barry Yelverton (1736–1805) was MP for Donegal in 1774; Chief Baron of the Court of Exchequer in 1783 and created Baron Avonmore in 1795. He was elevated to Viscount of Ireland and Baron of the United Kingdom in 1800.
7. Tom Pottinger to Eldred Pottinger. Diver, *The Hero of Herat*, 1912, p. 275.
8. Eldred Pottinger to Thomas Pottinger, 3 December 1838, PRO NI/1584A.
9. Henry Pottinger to Eldred Pottinger, 7 December 1838. Diver, *op. cit.*, p. 240.
10. Anne Hocking to Mrs Pottinger, 21 October 1840, Mr J. Platt, private collection.
11. Kaye, *op. cit.*
12. PRO FO 705/110.

CHAPTER TWO

1. Mountstuart Elphinstone, *An Account of the Kingdom of Caubul*, 1815, OUP edition, 1972, p. 266.

2.   Ibid., p. 229.

3.   Jonathan Duncan (1756–1811), Resident at Benares, 1788, where he was the first to combat infanticide. Governor of Bombay, 1795–1811. Sympathetic to petty chiefs whom he recognized as sovereign princes.

4.   IOR Selections from Records of Commissioner in Sind, File 203, p. 500.

5.   Crow to Duncan, 7 May 1800. IOR Home and Misc. Series. Vol. 333, pp. 393–449.

6.   Sir Gilbert Elliot, first Earl of Minto (1751–1814), Governor-General of India, 1807–13. In a varied career he was MP for Morpeth from 1776–84, for Berwick from 1786–90, and then for Helston, Cornwall in 1790. He was Viceroy of Corsica from 1794–6, and Minister at Vienna in 1796.

7.   Minto to Col. Bray, 11 October, 1807. Minto, *Life and Letters, 1807–14,* p. 81.

8.   IOR Board's Secret Letters, 2 March 1808.

9.   Sir Harford 'Baghdad' Jones Brydges (1764–1847), Envoy to Persia, 1807–11. As Harford Jones, created Baronet in 1807. Took name of Brydges, 1826.

10.   Minto to Ghulamali Khan, 10 October 1808. IOR Secret and Separate Branch Proceedings, No. 7.

11.   Henry Pottinger, *Travels in Beloochistan and Sinde,* 1816, p. 339.

12.   Ibid., p. 365.

13.   Ibid., p. 367.

14.   Ibid., p. 372.

15.   Smith to Edmonstone, 1 October. 1809. IOR Home and Misc. Series, Vol. 591, pp. 359–81.

16.   Ibid.

17.   Pottinger, *op. cit.,* p. 376.

18.   Elphinstone, *op. cit.,* pp. 229–30.

CHAPTER THREE

1.   Mountstuart Elphinstone, *An Account of the Kingdom of Caubul, 1815,* OUP edition, 1972, Vol. II, p. 223, footnote.

2.   Elliott D'Arcy Todd (1808–45), Lieutenant in the Bengal Artillery; in 1836 he took despatches from Herat to Simla by Kandahar and Peshawar; in 1841 he was political agent at Herat, which he abandoned because of devious activity of Shah Kamran; he was killed at the battle of Ferozeshah.

3.   Henry Pottinger, *Travels in Beloochistan and Sinde,* 1816, p. 6.

4.   Sir John Macdonald Kinneir (1782–1830), Lt.-Col. in the East India Company's service; a traveller and diplomat, travelled in Persia, Armenia, and Kurdistan, 1813–14.

5,   Pottinger, *op. cit.,* p. 29.

6.   Ibid., p. 290.

7.   General Sir Thomas Willshire, Bt. (1789–1862); he commanded the Bombay Division in 1839 and served with distinction in the Afghan campaign, capturing Khelat in 1839.

8.   Pottinger, *op. cit.,* p. 63.

9. Ibid., p. 136.
10. Ibid., p. 223.
11. Ibid., p. 306.
12. Ibid., p. 212.

CHAPTER FOUR

1. Quoted Kaye, *Lives of Indian Officers*, 1889 edition, Vol. I, p. 374.
2. Quoted Kaye, Ibid. In this letter Elphinstone adds that Pottinger's *Travels in Beloochistan and Sinde*, which he edited, had just been sent to the publisher.
3. Pottinger to Chief Secretary Warden, 23 July 1815. English Records of Maratha History, Vol. II, letter 166, p. 375.
4. Quoted Kaye, *op. cit.*, Vol. II, pp. 381–2.
5. Elphinstone to Captain Agnew, undated. Quoted Kaye, *op. cit.*, p. 383.
6. Pottinger to Editor, *Dublin University Magazine*, 2 November 1846. This, Pottinger's account of his action, was written thirty years later from 67 Eaton Place, in order to correct a slightly different version that had appeared in the magazine.
7. Elphinstone, 11 November 1817. Quoted Kaye, *op. cit.*, p. 387.
8. J. Grant Duff, *History of the Mahrattas*, 1826, p. 345.
9. Secretary to the Governor-General to Elphinstone, 14 July 1818. *English Records of Maratha History*, Vol. II, letter 141, p. 431.
10. Hastings to Secret Committee of Court of Directors, 21 August 1820. Ibid., letter 149, p. 495.
11. Elphinstone to Governor-General, 18 June 1818. Ibid., letter 138, pp. 403–10.
12. Elphinstone to Jenkins, 17 January 1819. Quoted Kaye, *op. cit.*, Vol. II, p. 397.
13. Elphinstone to Governor-General, 18 June 1818, *English Records of Maratha History*, letter 138, p. 410.
14. Secretary to Governor-General to Elphinstone, 26 September 1818. Ibid., letter 146, p. 477.
15. Elphinstone to Pottinger, undated, 1818, FO 705/26.
16. Elphinstone to Pottinger, 24 October 1822. FO 705/27.

CHAPTER FIVE

1. Moira in Council to Warden, 29 July 1820, IOR Bengal Secret and Political Proceedings, No. 9.
2. Warden to Metcalfe, 13 November 1820. Ibid., No. 4.
3. Edward Law, Lord Ellenborough, *A Political Diary, 1828–30*, Vol. II, p. 92.
4. James Burnes, *A Narrative of a Visit to the Court of Sinde*, published 1831, pp. 120–1.
5. IOR, Board's Secret Drafts, No. 208, 12 January 1830.
6. Norris to Burnes, 4 December 1830. IOR Bengal and Secret Consultations, 31 December 1830, No. 7.
7. Metcalfe, Minute. IOR Secret Letters, 30 October, 1830.

8. Alexander Burnes, *Travels into Bokhara*, etc., 1834.
9. Burnes to Pottinger, 23 February 1831. IOR Bengal Secret Letters.
10. Pottinger to Norris, 20 March 1831, Ibid.
11. IOR Bengal Secret and Political Proceedings, 25 November 1831, No. 21.
12. Pottinger to Bombay Government, 9 September 1831, Ibid. No. 6.
13. Burnes, *op. cit.*, Vol. II, pp. 199–201.
14. Bengal Govt to Clare, 22 October 1831. IOR Bengal Secret Letters, 9 December 1831. Enclosure 35.
15. Pottinger to Prinsep, FO 705/12 p. 6.
16. Ibid., p. 10.
17. Ibid., p. 202.
18. Pottinger to Bombay Government, 2 July 1832, IOR Secret Letters.
19. Pottinger's remarks, 4 July 1883. IOR Bengal Secret and Political Consultations, 10 October 1833. No. 13.
20. Clare to Bentinck, 10 March 1832. Bentinck papers.
21. Bentinck, Despatch, 5 March 1834, IOR Secret Letters.

CHAPTER SIX

1. Priscilla Napier, *I have Sind; Charles Napier in Sind 1841–4*, 1990, p. 30.
2. Kaye, *Lives of Indian Officers*, 1889 edition, Vol. I, p. 435.
3. Burnes to Pottinger, 7 December 1835, and Pottinger to Bombay Government, 17 December 1835. NAI, Foreign Dept, Political Consultations. Cited Robert Huttenback, *British Relations with Sind*, 1962.
4. Bombay Government to Governor-General's Office, 29 February 1836. Ibid.
5. W.J. Eastwick, *Tracts on India*, 1844, p. 19.
6. Macnaghten to Bombay Government 20 June 1836. IOR Secret Letters, 26 September 1836, Encl. 7.
7. Macnaghten to Pottinger, 26 September 1836. Parliamentary papers, 1843 Vol. XXXIX, p. 5.
8. Metcalfe to Auckland, 15 October 1836. Auckland papers, 37689 fos 98–101.
9. Colvin to Pottinger, and to Burnes, 3 November 1836. Also Burnes to Colvin, 6 November 1836. Auckland papers, 37690 fos 43–5.
10. Macnaghten to Pottinger, 1 May 1837. IOR Secret Letters, Encl. 9.
11. Macnaghten to Pottinger, 19 June 1837. Ibid., Encl. 93.
12. Auckland, Minute of 25 December 1836. Auckland papers, 37690, fos 19–22.
13. Macnaghten to Pottinger, 19 June 1837. IOR Secret Letters, Encl. 93.
14. Pottinger to Macnaghten, 3 June 1837. Ibid., Encl. 3.
15. Macnaghten to Pottinger, 27 December 1837. Ibid., No. 22.
16. Macnaghten to Pottinger, 25 September 1837. Ibid., Encl. 19.
17. Macnaghten to Pottinger, 21 February 1838. Ibid., No. 4.
18. Governor-General to Secret Committee, 23 April 1838. Ibid., No. 6.
19. Auckland, Minute of 14 June 1837. Auckland papers, 37691 fos 57–60.

CHAPTER SEVEN

1. Macnaghten to McNeill, 10 April 1837: also Minute by Governor-General, 7 September 1837. IOR Secret Letters, No. 3. Encl. 58.
2. Simla Manifesto, 1 October 1838, para. 10. Reproduced in George Pottinger, *The Afghan Connection*, 1983, p. 209.
3. Ibid., paras. 11 and 13.
4. Parliamentary Papers, 1843, XXXIX, p. 65.
5. Macnaghten to Pottinger, 13 August 1838. IOR Secret Letters, No. 186.
6. Pottinger to Macnaghten, 13 August 1838, and 24 September 1838. IOR Secret Letters, Encl. 83.
7. Auckland to Carnac, 12 October 1838. Auckland papers, 37694, fo. 67.

Sir James Rivett Carnac (1785–1846) was Chairman of the East India Company, 1836–7, and Governor of Bombay, 1838–41.

8. Colvin to Pottinger, 11 September 1838. Auckland papers, 37694, fo. 44.
9. Macnaghten to Pottinger, 19 November 1838. IOR Secret Letters, No. 31.

CHAPTER EIGHT

1. Auckland to Pottinger, 21 November 1838: Colvin to Pottinger, same date. Auckland papers, 37694, fos 125–6.
2. Pottinger to Eastwick, 13 January 1839. IOR Secret Letters, Encl. 7.
3. Parliamentary papers, 1843, Vol. XXXIX, pp. 1–2.
4. James Outram, *Rough Notes of the Campaign*, etc., 1840, p. 31.
5. Ibid., p. 160.
6. Pottinger to Maddock, 6 July 1839. IOR Secret Letters, No. 32, 19 September 1839, Encl. 4.
7. Ibid.
8. Cotton to Auckland, 25 June 1839. Parliamentary papers, 1843, Vol. XXXIX, p. 127.
9. Auckland to Cotton, 28 January 1839. Auckland 37695, fos 31–2.
10. Nott to Charles Nott, 7 February 1839. Nott, *Memoirs and Correspondence, 1854*, Vol. I, p. 102.
11. Outram, *op. cit.*, p. 39.
12. Auckland to Pottinger, 22 February 1839. Auckland papers, 37695, fos 81–2.
13. Major-General William George Keith Elphinstone (1782–1842) was a physically impaired, and totally inept, commander at Kabul. He died on the retreat. Not to be confused with Mountstuart Elphinstone.
14. Parliamentary papers, 1843, Vol. XXXIX, p. 127.
15. Ibid., p. 369.
16. Auckland to Macnaghten, 28 February 1839, Auckland papers, 37695, fos 97–8.
17. Auckland to Faish, 3 March 1839, Auckland papers, 37695, fo. 104.
18. Auckland to Hobhouse, 12 March 1839, Broughton papers, 36473, fos 436–44.
19. Quoted Priscilla Napier, *I have Sind*, etc., 1990, pp. 29–30.
20. Auckland to Outram, 1 December 1839, Auckland papers, 37697, fo. 6.

21.   Quoted, *Oxford History of India*, 3rd edition, 1958, p. 609.

22.   Napier, *op. cit.*, p. 232.

23.   Pottinger, at Bombay on his homeward journey, did, however, receive Napier's letter of 14 August 1844, written from Karachi. Napier regretted that he could not get to Bombay, but asked whether Pottinger had written the offending letter. Pottinger did not reply until 7 December when he was back in England. He said his remarks had 'no relation' to Napier, but that he had a 'perfect right' to express a private opinion. His tone was not apologetic. FO 705/36.

24.   Sir Algernon Law (ed.), *India under Lord Ellenborough*, 1926, p. 101.

25.   Ibid., footnote. The private letter was addressed to Captain Del Hoste, who had served in Sind. Pottinger admitted it had been 'most unjustifiably' published. FO 705/36.

26.   Napier, *op. cit.*, p. 30.

CHAPTER NINE

1.   Chests, often made of mango wood, contained opium weighing between 120 and 160 lbs.

2.   D. Butter, *Journal of the Asiatic Society of Bengal*, March, 1836, pp. 171–9.

3.   William John Napier (1786–1834), eighth Baron Napier. Before his misfortune at Canton, he had been a naval captain, and had published a treatise on sheep breeding.

4.   Parliamentary Correspondence relating to China, 1840, vol. XXXVI, p. 5.

5.   Hansard, 3rd series, Vol. 53, col. 818.

6.   Hansard, 3rd series, Vol. 54, col. 34.

7.   Sir George Elliot (1784–1863), present at the battle of Cape St Vincent and the Nile; highly thought of by Nelson; secretary of the Admiralty, 1834–5; Commander-in-Chief at the Cape of Good Hope, 1837–40; joint Plenipotentiary in China, 1840; promoted to Admiral in 1853.

8.   Palmerston to Elliot, 21 April 1841, FO 17/45.

9.   *Letters of Queen Victoria*, ed. A.C. Benson and Viscount Esher, 1907, Vol. I, p. 329.

10.   Though Elliot and Kishen were dismissed for their Canton negotiations, they both enjoyed later careers in other countries, Elliot as Consul General in Texas, and later as Governor of Bermuda, Trinidad and St Helena, and Kishen as the Imperial Emissary at Lhasa.

CHAPTER TEN

1.   *Canton Press*, 31 July 1841.

2.   Auckland to Pottinger (private), 24 June 1841, Auckland papers, 37715.

3.   *Field Officer*, 'The Last Year in China', 1843, Letter XV.

4.   W.D. Bernard, *Narrative of the voyages and services of the 'Nemesis'*, 1840–3, 1844, Vol. II, p. 115.

5. E.J. Eitel, *Europe in China*, 1895, pp. 179–80.

6. Palmerston to Admiralty, 5 June 1841, Encl. Adm 1/5501,

7. The *Times*, 9 November 1841.

8. R.S. Rait, *Life and Campaigns of Hugh, Viscount Gough*, 1903, p. 224.

9. Armine, S.H. Mountain, *Memoirs and Letters*, 1857, p. 194.

10. Ibid., p. 204.

11. Rait, *op. cit.*, p. 235.

12. J. Elliot Bingham, *Narrative of the Expedition to China*, 1842, Vol. I, pp. 285–90.

13. Pottinger, Memorandum, 14 October 1841, quoted A. Phillimore, *The Last of Nelson's Captains*, 1891, pp. 328–9.

14. Rait, *op. cit.*, p. 236.

15. Auckland to Pottinger, 12 February 1841, quoted ibid., p. 237.

16. Lt. Alexander Murray, *Doings in China*, 1843, pp. 73–4.

17. Peel to Wellington, 6 October 1841 Wellington papers (private).

CHAPTER ELEVEN

1. Auckland to Ellenborough, 20 December 1841, Auckland papers, 37717, *China Book*, Vol. III.

2. Auckland to Parker, 6 December 1841. Augustus Phillimore, *Life of Parker*. 1876–80, Vol. II, pp. 465–7.

3. *Times*, 23 November 1842.

4. Aberdeen to Pottinger, 4 November 1841, FO 17/53.

5. Pottinger to Aberdeen, 20 March 1842, FO 17/60. Quoted G.B. Endacott, *History of Hong Kong*, 1958, p. 21.

6. Pottinger to Ellenborough, 3 May 1842, FO 17/56.

7. Ellenborough, *Memorandum on Modifications to Instructions to Pottinger*, 29 October 1841. Ellenborough Papers 30/12/26/3.

8. Pottinger to Aberdeen, 8 March 1842, FO17/56.

9. Pottinger to Aberdeen, 3 May 1842, ibid.

10. Quoted E.J. Eitel, *Europe in China*, 1895, p. 184.

11. Matheson to J.A. Smith, 8 September 1841. J. Matheson, Private Letter Books, Vol. 7, Jardine Matheson Archive.

12. Peter Ward Fay, *The Opium War, 1840–42*, 1975, p. 331.

13. William Vesey, Baron Fitzgerald and Vesey (1783–1843) had been Chancellor of the Irish Exchequer, 1812–16, and President of the Board of Trade in 1828. He presided over the Board of Control from 1841–43.

14. Wellington, Memorandum, 19 June 1842, Wellington papers, Royal Commission on Historical Manuscripts.

15. Wellington, Memorandum, 1 February 1842, enclosed with letter to Ellenborough, 2 February 1842. *Op. cit.*

16. Stanley to Ellenborough, 3 February 1842. Lord Charles Colchester, (ed.) *Indian Administration of Lord Ellenborough*, 1874, pp. 214–7.

17. Ellenborough to Gough, 25 March 1842, enclosed in J. Stephen to H.U. Addington, (Foreign Office), 2 July 1842, FO 17/63.

CHAPTER TWELVE

1. Pottinger to Gough, 12 April 1842. A. Phillimore, *Life of Parker, 1876–80*, Vol. II, p. 471.

2. Lt. Alexander Murray, *Doings in China*, 1843, pp. 140–2.

3. John Ouchterlony, *The Chinese War*, etc., 1844, p. 238.

4. Pottinger to Aberdeen, 22 March 1842, FO 17/56.

5. *Dublin University Magazine clxvi*, October 1846, pp. 426–42, a long essay on Pottinger's career up to the Treaty of Nanking. Sir Henry wrote to the editor correcting one inaccuracy (not this reference), which implies that he accepted the rest of the article as a true version of what happened.

6. Captain Granville G. Loch, *The Closing Events of the Campaign in China*, 1843, p. 42. Loch (1813–53) was an adventurous Naval officer. Prominent in the Second Burmese War, he was shot while attacking Donabew.

7. Colin Campbell (1792–1863), Baron Clyde, was appointed Field Marshal in 1862. After a career stretching from the Peninsular to the Crimean Wars, he became Commander-in-Chief, India in 1857, and suppressed the Mutiny in 1857–8. (The son of a Glasgow carpenter, his real name was Macliver.)

8. R.S. Rait, *Life and Campaigns of Gough*, 1903, Vol. I, p. 272.

9. Rait, *op. cit.*, p. 277.

10. J. Ouchterlony, *The Chinese War*, 1844, p. 426.

11. Sir Henry Keppel (1809–1904), A *Sailor's Life with Four Sovereigns*, 1899, Vol. I, p. 269. Appointed Admiral of the Fleet in 1877, Keppel had been second in command, China Station in 1856, and Commander-in-Chief there in 1866. He was an intimate friend of Edward VII.

12. Pottinger to Gough, 1 July 1842. Phillimore, *op. cit.*, Vol. II, p. 473.

13. Rev. Karl Friedrich August Gutzlaff was one of the most intriguing figures in the Opium War. He came from Pomerania and worked on Java and at Bangkok, before reaching China on board an opium ship. Unusually fluent in Chinese, he later combined vigorous evangelism with selling opium and official work for Her Majesty's Government. He acted as civil magistrate during the occupation of Ningpo.

14. John, the son of Dr Robert Morrison, the celebrated missionary and lexicographer, had been employed as an interpreter since the time of the Napier fiasco. Robert Thom had been on Elliot's expedition. The lot of an interpreter could be hazardous, and Thom had a narrow escape at Amoy.

15. *Dublin University Magazine, op. cit.*, pp. 426–42.

16. S. Lane-Poole, *Sir Harry Parkes in China*, 1901, pp. 27–8. Parkes (1828–85) had an eventful diplomatic career. Arrested during negotiations at the end of the Third Chinese War in 1860, he was confined in chains. He was Minister to Japan in 1865, and to China in 1883.

17. Loch, *op. cit.*, pp. 172–3.

18. Sir George Charles D'Aguilar (1784–1855), served against the Marathas; sent by Governor-General Bentinck on a mission to Constantinople. A martinet, he wrote manuals on military discipline.

CHAPTER THIRTEEN

1. *Edinburgh Review*, January 1860, pp. 103–4.
2. Quoted E.J. Eitel, *Europe in China*, 1895, p. 187.
3. Peel to Stanley, 23 November 1842, Peel 40467, FO 303.
4. Stanley to Queen Victoria, 23 November 1842, *Victoria, Letters*, Vol. I, pp. 440–2.
5. *Times*, 22 November 1842.
6. Palmerston to Pottinger, 31 May 1841. Reproduced in H.B. Morse, *The International Relations of the Chinese Empire*, 1910, Appendix K, pp. 655–9.
7. Aberdeen to Pottinger, 4 November 1841, FO 17/53.
8. Stanley to Pottinger, 31 January 1842, S/9/3, India Office Archive.
9. Pottinger to Aberdeen, 20 March 1842, FO 17/60.
10. Pottinger to Aberdeen, 29 August 1842, FO 17/57.
11. Aberdeen to Pottinger, 4 January 1843, FO 17/74.
12. Stanley to Pottinger, 3 June 1843, FO 17/75.
13. G.B. Endacott, *A History of Hong Kong*, 1958, p. 37.
14. Davis to Stanley, 24 July 1844, No. 42, CO 129/6.
15. Council Minutes CO 131/1.
16. Pottinger to Stanley, 13 November 1843, CO 129/2, No. 23.

CHAPTER FOURTEEN

1. Pottinger to Ellenborough, 12 September 1842. Aberdeen papers, 43198.
2. Pottinger to Aberdeen, 20 December 1842, FO 17/59.
3. Draft No 46 to Pottinger, 1 April 1843, FO 17/64.
4. Pottinger to Aberdeen, 6 February 1843, FO 17/66.
5. Pottinger to Aberdeen, 20 March 1843. FO 17/66.
6. Pottinger to Aberdeen, 10 March 1843, FO 17/66.
7. Pottinger to Aberdeen, 13 June 1843, No. 90. CO 129/3.
8. Proclamation, 22 July 1843. D1584/5/1 PRO NI.
9. G.B. Endacott, *History of Hong Kong*, 1958, p. 25.
10. E.J. Eitel, *Europe in China*, 1895, p. 200.
11. Palmerston's earlier letter to Pottinger. See Note 6 to Chapter Thirteen.
12. Pottinger to Aberdeen, 27 June 1843, D1584/5/5.
13. A. Cunnynghame, *An ADC's Recollection of Service in China*, 1844, Vol. II, p. 56.
14. Pottinger to Aberdeen, 20 March 1843, FO 17/66.
15. Aberdeen to Pottinger, 4 January 1843, FO 17/64.
16. Ibid.
17. Peel to Stanley, 15 December 1842. Peel papers, 40467.
18. Ellenborough to Aberdeen, 17 November 1842. Aberdeen papers, 43198.
19. Temple, 6 March 1869, Temple papers, EUR F86.
20. Campbell, *Memoirs of my Indian Career*, 1893, Vol. II, p. 297.
21. Pottinger to Aberdeen, 3 November 1843, FO17/70.
22. Lay to Pottinger, 1 April 1844, FO 17/81.

23. Aberdeen to Pottinger, 4 January 1843. No. 4, CO 129/3.

24. See Note 18 to Chapter Twelve.

25. Palmerston to Admiralty, 2 June 1841, and Auckland to Hobhouse, 11 August 1841. Parliamentary papers, 1843, Vol. XXX, pp. 618 and 621.

26. A. Phillimore, *The Last of Nelson's Captains*, 1891, p. 313.

27. Ibid., p. 318.

28. Ibid., p. 341.

29. Ibid., pp. 347–8.

30. Ibid., p. 355.

31. Parker to Secretary of Admiralty, 12 August 1843, FO 17/75.

32. Pottinger to Aberdeen, 18 July 1843, (no. 84), enclosing No. 3, Pottinger to Parker, same date, FO 17/68.

33. Parker to Keppel, 4 August 1843. Phillimore, *op. cit.*, p. 382.

34. Ibid.

35. Parker to Secretary of Admiralty, 14 and 24 October 1843, Adm. 1/5630.

36. Parker to Admiralty, 26 July 1843. Phillimore, *op. cit.*, p. 379.

37. Aberdeen to Pottinger, 6 February 1844, FO 17/77.

38. Pottinger to Aberdeen, 18 July 1843 (No. 84), enclosing No. 3, Pottinger to Parker, same date, FOI 17/68.

39. Pottinger to Aberdeen, 1 March 1844, FO 17/80.

40. Parker to Admiralty, 16 November 1843, Adm. 1/5530.

41. Pottinger to Aberdeen, 16 March 1844, FO 17/80.

42. Cochrane to Admiralty, 20 June 1844, Adm. 1/5539.

43. Quoted, E.J. Eitel, *Europe in China*, 1895, p. 192.

44. Notification, 8 November 1838, Parliamentary papers, 1839, Indian Papers, 1.

45. Lady Sale, *Journal of the Disasters in Afghanistan*, 1843, entry for 15 November 1841.

46. Eldred Pottinger's career is narrated in detail in Kaye, *Lives of Indian Officers*, 1880, and G. Pottinger, *The Afghan Connection*, 1983.

47. E. Pottinger to J. Pottinger, 23 August 1843, Pottinger papers, D 1584A/1/3.

CHAPTER FIFTEEN

1. Rev. George Smith, *A Narrative of an Exploratory Visit to the Consular Cities of China*, 1847, p. 509.

2. Hansard, 17 March 1843, Vol. 67, Col. 1078 Lords.

3. Capt A. Cunnynghame, *An ADC's Recollection of Service in China*, 1844, Vol. II, p. 86.

4. G.B. Endacott, *History of Hong Kong*, 1958, p. 75.

5. Aberdeen to Peel, 17 October 1844, Peel papers, 40454 fo. 278.

6. Aberdeen to Peel, 22 October 1844, Ibid., fo. 292.

7. Aberdeen to Peel, 27 December 1844, Peel papers, 40453, fo. 305.

8. Hansard, 7 February 1843, Vol. 66, Col. 221.

9. Sir George Thomas Staunton (1781–1859), writer on China. He accompanied Lord Macartney's Chinese embassy in 1792; and was at Canton, 1798–1817. An

interpreter, he introduced vaccination to China in 1805. He was co-founder of Royal Asiatic Society in 1823. His works include *Fundamental Laws*, 1810 – the first Chinese book to be rendered in English.

10.   Joseph Hume (1777–1855), was a radical politician. He served in East India Company's medical service, 1797–1807 and was MP for various constituencies before sitting for Montrose, 1842–55. A friend of Alexander Burnes. Though he pressed for a pension for Pottinger, he was a very vocal proponent of economy in public expenditure.

11.   Hansard, 14 February 1843, Vol. 66, cols 571–4.

12.   Hansard, ibid., cols 538–544.

13.   Hansard 3 May 1843, Vol. 68, col. 1241.

14.   Hansard, 2 April 1844, Vol. 69, cols 1753–4.

15.   Hansard 3 June 1845, Vol. 80, col. 1386.

16.   P&O Archive; National Maritime Museum letter to the author of 1 December 1994.

17.   *Times*, 22 April 1846.

18.   John Cam Hobhouse (1786–1869), Baron Broughton De Gyfford, statesman. He was Byron's friend and executor and Secretary for War, 1832–3, and Chief Secretary for Ireland, 1833. He was twice President of the Board of Control, in 1835–41, and 1846–52 and was said to have invented the phrase 'His Majesty's Opposition'.

19.   Hansard, 3 June 1845, Vol. 80, cols 1374–94.

20.   Hansard, 16 June 1845, Vol. 81, col. 615.

CHAPTER SIXTEEN

1.   Grey, *The Colonial Administration of Lord John Russell*, 1853, Vol. II, p. 203. Sir Henry George Grey, Viscount Howick, succeeded his father as third Earl Grey in 1845, and became active leader of his party in House of Lords. Secretary for the Colonies from 1846–52. He strongly advocated transportation of convicts and opposed Gladstone's Home Rule policy.

2.   Sir Peregrine Maitland (1777–1854), joined the army in 1792 and served in Flanders from 1794–8; in Spain in 1809 and 1812; and at Waterloo. He was Lieutenant-Governor of Upper Canada from 1818–28, and of Nova Scotia from 1828–34; Commander-in-Chief of the Madras army from 1836–8; Governor, Cape of Good Hope 1844–47; promoted to General, 1846.

3.   Grey to Pottinger, 26 August 1846, Grey papers, University of Durham.

4.   Grey, *The Colonial Administration of Lord John Russell*, 1853, Vol. II, p. 198.

5.   Grey to Pottinger, 14 September 1846, Grey papers.

6.   Grey, Journal, entry for 6 December 1846, ibid.

7.   Parliamentary papers, 1847–8, Vol. 43, pp. 2–4.

8.   *Grahamstown Journal*, 6 February 1847.

9.   Henry Frederick Berkeley (1785–1857), served in Peninsula and at Waterloo. He was promoted to Lieut.-General before leaving for Cape with Pottinger. Commander-in-Chief of the Madras army from 1847; he was later MP for

Devonport. He was described as 'yielding and easy-tempered' by S.M. Mitra, in *Life and Letters of Sir J. Hall*, 1911, p. 194.

10.   Henry Somerset (1794–1862), served in Peninsula and at Waterloo. He commanded the Cape Mounted Rifles, 1827–50. He was thought to be a friend of coloured people, but to have the interests of white colonists at heart. He was nephew of the first Lord Raglan.

11.   Proclamation, 3 March 1847; *Cape of Good Hope Gazette*, 18 March 1847.

12.   Pottinger to Berkeley, 26 March 1847, Brenthurst Library papers fo. 6266/9.

13.   Pottinger to Berkeley, 5 April 1847, ibid., fo. 6266/19.

14.   Grey, *op. cit.*, Vol. II, p. 200.

15.   Grey to Pottinger, 14 July 1847, fo. 6272/51.

16.   Pottinger to Berkeley, 23 May 1847, fo. 6266/58.

17.   Pottinger to Grey, 16 May 1847, GH 23/17, Cape Archives.

18.   Pottinger to Grey, 16 May 1847, Grey papers.

19.   Pottinger to Berkeley, 3 December 1847, fo. 6208/140.

20.   Sir George Cory, *The Rise of South Africa*, 1930. Vol. V, p. 20.

21.   *Grahamstown Journal*, 15 June 1847.

22.   Pottinger to Berkeley, 20 June 1847, fo. 6267/71.

23.   Pottinger to Calderwood, 16 August 1847, fo. 6267/84b.

24.   Proclamation by Governor, 27 August 1847, fo. 6272/63.

25.   Berkeley to Pottinger, 2 September 1847, fo. 6273/79d.

26.   Pottinger to Berkeley, 3 September 1847, fo. 6267/87.

27.   Somerset, Memorial, 5 August 1847, fo. 6272/57.

28.   Pottinger to Berkeley, 9 September 1847, fo. 6267/89.

29.   Berkeley to Pottinger, 22 September 1847, fo. 6273/49a.

30.   Somerset to Berkeley, 22 September 1847, fo. 6273/49b.

31.   Pottinger to Berkeley, 24 September 1847, fo. 6267/95 and 97.

32.   Grey to Pottinger, 26 July 1847, fo. 6272/54.

33.   Grey to Pottinger, 25 July 1847, private, Grey papers.

34.   Pottinger to Grey, 23 August 1847, Grey papers.

35.   S.M. Mitra, *Life and Letters of Sir J. Hall*, 1911, p. 194.

36.   Pottinger to Berkeley, 20 October 1847, fo. 6267/119.

37.   Pottinger to Berkeley, 25 October 1847, fo. 6267/124.

38.   Berkeley to Pottinger, 27 November 1847, fo. 6273/70c.

39.   Pottinger to Grey 22 November 1847, fo. 6268/137.

40.   Parliamentary Papers, 1847–8, Vol. 43, p. 157.

41.   Berkeley to Pottinger, 16 November 1847, fo. 6273/72.

42.   Pottinger to Grey, 30 October 1847, private, Grey papers.

43.   Sir George Cory, *op. cit.*, Vol. V, p. 96.

44.   *South African Commercial Advertiser*, 29 December 1847.

45.   Grey to Pottinger, 18 March 1848, private, Grey papers.

46.   *Cape Frontier Times*, 1 August 1848.

47.   Grey, *op. cit.*, Vol. II, p. 200.

48.   *Advertiser and Mail* (Cape Town) 28 April 1866, letter signed 'Tancred'.

49.   G.M. Theal, *History of South Africa from 1795 to 1872*, 1908, Vol. 3, p. 52.

50.   Sir George Cory, *op. cit.*, p. 95.

CHAPTER SEVENTEEN

1. Sir Penderel Moon, *The British Conquest and Dominion of India,* 1989, p. 276.

2. Ibid., p. 751.

3. George Hay, eighth Marquis of Tweeddale (1787–1876), served in Sicily in 1806, the Peninsula from 1807–13, and in America in 1813. He was wounded at Busaco, Vittoria, and Niagara, where he was captured. He became Governor of Madras from 1842–8 and Field Marshal in 1875.

4. '*A Visit to Madras in the year 1811*', published in 1821, p. 8.

5. Ibid., p. 15.

6. Ibid., p. 28.

7. Pottinger to Lushington, 14 January 1849, MSS EUR F213/24, p. 12. Sir James Law Lushington (1779–1859), entered the Madras army in 1797, and rose to be General and Chairman of the East India Company from 1838–9. His brother Stephen Rumbold Lushington (1776–1868), was Governor of Madras from 1827–35.

8. Pottinger to Hobhouse, 22 April 1848, F213/23 p. 34. For Hobhouse, see Note 18 to Chapter Fifteen.

9. Ibid., p. 270.

10. Pottinger to Hobhouse, 26 December 1848, ibid., p. 334.

11. Pottinger to Melville, 24 January 1849, F 213/24 p. 14.

12. Sir William Sampson Whish (1787–1853), was Lieutenant in the Bengal Artillery in 1804; he rose to be Lieutenant-General in 1851; commanded the Multan field force in 1848 and took part in the siege of Mulraj 1848–9.

13. Pottinger to Hobhouse, 13 November 1848. F213/23 p. 270.

14. Pottinger to Hobhouse, 26 December 1848, ibid., p. 337.

15. Pottinger to Hobhouse, 14 February 1849, F213/24 p. 44.

16. Moon, *op. cit.,* p. 616, note 9.

17. Pottinger to Hobhouse, 13 November 1848 F213/23 p. 270.

18. Pottinger to Lushington, 14 January 1849 F213/24 p. 11.

19. Madras Despatches, 2 October 1850, E/4/974, ff. 227–8.

20. Madras Despatches, 7 October 1851, E/4/975, f. 731.

21. Warrant FO 705/110.

22. Pottinger to Galloway, 26 September 1849, F213/24 p. 260. Sir Archibald Galloway (1780?–1850), entered the Bengal Native Infantry in 1800; rose to be Major-General in 1841 and Chairman of the East India Company in 1849. Published works include *Notes on the Siege of Delhi,* 1804.

23. Pottinger to Hobhouse, 11 March 1849, F213/24 p. 88.

24. Madras Despatches, 2 June 1852, E/4/976, f. 1068.

25. Pottinger to Hobhouse, 27 December 1849, F213/24 p. 248.

26. Pottinger to Galloway, 20 August 1849, F213/24, p. 224.

27. Dalhousie to Hobhouse, 23 October 1850, F213/25 p. 172. Dalhousie's view is not surprising since Pottinger had earlier written to him, 'I hope you will not have thought me inattentive or remiss in not writing more regularly to you. I had nothing whatever to communicate.' Pottinger to Dalhousie, 17 January 1849, fo. 704/89 f. 34.

28.   George Francis Robert, third Baron Harris (1810–72) was Governor of Trinidad in 1846 and Governor of Madras from 1854–9.

EPILOGUE

1.   William lost no chance to write on his brother's behalf, e.g. his letter (undated) to the Royal Geographical Society (PRO NI 1584/5/5). For other views on Henry's claim to a peerage, see *Dublin University Magazine*, clxvi, October 1846, p. 426. For Parliamentary proceedings, see Chapter XV.

2.   John Brooke-Little to author, 21 September 1994.

3.   Ibid.

4.   Reference in Fred's diary, FO 705/124.

5.   *Bombay Calendar and Almanac*, 1839, 2nd ed., p. 176.

6.   G.O. Trevelyan, *The Competition Wallah*, 1864, p. 19.

7.   Lt. Henry Pottinger to John Pottinger, undated, 1839. PRO NI D1584/2/1. In the same letter the young officer reports that his Uncle Henry has given him 400 rupees to buy a horse.

8.   Anne Hocking to her Mother, 21 October 1840, Private Collection, Mr J. Platt.

9.   Pottinger to Hobhouse, August 1849, F213/24 p. 233.

10.   Most of his poetry consists of light, occasional, verses, but he sometimes tries to be more serious – and pretentious. This is an example:

Scepticism

Hence! Fiend, whose gorgon eye would fain,

I feel, convert my soul to stone! –

Congeal, at once, my breast and brain,

As cold and callous as thine own.

11.   Rolf Boldrewood, *Robbery under Arms*, 1888.

12.   Entries in Fred's Diary, F705/124.

13.   Boldrewood, *op. cit.*

14.   *The Field*, 22 May 1937, p. 1342.

15.   Extracted from *Australian Daily Mirror*, April–May 1949. In another more fanciful account, Fred's pistol went off when he jumped down from the coach to pick a wayside flower for a young passenger.

16.   *Dublin University Magazine*, clxvi, October 1846, p. 442.

Sources

MANUSCRIPT SOURCES

British Library, India Office Collection
Broughton papers MSS EUR F 213/23–5
Campbell papers MSS EUR E 349
Elphinstone papers MSS EUR F 88
Madras Despatches E/4/972–981
Temple papers MSS EUR F 86
Bengal Secret Proceedings, 1820–6
Bengal Secret and Separate Consultations, 1808–34
Bengal Secret and Political Consultations, 1820–3
Bengal Secret and Separate Proceedings, 1808–34
Bengal Secret Letters and Enclosures, 1808–32
Board of Control's Collections, 1799–1844
Board of Control Letter Books
Bombay Secret Proceedings, 1820–6
Indian Political and Foreign Consultations, 1806–8
Indian Secret Consultations, 1837
Indian Secret Letters to England and Enclosures, 1832–44
Indian Secret Proceedings, 1830–8
Letters from the Board of Control to the East India Company, 1829–44
Letters from the East India Company to the Board of Control, 1843–4

British Museum
Aberdeen papers Add MSS 43198
Auckland papers Add MSS 37690–37708, 37715, 37717
Broughton papers Add MSS 36473–4

Palmerston papers Add MSS 48535

Peel papers Add MSS 40428, 40453–5, 40467–8

Public Record Office, London

Ellenborough papers PRO 30.12

Pottinger papers FO 705

Admiralty Records Ad 19 and 46

Colonial Office Records CO 129 and 403

Foreign Office Records FO 17, 223, 228

Public Record Office, Northern Ireland, Belfast

Pottinger papers D 1584/5/1–5

Official Records

Correspondence relating to Affairs of Persia and Afghanistan, Palmerston's annotated copy, PRO FO 539.1 and .2

Parliamentary papers, especially 1840 xxxvi and xxxvii, 1842 xlv; 1843 xxxvii, xxxix; 1847 xxviii, and 1847–8 xliii

Hansard for relevant dates

Contemporary Newspapers and Periodicals

Morning Chronicle

The Times

Edinburgh Review

Dublin University Magazine

Cape Frontier Times

Grahamstown Journal

South African Commercial Advertiser

PUBLICATIONS

Abbot, J. *Sind; a restatement,* 1924

Archbold, W.A.J. (ed.) *Cambridge History of the British Empire,* Vol. IV, 1921

Arnold, Sir E. *Dalhousie's Administration of India,* 2 Vols., 1862–5

Ascoli, F.D. *Early Revenue History of Bengal,* 1917

Beeching, Jack. *The Chinese Opium Wars,* 1975

Bingham, J. Elliott. *Narrative of the Expedition to China,* 2 Vols., 1842

Boldrewood, Ralph. *Robbery under Arms,* 1888

Burnes, Sir Alexander. *Travels into Bokhara,* 1834

Burnes, James. *A Narrative of a Visit to the Court of Sinde,* 1831

Calderwood, Henry. *Caffres and Caffre Missions,* 1858

Coates, Austin. *Prelude to Hong Kong,* 1966

Colchester, Lord Charles (ed.) *The Indian Administration of Lord Ellenborough,* 1874

Cordeur Basil le and Sanders, Christopher. *The War of the Axe,* limited edition, 1981

Cory, Sir George E. *The Rise of South Africa from 1795 to 1872,* Vol. V, 1930

Costin, W.C. *Great Britain and China 1833–60,* 1937

Cunnynghame, Captain Arthur. *An ADC's Recollections of Service in China,* 2 Vols., 1844

—— *The Hero of Herat,* 1912

—— *Judgment of the Sword,* 1913

Dodwell, H.H. (ed.) *Cambridge History of India,* 1922–53

Dodwell, H.H. *The Nabobs of Madras,* 1926

Duff, Grant J. *History of the Mahrattas,* 1826, revised edition 1921

Eames, J.B. *The English in China* (1600–1843), 1909

Eastwick, Captain W.J. *Speeches on the Sinde Question 1844,* 1863

Eitel, E.J. *Europe in China: the history of Hong Kong,* 1895

Ellenborough, First Earl of. Secret despatches, selection, 1926

Ellenborough, First Earl of. *A Political Diary 1828–30,* 2 Vols., 1881

Elliot, Admiral Sir George. *Memoir, etc.,* 1863

Elphinstone, Mountstuart. *An Account of the Kingdom of Caubul,* 1816

Endacott, G.B. *Government and People in Hong Kong 1841–1962,* 1964

Endacott, G.B. *A History of Hong Kong,* 1958

Fairbank, J.K. *Trade and Diplomacy on the China Coast 1842–54,* 2 vols., 1953

Fay, Peter Ward. *The Opium War 1840–42*, 1975

'Field Officer', *The Last Year in China*, 1843

Forrest, Sir G.W. *Selections from Minutes of Elphinstone*, 1884

Fortescue, Sir J.W. *History of the British Army*, Vol. XII, 1927

Graham, Gerald S. *The China Station: War and Diplomacy 1830–60*, 1978

Greenberg, Michael. *British Trade and the Opening of China 1800–42*, 1951, reprinted 1970

Gopal, Sarvepalli. *British Policy in India 1858–1905*, 1965

Gough, Sir Hugh. *Old Memories*, 1897

Gupta, P.C. *Baji Rao II and the East India Company*, 1939

Heber, Reginald. *Narrative of a Journey through the Upper Provinces of India, 1824–5*, 1828

Hibbert, Christopher. *The Dragon Wakes*, 1970

Holt, Edgar. *The Opium Wars in China*, 1964

Huttenback, Robert. *British Relations with Sind 1799–1843*, 1962

Imlah, A.H. *Lord Ellenborough*, 1939

Jocelyn, Viscount. *Six Months with the Chinese Expedition*, 1841

Kaye, Sir J.W. *The Administration of the East India Company*, 1853

—— *History of the War in Afghanistan*, 1851, revised edition 1874

—— *Life and Correspondence of Lord Metcalfe*, 1854

—— *Lives of Indian Officers*, 1880; revised edition 1889

Kaye, Third Earl. *The Colonial Policy of Lord John Russell*, 1853

Lane-Poole, Stanley. *Sir Harry Parkes in China*, 1901

Law, Sir Algernon (ed.) *India under Lord Ellenborough 1842–4*, 1926

Loch, Captain Granville G. *The Closing Events of the Campaign in China*, 1843

Mackenzie, K.S. *Narrative of the Second Campaign in China*, 1842

Macrory, Sir Patrick. *Signal Catastrophe*, 1966

Malcolm, Sir John. *Political History of India 1784–1823*, 1826

Mill, James. *History of British India*, 1817, fifth edition, 1858

—— *A Visit to Madras in the year 1811*, 1821

Mitra, S.M. *Life and Letters of Sir John Hall*, 1911

Mountain, Armine S.H. *Memoirs and Letters*, 1857

Moon, Sir Penderel. *The British Conquest and Dominion of India*, 1989

Morrell, W.P. *British Colonial Policy in the Age of Peel and Russell*, 1930

Morse, H.B. *The International Relations of the Chinese Empire*, 1910

Napier, Priscilla. *I have Sind; Charles Napier in India 1841–4*, 1990

Norris, J.A. *The First Afghan War*, 1967

Ouchterlony, John. *The Chinese War*, 1844

Outram, James. *Rough Notes of the Campaign in Sinde and Afghanistan in 1838–9*, 1840

Parkinson, Northcote C. *Trade in the Eastern Seas 1793–1813*, 1937

Phillimore, Sir A. *The Last of Nelson's Captains*, 1891

Phillimore, Sir A. *Life of Admiral Sir W. Parker*, 3 Vols., 1876–80

Pope-Hennessy, J. *Half Crown Colony*, 1969

Pottinger, George. *The Afghan Connection*, 1983

Pottinger George and Macrory, Sir Patrick. *The Ten-Rupee Jezail*, 1993

Pottinger, Henry. *Travels in Beloochistan and Sinde*, 1816

Prinsep, H.T. *History of Transactions under Marquess of Hastings 1813–23*, 1825

Rait, Robert S. *Life and Campaigns of Hugh, Viscount Gough*, 1903

Sale, Lady. *Journal of the Disasters in Afghanistan 1841–2*, 1843, revised edition, ed. Sir Patrick Macrory, 1969

Sardesai, G.S. (ed.) *English Records of Maratha History; Poona Affairs* Vol. I, 1950, and Vol. II, 1953

Shore, F.J. *Notes on Indian Affairs*, 1837

Smith, Revd. George. *Narrative of Exploratory Visit to China, etc.*, 1847

Spear, T.G.P. (ed.) *Oxford History of India*, 3rd ed. 1958

Theal, George McCall. *History of South Africa 1795–1872*, vol. 3, 1908

Trevelyan, Sir G.O. *The Competition Wallah*, 1864

Trotter, L.J. *History of India 1836–80*, 1886

Waley, Arthur. *The Opium War through Chinese eyes*, 1958

Ward Sir Adolphus and G.P. Gooch. (eds) *Cambridge History of British Foreign Policy 1783–1919*, Vol. II, 1923

Index

LC 11-8-91	